G000044066

2018 STANDARD CATALOG OF

CRYPTOCURRENCIES

2018 STANDARD CATALOG OF
CRYPTOCURRENCIES

Mateo Marin   Daniel F. Wehleit

NORMAL BOOKS

THE BRANDS & TECHNOLOGIES
are delivered by our selected cryptocurrencies.

CONCEPT AND EDITORIAL
Mateo Marin & Daniel F. Wehleit

DESIGNED BY
Daniel F. Wehleit

PRODUCTION
Mateo Marin

EDITED BY
Jason Brett Serle

EDITORIAL ASSISTANT
Eliot Eden

SPECIAL THANKS TO
Digibyte and NEM Foundation

PUBLISHED BY
NormalBooks, Wrangelstrasse 86, 10999 Berlin, Germany
More information at www.normalbooks.io

PRINT PRODUCTION
MEDIALIS Offsetdruck GmBH,
Heidelberger Strasse 65/66
12435 Berlin, Germany
www.medialis.org

ISBN 978-84-697-8303-0
First Edition Published March 2018.

Contents

Introduction

Welcome to the 2018 Standard Catalog of Cryptocurrencies.

The first of its kind, here you can discover 100 cryptocurrencies and learn about everything, from their fascinating history to their unique features.

Since the birth of Bitcoin in 2009, the number of altcoins has grown at an astonishing rate. Some have risen to the very top of the cryptocurrency pile while others have fallen away, never to be seen again.

Cryptocurrency is ever-evolving, making it at times, hard to keep up with the constant developments and latest trends. This book is for anyone and everyone with an interest in cryptocurrency. Whether a newcomer to the world of crypto or an experienced trader, there is something here for you.

Each coin featured in the 2018 Standard Catalog of Cryptocurrencies has been extensively researched, providing you with all of the essential information. From the very origins of the coin to the people behind it, it's a great way to learn about new coins, as well as revisit some of your favorites. At the back of the book, you'll find a glossary which is packed full of all of the key cryptocurrency terms.

Just as important as the information on each cryptocurrency is the presentation itself. Each coin is featured with its own unique logo, and colorful infographics serve to better demonstrate what a particular coin is about. We hope that this makes the book as pleasing to the eye as it is to the mind.

So with that, we hope you enjoy this book. We feel it's a great way to learn about cryptocurrencies, discover potential investments, or to just absorb yourself in this fascinating technology.

WHAT ARE ALTCOINS?

A very common word in the world of cryptocurrency, is 'altcoin' or simply 'alt', and is essentially any cryptocurrency coin other than Bitcoin. The term altcoin is derived from the words 'alternative' and 'coin'. In the years since Bitcoin was introduced, hundreds of altcoins have been created. Some have gone on to have great success while others have disappeared as quickly as they entered the market.

In order to understand why altcoins exist, we have to accept that Bitcoin isn't perfect. It may be the reigning and undisputed king of cryptocurrency but nothing lasts forever. Technology is ever-advancing and this is where altcoins come in. Altcoins aim to offer an improvement on Bitcoin or at the very least, a key difference. This could be in the way that the coin is mined, for example.

As you explore the many coins in this book, you'll find that they vary a great deal in terms of their history, features, uses, and fundamental driving philosophies. This is what makes cryptocurrency so interesting. Let's take a look at a couple of examples of altcoins and how they aim to improve upon Bitcoin. Litecoin (LTC) was launched in 2011 by a former Google software engineer by the name of Charlie Lee. One Bitcoin problem it improves upon is transaction speed, which makes LTC a much more practical choice when it comes to everyday transactions.

Another popular altcoin is Monero (XMR). Launched in 2014, Monero was designed to offer the privacy that Bitcoin lacks. While Bitcoin offers anonymity in that wallets are not linked to personal information, it's still possible to see how much Bitcoin people are sending and receiving and how much Bitcoin is in a certain wallet. This is not the case with Monero where transactions are virtually impossible to trace.

So if some altcoins are improving on aspects of Bitcoin, why is Bitcoin still the number one cryptocurrency with by far the biggest market cap? Well, it was the very first cryptocurrency and that counts for a lot. You only have to look at Bitcoin's incredible rise over the years to see why it's an attractive proposition for investors, both experienced and newcomers alike.

Chances are that if you ask a random person on the street about Ethereum, Litecoin or Monero they won't have even heard of them yet. However, while cryptocurrency is still very much in its infancy, awareness is growing around Bitcoin. Brand awareness is a powerful thing. If Bitcoin is to be dethroned in the future, it will require altcoins to gain a lot more mainstream exposure.

The term 'altcoin' is derived from the words 'alternative' and 'coin' and is essentially any cryptocurrency coin other than Bitcoin.

HOW TO USE THIS BOOK

WHAT DOES IT ALL MEAN?

All the cryptocurrencies featured in this book have a fact sheet with technical details about the coin. The data displayed was taken from Coinmarketcap.com on January 7, 2018. Under the main logo of the coin you will find the following details:

Currency Code: Every cryptocurrency has a code or ticker symbol that is used to trade on the exchanges. Most of the cryptocurrencies have a 3 letter code, but some have 4 or 5 letters.

Launch Date: This is the date when the coin was first announced or launched.

Market Cap: The current valuation of the cryptocurrency in US Dollars - $USD.

Max. Supply: The maximum number of minted or mined coins that can exist on the blockchain of that particular coin.

Circulating Supply: The current amount of coins circulating that have been either mined or minted.

Consensus Mechanism: The protocol by which the blockchain confirms the transactions for that particular coin. The most commonly used are proof-of-work (PoW) and proof-of-stake (PoS).

Hashing Algorithm: The mathematical algorithm used to process and confirm the transactions of the blockchain.

Block Time: The amount of time it takes for a block to be confirmed on the blockchain.

URL: The official homepage for the project where you can find additional information.

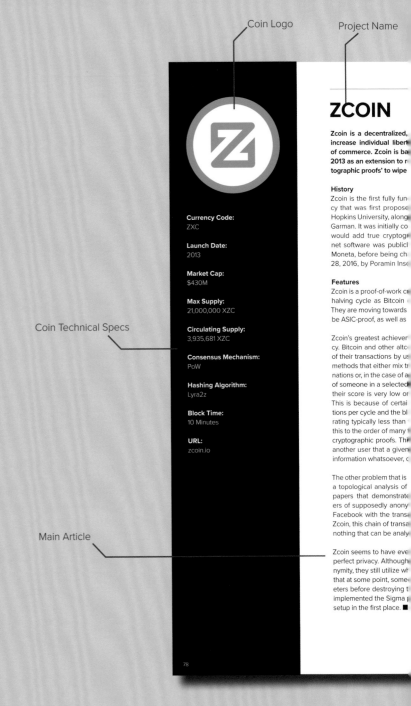

Coin Logo

Project Name

ZCOIN

Zcoin is a decentralized,
increase individual libert
of commerce. Zcoin is ba
2013 as an extension to r
tographic proofs' to wipe

History
Zcoin is the first fully fun
cy that was first propose
Hopkins University, along
Garman. It was initially co
would add true cryptogr
net software was publicl
Moneta, before being ch
28, 2016, by Poramin Inse

Features
Zcoin is a proof-of-work c
halving cycle as Bitcoin
They are moving towards
be ASIC-proof, as well as

Zcoin's greatest achiever
cy. Bitcoin and other alto
of their transactions by us
methods that either mix tr
nations or, in the case of a
of someone in a selected
their score is very low or
This is because of certai
tions per cycle and the bl
rating typically less than
this to the order of many
cryptographic proofs. The
another user that a given
information whatsoever, c

The other problem that is
a topological analysis of
papers that demonstrate
ers of supposedly anony
Facebook with the transa
Zcoin, this chain of transa
nothing that can be analy

Zcoin seems to have eve
perfect privacy. Although
nymity, they still utilize wh
that at some point, some
eters before destroying t
implemented the Sigma
setup in the first place. ∎

Coin Technical Specs

Currency Code:
ZXC

Launch Date:
2013

Market Cap:
$430M

Max Supply:
21,000,000 XZC

Circulating Supply:
3,935,681 XZC

Consensus Mechanism:
PoW

Hashing Algorithm:
Lyra2z

Block Time:
10 Minutes

URL:
zcoin.io

Main Article

78

cryptocurrency whose mission is to
eing financial privacy and freedom
ocoin protocol - originally created in
tcoin and uses 'zero-knowledge cryp-
en transactions.

entation of Zerocoin, a cryptocurren-
D. Green, a professor at the Johns
ate students - Ian Miers and Christina
extension to the Bitcoin protocol that
ity to Bitcoin transactions. The test-
December 19, 2015, with the name,
for its official release on September
so the founder of Vertcoin.

at uses the same mining method and
different hashing algorithm - Lyra2z.
TP (Merkle Tree Proofs), designed to
ets through the high use of memory.

n in the area of anonymity and priva-
ave aimed to improve the anonymity
mixers or ring signatures. These are
others to hide their origins and desti-
require the endorsed digital signature
e problem with these methods is that
y set - a measure of a coin's privacy.
ations due to the number of transac-
le they demonstrate a traceability set
tion, Zcoin has managed to increase
ks to their system of zero-knowledge
method by which one user proves to
ue, without communicating any other
ct that it is true or not.

stem is due to the inability to perform
history. There are multiple research
gical analysis can identify the own-
comparing a separate network like
a cryptocurrency's blockchain. With
mply does not exist. There is literally

urther than this in their drive towards
e setups provide a great deal of ano-
'trusted setup'. This basically means
trusted to generate the initial param-
improve on this situation, Zcoin has
oes away with the need for a trusted

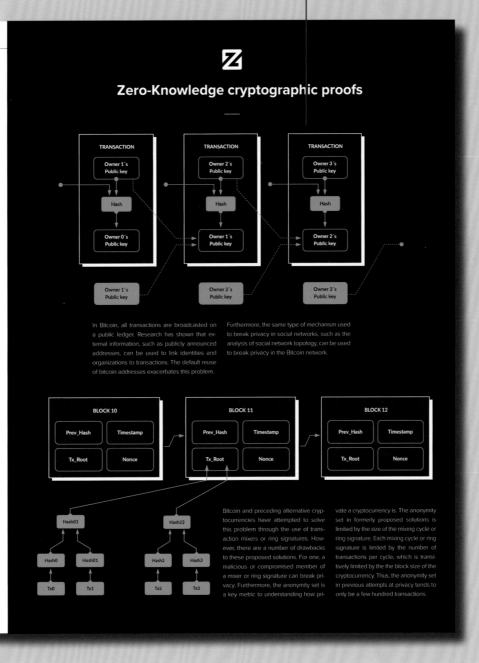

Zero-Knowledge cryptographic proofs

In Bitcoin, all transactions are broadcasted on a public ledger. Research has shown that external information, such as publicly announced addresses, can be used to link identities and organizations to transactions. The default reuse of bitcoin addresses exacerbates this problem.

Furthermore, the same type of mechanism used to break privacy in social networks, such as the analysis of social network topology, can be used to break privacy in the Bitcoin network.

Bitcoin and preceding alternative cryptocurrencies have attempted to solve this problem through the use of transaction mixers or ring signatures. However, there are a number of drawbacks to these proposed solutions. For one, a malicious or compromised member of a mixer or ring signature can break privacy. Furthermore, the anonymity set is a key metric to understanding how private a cryptocurrency is. The anonymity set in formerly proposed solutions is limited by the size of the mixing cycle or ring signature. Each mixing cycle or ring signature is limited by the number of transactions per cycle, which is transitively limited by the the block size of the cryptocurrency. Thus, the anonymity set in previous attempts at privacy tends to only be a few hundred transactions.

BLOCKCHAIN
What it is and why it matters

In the eyes of many within the crypto space, the blockchain is one of the greatest inventions of the 21st century.

Originally created for Bitcoin by Satoshi Nakamoto, the blockchain has evolved so much that there are a rapidly increasing number of uses for this innovative technology. In conjunction with cryptocurrency, the blockchain is seen as having the potential to transform the very way our economy, businesses, and government systems function.

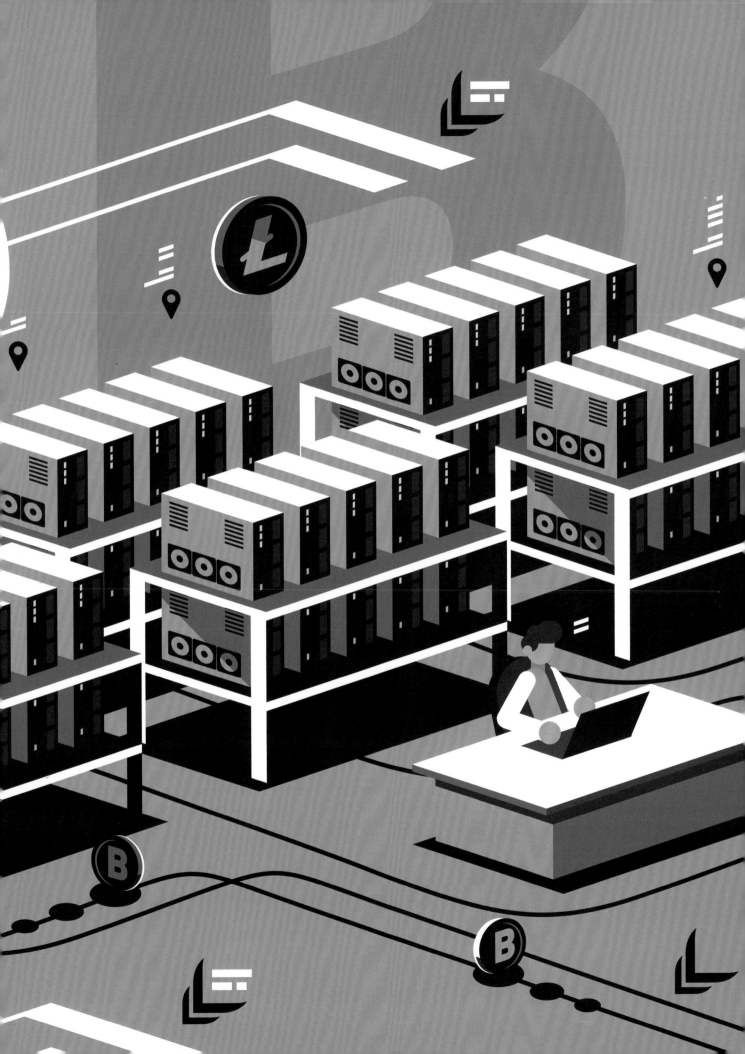

THE FUTURE FOR BITCOIN

Whether you're a bitcoin bull or bear, no one can deny the incredible surge in the cryptocurrency over the past year. Seen as too volatile for some investors and lacking the safeguards afforded to most financial assets, bitcoin remains a contentious issue in the trading world. Yet despite warnings of a speculative bubble, interest in bitcoin shows no sign of abating, as hedge funds step up their investments and other companies attempt to bring cryptos into the mainstream. With strategists and hedge fund managers predicting a further run in bitcoin in the short term at least, what does 2018 hold for its seemingly unstoppable appreciation?

$11,624

value of one bitcoin on December 4, 2017, compared with $752 a year earlier

1,028%

increase in the value of bitcoin against the US dollar in 2017 alone

DIGITAL CURRENCY

IOT

GOVERNANCE

HEALTHCARE

FINANCE

DATA STORAGE

ONLINE VOTING

INSURANCE

HOW DOES
BLOCKCHAIN
WORK

In order to better understand block-chains, it's important to look first at the problems they solve. Why do we have money?

We have it in order to facilitate trade. As societies grew and trade became increasingly long-distance, third-parties such as banks, governments and corporations came about with the original intention of facilitating trade and approving our transactions. This has helped us to ease some of the uncertainty surrounding trade by creating standardized procedures and regulations to ensure that both sides honor an agreement or contract.

Over time, the third-parties we employ to facilitate our trade have migrated online, saving us and themselves time and money. However, where there is money, there is greed. In order for middlemen to carry out this work, we have to pay fees to them. What's more, we have to sacrifice our anonymity, and to some extent our privacy, in order to use their services.

How can we trust that they are acting responsibly with this information?

How can we know that records will not be lost or even tampered with?

 A transaction is requested

 The transaction is broadcasted to a network of nodes

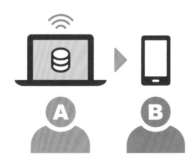

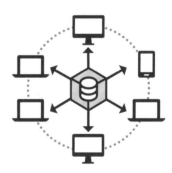

 The transaction is unified with other transactions as a block of data.

 The new block is added to the blockchain in a transparent and unalterable way.

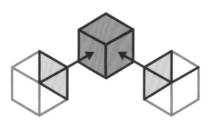

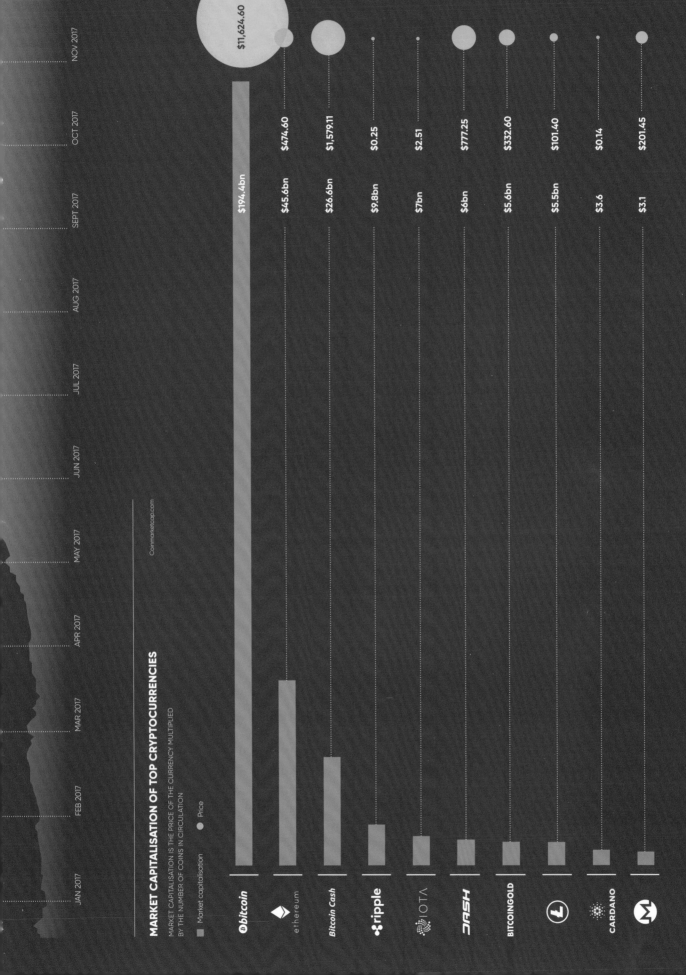

MARKET CAPITALISATION OF TOP CRYPTOCURRENCIES

MARKET CAPITALISATION IS THE PRICE OF THE CURRENCY MULTIPLIED
BY THE NUMBER OF COINS IN CIRCULATION.

■ Market capitalisation ● Price

Coinmarketcap.com

bitcoin — $11,624.60 — $194.4bn

ethereum — $474.60 — $45.6bn

Bitcoin Cash — $1,579.11 — $26.6bn

ripple — $0.25 — $9.8bn

IOTA — $2.51 — $7bn

DASH — $777.25 — $6bn

BITCOINGOLD — $332.60 — $5.6bn

L — $101.40 — $5.5bn

CARDANO — $0.14 — $3.6

M — $201.45 — $3.1

JAN 2017   FEB 2017   MAR 2017   APR 2017   MAY 2017   JUN 2017   JUL 2017   AUG 2017   SEPT 2017   OCT 2017   NOV 2017   DEC 2017

$1,000 $0

RACONTEUR

BITCOIN LEADS THE WAY IN CRYPTOCURRENCY USAGE

PERCENTAGE OF WALLETS, EXCHANGES AND PAYMENT SERVICE PROVIDERS THAT SUPPORT THE FOLLOWING

A	B	C
Bitcoin	Ethereum	Litecoin
98%	**33%**	**26%**

D	E	F
Ripple	Dogecoin	Ethereum Classic
13%	**11%**	**10%**

G	H	I
DASH	Monero	Other
9%	**8%**	**16%**

University of Cambridge/Visa 2017

University of Cambridge/Visa 2017

IN THE PRESS...

People need to start taking this seriously... Within five years, it's going to catch Apple which has a $800-billion market cap

STANDPOINT RESEARCH FOUNDER RONNIE MOAS

Gold has value solely because people say it has value; bitcoin is built on an amazing technology, there's a limited supply of it

HEDGE FUND MANAGER MIKE NOVOGRATZ

Bitcoin remains the greatest form of money mankind has ever seen, and we remain dedicated to protecting and fostering its growth worldwide

COALITION OF BITCOIN DEVELOPERS IN A STATEMENT FOLLOWING THE CANCELLATION OF A SO-CALLED BITCOIN 'FORK' TO CREATE A NEW VERSION OF BITCOIN

Given that number of users haven't exceeded 0.1 per cent of the global population, there's still more potential for this momentum trade to continue. Whether the price will be justified in the foreseeable future depends on the adoption and the application of the new currency, but so far it still looks unstoppable

FXTM CHIEF MARKET STRATEGIST HUSSEIN SAYED

There is a big difference between a digital currency and a traditional currency... Traditional ones are supported by governments that have armies and tax men that can make people follow their rules, and digital ones don't. But that doesn't invalidate digital currencies at all

MAN GROUP CHIEF EXECUTIVE LUKE ELLIS

BITCOIN FUTURES

The CME Group in October announced plans to introduce bitcoin futures, paving the way for the development of the digital currency as a more established asset class, spurring even more interest in recent months. CME Group chairman Terry Duffy explains that because bitcoin is a "new, uncharted market that will continue to evolve", the bitcoin futures contract will be subject to a variety of risk management tools such as an initial margin of 35 per cent and intraday price limits.

CME Group confirms bitcoin futures will be open for trading on December 18

Bitcoin developers and miners cancel an upgrade to the underlying software

CME Group announces plans to launch bitcoin futures pending regulatory review

SURGE CONTINUES FOR BITCOIN

YEAR-TO-DATE RISE IN BITCOIN AS OF DECEMBER 4, 2017

$10,000
$9,000
$8,000
$7,000
$6,000
$5,000
$4,000
$3,000

In reality, it all comes down to trust. With blockchains, we can further ease our uncertainty because it solves many of the problems that arise when dealing with third-parties.

So what is the blockchain?

To put it simply, a blockchain is a public ledger with information that is stored on a network of personal computers. Millions of people use their personal computers to hold bundles of records submitted by others known as blocks.

These blocks are linked to previous blocks, forming what is known as the blockchain.

The blockchain is home to a record of all cryptocurrency transactions which can be accessed by anyone, anywhere.

This means that the blockchain is decentralized and doesn't belong to any one person or entity. Information is distributed, offering greater transparency and reducing the need to trust in any one party. Cryptography

is used to prevent records from being altered. With so many people helping to run it, it's almost impossible for a hacker to take down the network or corrupt it.

On the blockchain, all records of ownership are tracked, ensuring that a coin cannot be spent twice or owned by more than one person. People can do this on their personal computers, earning a small fee in the process. These people are called miners and they also work to create the currency by mining it.

Needless to say, the advantages presented by the blockchain can save a great deal of time and money which is why blockchain technology is increasingly popular. By exploring this book, you'll find out the many ways in which the blockchain is being put to good use.

To put it simply, a blockchain is a public ledger with information that is stored on a network of personal computers. Millions of people use their personal computers to hold bundles of records submitted by others known as blocks. These blocks are linked to previous blocks, forming what is known as the blockchain.

The network validates the transaction using known algorithms

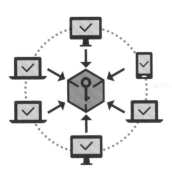

VALIDATION MAY INCLUDE

SMART CONTRACTS

CRYPTOCURRENCY

OTHER RECORDS

The transaction is complete

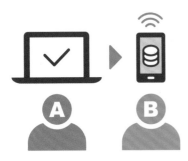

BENEFITS OF THE BLOCKCHAIN

TRANSPARENCY AND TRACKING

SIMPLER AND FASTER

REDUCED COSTS

INCREASED TRUST

2018 STANDARD CATALOG OF
CRYPTOCURRENCIES

"BITCOIN IS A TECHNOLOGICAL TOUR DE FORCE."

BILL GATES, MICROSOFT CO-FOUNDER

Currency Code:
BTC

Launch Date:
2009

Market Cap:
$287,582M.

Max. Supply:
21,000,000 BTC

Circulating Supply:
16,786,978 BTC

Consensus Mechanism:
PoW

Hashing Algorithm:
SHA-256

Block Time:
10 minutes

URL:
bitcoin.org

BITCOIN

The first decentralized digital currency, Bitcoin was founded in 2009 by a person going by the name of Satoshi Nakamoto. Though he has claimed to be a Japanese man born in 1975, his true identity is the source of constant speculation. On August 18, 2008, the website Bitcoin.org was created and in November of the same year, Satoshi Nakamoto first described Bitcoin in an online paper titled Bitcoin: A Peer-to-Peer Electronic Cash System.

History

In January 2009, the first Bitcoin software was released and the Bitcoin network came into existence along with the very first units of Bitcoin. Satoshi Nakamoto collaborated on Bitcoin with other developers until 2010 when he handed over the reigns. Since its inception in 2009, the price of a single Bitcoin has grown from just a few cents to over $13,000 at the time of writing.

One issue that Bitcoin has encountered over the years is conflicting perspectives on how it should develop. This has lead to two hard forks. First, there was the creation of Bitcoin Cash on August 1, 2017, followed shortly after by Bitcoin Gold on October 23. Since then there have been a whole host of other forks, however, Bitcoin has remained the most popular cryptocurrency on the market.

Features

Many of the features of Bitcoin have since been implemented by other cryptocurrencies. In fact, many have improved on Bitcoin in some respects thanks to advances in technology. We've since seen the birth of coins with faster transactions, lower fees, and more economical mining methods. Nevertheless, Bitcoin was the very first cryptocurrency and introduced a number of incredibly important features.

A core component of Bitcoin was the very first distributed blockchain. Seen by many as one of the greatest inventions of the 21st century, the blockchain is a form of public ledger. There you can find a record of all of the Bitcoin transactions and even how much Bitcoin a particular wallet has. Due to this, Bitcoin offers a great deal of transparency, and yet at the same time, there is relative anonymity since no personal information is attached.

In order for a Bitcoin transaction to be successful, it must be confirmed by the network. Miners earn a fee for approving these transactions. As with the blockchain, Bitcoin introduced the concept of mining a digital currency, much like mining for valuable minerals or other materials. By verifying transactions and finding new blocks, miners play a very important role in maintaining the Bitcoin network.

Another essential feature that Bitcoin introduced to cryptocurrency as a whole was the crypto wallet; a safe place to hold or store Bitcoins. The very first wallet for Bitcoin was part of Bitcoin Core, the reference client of Bitcoin. Nowadays there are many types of Bitcoin wallets available including desktop wallets, web wallets, and even brain wallets. This is another example of Bitcoin laying the foundations for cryptocurrency as a whole. ∎

Introduced to the world in 2009, Bitcoin was the very first cryptocurrency. Even today it remains the biggest and most popular cryptocurrency available. Combined with the invention of the blockchain, Bitcoin has paved the way for the many coins found in this book.

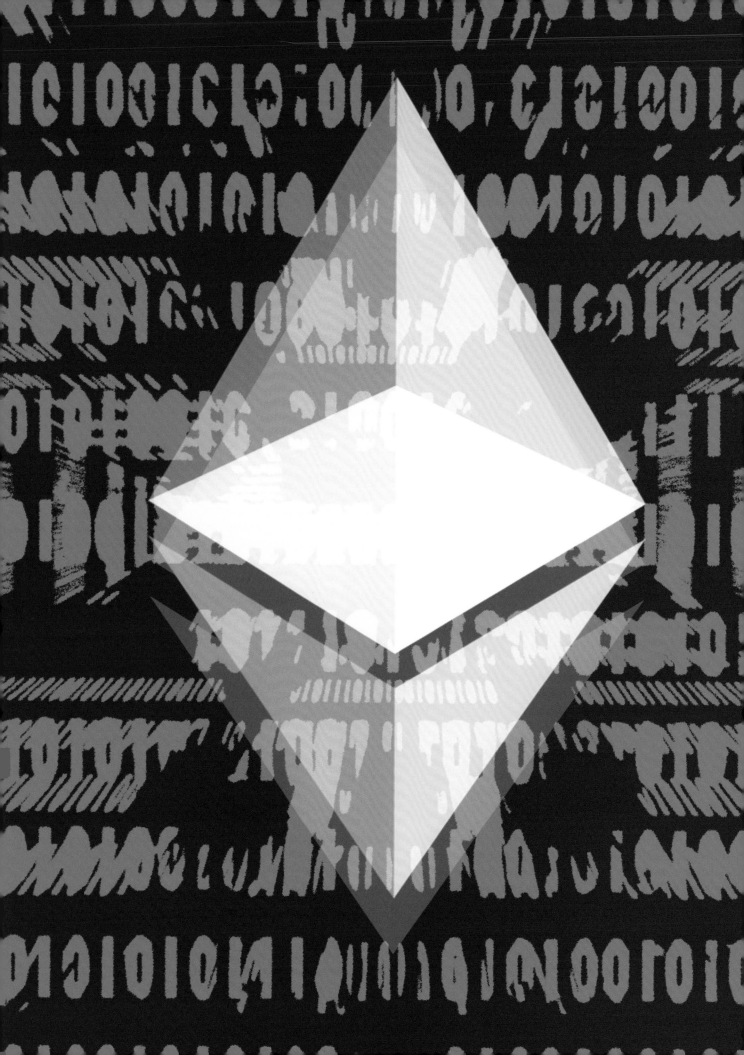

ETHEREUM

Ethereum is a decentralized platform that runs applications known as smart contracts. These apps run on the Ethereum blockchain exactly as programmed, without any downtime, censorship, fraud or third-party interference.

History

Ethereum was created by Vitalik Buterin, a programmer involved with Bitcoin, who in 2013 released a white-paper detailing the design and reasoning behind the Ethereum protocol and smart contracts. A token pre-sale was conducted in July 2014 and raised over $14 million.

In June 2016 Ethereum was split into two groups: Ethereum and Ethereum Classic. The split came after the funding of the DAO project which raised $150 million in Ether (the cryptocurrency of the Ethereum network). Shortly after the fundraising, the DAO was compromised and a valid action in the code was executed to withdraw the funds to an account that was under the control of the attacker. As a result, the Ethereum community took a vote as to whether or not the history of the blockchain should be tampered with to allow the funds to be returned to investors. Out of this vote, Ethereum Classic was born to retain the complete history of the original chain, including the compromise, while Ethereum continued with a modified history, returning the funds to the investors.

By June 2017 Ethereum had briefly crossed the $400 mark after bullish momentum encouraged by an endorsement of Ethereum by the Russian government.

Features

Ethereum's primary function is to enable developers to build and deploy decentralized applications. Ethereum has two main features: smart contracts and the Ethereum Virtual Machine (EVM) that allows for decentralized applications (Dapps) to be created for almost any purpose.

A smart contract is a code that handles the exchange of money, content, property or anything that can be assigned a value. Smart contracts operate by automatically executing when certain parameters are met which are verified by the blockchain. The Ethereum blockchain ensures that the code cannot be interfered or tampered with through censorship, downtime, fraud or third-party manipulation. Smart contracts can be coded in a variety of languages on the Ethereum blockchain which has a much wider scope than other blockchains, allowing for a huge range of applications.

EVM is Turing-complete software running on the Ethereum network. This means that, given the necessary time and memory, it has the ability to execute any algorithm. EVM enables blockchain applications to be created easily and efficiently without the need for an entirely new blockchain for each application. Its purpose is to allow smart contract builders to execute their code before releasing it to the main chain so they can find errors and bugs and learn how to create more powerful and effective smart contracts.

Ethereum can also be used to create Decentralized Autonomous Organizations (DAO). A DAO is run by programming code that is stored within smart contracts on the Ethereum blockchain. DAOs run transparently and independently of human influence and are designed to replace the structure of a traditional organization, removing the need for centralized control. ∎

Currency Code:
ETH

Launch Date:
2013

Market Cap:
$106,276M

Max. Supply:
Unlimited

Circulating Supply:
96,821,923 ETH

Consensus Mechanism:
PoW

Hashing Algorithm:
Ethash

Block Time:
15 seconds avg.

URL:
ethereum.org

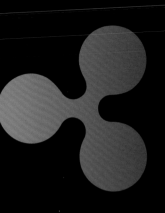

Currency Code:
XRP

Launch Date:
2014

Market Cap:
$123,601M

Max. Supply:
100,000,000,000 XRP

Circulating Supply:
38,739,144,847 XRP

Consensus Mechanism:
RPCA

Hashing Algorithm:
ECDSA

Block Time:
54 seconds

URL:
ripple.com

RIPPLE

Ripple is a digital currency network, real-time gross settlement system (RTGS), and remittance network, that aims to provide cheaper and faster global transactions. It is built upon a distributed open source internet protocol and consensus ledger, however, it has drawn some criticism over the question of centralization.

History

The origins of Ripple trace back to before even Bitcoin was born. In 2004, web developer Ryan Fugger came up with the idea of Ripplepay, which was introduced in 2005. The idea behind it was to have a decentralized monetary system, allowing people to create their own money. Some years later in 2011, this concept was further developed by Jed McCaleb, an American programmer. In this new digital currency system, transactions would be verified by consensus among members of the network. Working in conjunction with Chris Larsen, the two co-founded OpenCoin in 2012. There, they developed a new payment protocol which would enable instant and direct currency transfer between two parties and support all types of currencies. OpenCoin soon introduced a common ledger made up of validating servers. They also introduced their own currency by the name of XRP. This would allow financial institutions to transfer money with significantly lower fees and shorter waiting time. In September 2013, OpenCoin Inc. changed its name to Ripple Labs Inc. This coincided with the release of the Ripple reference server and client as free and open source software.

Ripple aimed to integrate with the existing network of banks. Indeed, Ripple's protocol has been adopted by a number of financial institutions since its introduction in 2013. In early 2014, the online-only Fidor Bank in Munich became the first bank to use Ripple. Since then, many other partnerships have followed, including UBS and Santander.

Features

While many cryptocurrencies have been created for specific purposes, XRP is one of the only digital assets especially designed for financial institutions and payment providers. It does this, in part, by acting as a bridge between fiat and crypto with a network designed to allow the seamless transfer of currency — whether dollars, euros, pounds, yen or Bitcoins.

One of the key features of Ripple is its consensus ledger. This common, shared ledger is a distributed database which holds the information for all of the Ripple accounts. Independent validating servers can belong to anyone, whether a bank or a market maker. They serve to manage the network by comparing transaction records. Essentially, the protocol requires users to rely on trust rather than the proof-of-work of Bitcoin. One of the pros and, at the same time, potential cons of Ripple, is the fact that the currency is unmineable with the full supply of coins already in existence and created by Ripple from its inception. This avoids the polemic unsustainability issues that other proof-of-work platforms suffer from and avoids certain centralization issues due to the consolidation of mining technology into the hands of just a few. Ripple, on the other hand, has already created all of its currency, and much of it, some 55 billion coins, currently sits in an escrow account. This situation leads to the potential for Ripple to stabilize the currency value if needed, by increasing the supply and releasing some of the currency held in escrow, however, it has also led to some questions about centralization and the possible manipulation of the Ripple market by the company themselves. ∎

BITCOIN CASH

A hard fork of Bitcoin, Bitcoin Cash was introduced to address scalability issues. When the Bitcoin community was unable to reach a consensus on raising its maximum limit of 1MB data per block (around 3 transactions per second), Bitcoin Cash was created as a means to implement these changes.

History

In July 2017, the Bitcoin community agreed on the Bitcoin Improvement Proposal (BIP) 91. This proposal sought to activate Segregated Witness (SegWit) for the Bitcoin main chain, but without increasing the block-size limit this was seen as delaying the issue of scalability, not solving it. Bitcoin Cash was announced with an 8MB scalable block-size limit with further research being conducted to reduce increasing fees and long confirmation times.

The hard fork was implemented on August 1, 2017. The transaction history of Bitcoin remained but all future transactions occurred on the new fork and all Bitcoin wallets holding Bitcoin at the time also became owners of Bitcoin Cash.

There have been a number of conspiracies surrounding the creation and development of Bitcoin Cash, one of the most persistent being the accusation against Bitcoin Cash that they are trying to fool people into thinking that they are Bitcoin. One case in point is Bitcoin Cash's use of the Bitcoin.com domain as its main page and the ambiguous use of the term Bitcoin on the site that would lead any crypto novice into thinking that they were on an official Bitcoin site rather than Bitcoin Cash.

There has also been much debate regarding a possible pump and dump scheme involving Chinese miners as well as the attempt by Bitcoin Cash to attack Bitcoin by offering far more attractive mining prospects to miners in order to lure them away from Bitcoin onto the Bitcoin Cash network. There have even been accusations that the people behind Bitcoin Cash caused the recent slow transaction times and expensive fees of Bitcoin by flooding the network with millions of redundant transactions.

Features

Bitcoin Cash features On Chain scalability with a default block-size of 8MB which means the system can be scaled with growth to prevent fee and confirmation issues as transactions increase.

It also features new transaction signatures that provide improved wallet security and replay protection. The development work is also decentralized and is carried out by several independent teams.

A new difficulty adjustment algorithm allows miners to migrate easily from the Bitcoin blockchain while, at the same time, providing protection against hashrate fluctuations.

Bitcoin Cash aims to fulfill the original promise of Bitcoin as "Peer-to-Peer Electronic Cash" by re-introducing low fees and reliable confirmations. ∎

Currency Code:
BCH

Launch Date:
2017

Market Cap:
$48,683M

Max. Supply:
21,000,000 BTC

Circulating Supply:
16,962 BTC

Consensus Mechanism:
PoW

Hashing Algorithm:
SHA-256

Block Time:
10 minutes

URL:
bitcoincash.org

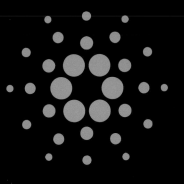

Currency Code:
ADA

Launch Date:
2017

Market Cap:
$26,227M

Max. Supply:
45,000,000,000 ADA

Circulating Supply:
25,927,070,538 ADA

Consensus Mechanism:
PoS

Hashing Algorithm:
Ouroboros

Block Time:
20 seconds

URL:
cardanohub.org

CARDANO

Cardano is an open source, decentralized public blockchain and cryptocurrency project. It is the first blockchain platform to evolve out of a scientific philosophy and to be built on peer-reviewed academic research. Cardano allows for complex programmable transfers of value in a secure and scalable fashion. The project was designed to protect the privacy rights of users, as well as taking into account the needs of regulators.

History

Towards the end of 2014, a group of cryptocurrency enthusiasts, investors and entrepreneurs initiated the Cardano project and approached Input Output HK (IOHK – a cryptocurrency and blockchain engineering company) to design and implement the project. The Cardano Foundation was created to supervise the development of Cardano, as well as represent users of the protocol. Additionally, a third entity known as 'Emurgo' was created to acquire for-profit partnerships on behalf of the Cardano project. IOHK, Cardano Foundation, and Emurgo are all separately owned and led. The project was officially launched on September 29, 2017.

Cardano was written in the Haskell programming language, considered to be one of the most secure programming languages available. Haskell was used to reduce the number of potential errors and to natively add security to the platform, using a technique called 'formal verification' to mathematically prove the correctness of the code.

Cardano did not begin with the traditional approach of a roadmap or a white-paper to outline the steps the project would take during its development. Instead, it adhered to a collection of design principles and engineering best practices to direct the development of the project. IOHK built a library of research papers and surveys, aiming to avoid common pitfalls within the cryptocurrency industry, such as a lack of protocol layering, the ignoring of mainstream cryptographic research when developing blockchain products, and not accommodating for future updates within a platform.

Features

The Cardano project is developed in layers. The value ledger is known as the Cardano Settlement Layer (CSL), the cryptographic proof-of-stake blockchain named 'Ouroboros' and powered by the ADA token. The Cardano team ensured that the protocol was provably secure, a mathematical method of proving the algorithm works as long as at least half of the nodes on the network are not compromised.

Ouroboros is modular and flexible by design, allowing for added functionality such as delegation, sidechains, alternate data structures for lightweight client structures and different forms of random number generation. Ouroboros also supports two sets of scripting languages, allowing for future protocols to be built on top of the layer.

The second layer is known as the Cardano Computation Layer (CCL), where the transactional information in the CSL (the record of movement and the conditions of the transactions) is processed. The CCL also runs Ouroboros, but allows for permissioned and permissionless ledgers, meaning different implementations of the blockchain can be created and managed by users, and developers can build dApps and smart contracts that run independently of the CSL, while meeting the regulatory requirements relevant to the use case. The CCL interacts with the CSL as a reference point, to ensure the integrity of the blockchain. ∎

LITECOIN

Often referred to as the silver to Bitcoin's gold, Litecoin is similar to Bitcoin in many respects. This open source cryptocurrency inspired by Bitcoin has some technical differences and improvements including lower transaction fees and faster payments.

History

The Litecoin network went live in October 2011, just a few days after it was released via an open source client on GitHub. The creator was Charlie Lee, a former Google software engineer. A fork of the Bitcoin Core client, Litecoin offered a number of differences such as decreased block generation time, an increased maximum number of coins and a different hashing algorithm.

In November 2013, cryptocurrency saw a huge spike in investment with many cryptocurrencies reaching all-time highs. Litecoin was no exception as its price surged from just $2 to $50 per coin. This price jump saw Litecoin attain a $1 billion market cap for the first time. Following this, Litecoin's price came back down to just a few dollars and remained there for several years. Not until 2017 did cryptocurrency really begin to take off and this is when Litecoin's price grew from around $4 to almost $90 at its peak.

In May 2017, Litecoin became one of the first cryptocurrencies to adopt Segregated Witness (SegWit), an implemented soft fork change. This is intended to solve the blockchain size limitation problem that has reduced the transaction speed of Bitcoin. In the very same month, Litecoin took part in the very first Lightning Network transaction which is a proposed solution to the scalability problem faced by Bitcoin.

Features

This peer-to-peer currency has a number of features that have set it apart and increased its popularity. In particular, Litecoin aims to be faster and lighter than Bitcoin. Litecoin's blockchain features a 2.5-minute block generation time compared to that of Bitcoin which is 10 minutes. The faster block time of Litecoin means quicker confirmations and transactions as a result. Another advantage of Litecoin is that it has low fees.

The mining of Litecoin features an algorithm called Scrypt which is generally seen as more accessible for new miners since ASICs are not required. This is in stark contrast to Bitcoin which has seen its mining difficulty increase so that CPUs and GPUs can no longer be used to mine it. It is, however, more memory intensive than the processor intensive SHA-256 algorithm used by Bitcoin.

Litecoin's use of the Lightning Network has led it to explore atomic swaps. This would allow for the decentralized exchange of cryptocurrencies without the need for third-party exchanges which charge fees. While this is still a work in progress, there have already been some successful atomic swaps. With such features in the pipeline, it's clear that Litecoin has a clear vision of where it's going and where it wants to be. Much of this is down to the founder Charlie Lee who is very prominent in the cryptocurrency world as well as on the social media scene. ∎

Currency Code:
LTC

Launch Date:
2011

Market Cap:
$16,400M

Max. Supply:
84,000,000 LTC

Circulating Supply:
54,649,548 LTC

Consensus Mechanism:
PoW

Hashing Algorithm:
Scrypt

Block Time:
2.5 minutes

URL:
litecoin.com

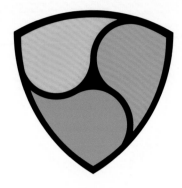

Currency Code:
XEM

Launch Date:
2014

Market Cap:
$15,034M

Max. Supply:
8,999,999,999 XEM

Circulating Supply:
8,999,999,999 XEM

Consensus Mechanism:
PoI (Proof of Importance)

Hashing Algorithm:
Eigentrust++

Block Time:
60 seconds

URL:
nem.io

NEM

NEM is the world's first Smart Asset blockchain. Built from the ground up for enterprise-grade performance, NEM's blockchain technology delivers a platform for management of almost any kind of asset: currencies, supply chains, notarizations, ownership records and more.

History

NEM was designed with the idea of creating a community-oriented crypto-currency from scratch. The NEM projected started in January 2014, with the first Alpha version released in June 2014 and the Beta released in October 2014. During the Alpha stage, there was community pressure to launch the product but the developers refrained, instead taking the time to test the network and build the foundation of NEM.

The stable release of the NEM platform occurred in March 2015. New features to NEM will come via Catapult which has been in development since 2016. Written in C++, it is an enhanced version of NEM designed to increase everything from flexibility and stability to scalability. This in turn is expected to offer better network performance and more enhanced features. The blockchain software of NEM is used in Mijin, a private and commercial blockchain that aims to make banking more secure while reducing the costs of banking institutions, as well as providing scalable blockchain solutions for other enterprise use cases. The developers of NEM are pseudonymous. This is in contrast to the key figures of the NEM foundation whose profiles are public.

NEM Foundation

The NEM.io Foundation is incorporated in Singapore as a company limited by guarantee. The sole purpose of the Foundation is to introduce, educate, and promote the use of the NEM blockchain technology platform on an international scale to all industries and institutions.

The business' ethos is to provide NEM's blockchain technology platform to enhance enterprise whilst being run by the people, for the people. NEM's team provides this through an array of support and education, from training events and service providers to technical support for the ecosystem.

Purpose of the NEM Foundation

NEM Blockchain for Every Industry
The Foundation details the opportunities in every industry to effectively store transaction, customer, and supplier data in a transparent immutable ledger.

NEM Blockchain for Governments
The Foundation is committed to work with Governments to further spread the use of NEM Blockchain Technology.

NEM Blockchain in Academia
The Foundation helps institutions to adopt NEM technology so they can enjoy the benefits of Blockchain technology.

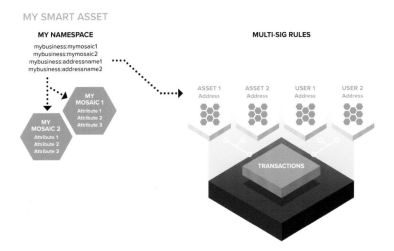

MY SMART ASSET

MY NAMESPACE

mybusiness:mymosaic1
mybusiness:mymosaic2
mybusiness:addressname1
mybusiness:addressname2

MULTI-SIG RULES

MY MOSAIC 1
Attribute 1
Attribute 2
Attribute 3

MY MOSAIC 2
Attribute 1
Attribute 2
Attribute 3

ASSET 1 Address

ASSET 2 Address

USER 1 Address

USER 2 Address

TRANSACTIONS

NEM Blockchain Architecture

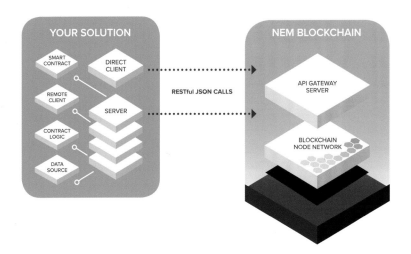

The NEM blockchain platform is built from a network of nodes, all running NEM's core node server software. In summary, these nodes provide a powerful, easy-to-use, stable, and secure platform where Smart Assets transactions are conducted, searched, and immutably logged to the blockchain ledger.

Features & Smart Asset System

NEM is built around a powerful system for customizing your use of the blockchain. We call it the "Smart Asset System", and it gives you the power to use NEM as if it were a custom blockchain built for your application and your assets. Rather than force you to write your own "smart contract" code from scratch or use off-blockchain methods of defining custom assets for your business, NEM gives you direct API access to a specialized set of tested and secure on-blockchain features.

Accounts

NEM Addresses are container assets on the blockchain that can represent a single object that must be unique and updatable. Addresses contain Mosaics. An Address could represent things like: a package to be shipped, a deed to a house, or a document to be notarized. Address assets become truly smart when configured with special rules – directly on the NEM blockchain – that define how they relate and control each other, as well as how their contents can be can be updated and transferred. One crucial rule type is multi-signatory control (often called "Multisig") that allows ownership of Address assets to be shared in a variety of ways between multiple parties, all on the blockchain.

Mosaics

Mosaics are part of what make the Smart Asset System unique and flexible. Mosaics are fixed assets on the NEM blockchain that can represent a set of multiple identical things that do not change. A Mosaic could be as simple as a token, but it could also represent a set of more specialized assets like: reward points, shares of stock, signatures, status flags, votes or even other currencies. Each Mosaic is defined by a variety of attributes such as name, description, quantity, divisibility, transferability and more.

Namespaces

Namespaces let you create a unique place for your business and your assets on the NEM blockchain. A Namespace starts with a unique name that you choose, similar to an internet domain name. You then have the ability to define your own subdomains, as well as names for your assets. This makes your assets unique, easy to use, and trustable.

Messages

NEM blockchain allows for transactions to include encrypted or plain messages.

Transactions

Transactions are how your Smart Assets are put into action. Transactions let you transfer Mosaics between Addresses, transfer or configure ownership of Addresses (including use of Multisig rules), send messages and more. NEMs blockchain includes a built-in consensus-driven timekeeping facility, so transactions are automatically and accurately time stamped.

The Blockchain Node Network

Each NEM node works with other nodes to build the peer-to-peer blockchain network. In sum, this network creates and supports the blockchain itself. The NEM node software verifies transactions, maintains a database, synchronizes with other nodes, and maintains stability and trustworthiness to create a network that is fast, secure, and scalable. Some of its distinguishing features include:

Proof of Importance (PoI)

NEM's consensus is built on a unique Proof of Importance algorithm, using a technique similar to Google's PageRank to prevent a variety of attacks on the trustworthiness of blockchain transactions. It serves the same purpose as typical Proof of Work (PoW) mechanisms used by Bitcoin and others, but is much more scalable and energy efficient. This allows nodes to run on almost any hardware while still providing an absolutely secure network that can scale without limit.

Eigentrust++

NEM implements a modified version of the Eigentrust++ algorithm that allows nodes to intelligently judge the "reputation" of other nodes and reject bad actors, as well as optimally balance loading across the network.

Spam protection

NEM nodes implement a built-in spam filter that prevents the network from being swamped by a flood of transactions, automatically ensuring throughput while not rejecting good transactions.

P2P time synchronisation

In order to be independent from any outside entity (like NTP) for time synchronization, NEM makes use of a custom time synchronisation protocol. This protocol ensures nodes are continuously synchronizing and thus achieve network time consensus. This warrants reliable timestamps, which is vital in blockchain technology.

Network Incentivization via Harvesting

Scaling of the public blockchain is self-incentivized by "harvesting". Anyone may create a public node, adding capacity to the network. That added capacity is rewarded by the node's ability to harvest the fees associated with any transaction they happen to process. Any given node's likelihood of harvesting is scaled by its accounts PoI "importance" score, not the amount of processing horsepower it has. User accounts can also participate in harvesting without setting up a node using "delegated harvesting".

Each node provides the API gateway that applications may use to access the blockchain and its features. This means that your application does not need to run any complex node software; all usage functionality is available through the API interface on each node in the network itself. This means that the blockchain can be used to create a variety of solution architectures with light-weight code in any language.

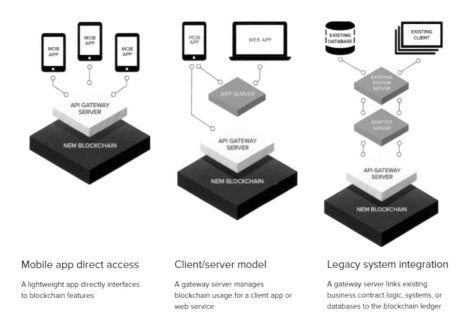

Mobile app direct access	Client/server model	Legacy system integration
A lightweight app directly interfaces to blockchain features	A gateway server manages blockchain usage for a client app or web service	A gateway server links existing business contract logic, systems, or databases to the blockchain ledger

BENEFITS OF XEM

XEM is the native currency of the NEM public blockchain. It is used to pay for transactions on this public blockchain in order to incentivize its network of public nodes that process and record transactions for businesses and users there. This means that XEM has real fundamental value as the currency of a functioning economy.

- **Perfect for storing value** - it has Zero Inflation
- **Scalable** - featuring High TPS
- **Harvestable** - making it a great passive income stream
- **Efficient** - with negligible electricity and hardware costs
- **Fair** - all coins are distributed equally
- **High demand** - for its business usage

Currency Code:
XLM

Launch Date:
2014

Market Cap:
$12,666M

Max. Supply:
N/A

Circulating Supply:
17,877,823,816 XLM

Consensus Mechanism:
SCP

Hashing Algorithm:
N/A

Block Time:
3.5 seconds

URL:
stellar.org

STELLAR LUMENS

Stellar Lumens is a native digital currency of the Stellar payment network, a network that facilitates money transfer around the world in a fast and secure manner with nearly zero fees. Based on blockchain technology and the proof-of-stake (PoS) algorithm, the network offers an open source, distributed platform that links users, payment systems, and banks. The network mainly focuses on the developing world.

History
The Stellar network was launched in 2014 by Jed McCaleb (founder of Ripple and Mt. Gox) and Joyce Kim with 100 billion Stellars – the original name of the network's digital currency. The network was initially based on the Ripple protocol, and following numerous modifications to critical consensus code, the network forked. One of the co-founders, Joyce Kim, attributed the event to flaws in the Ripple protocol, though Ripple refuted the claims. In 2015, the Stellar Foundation launched an upgraded network based on an entirely new consensus algorithm.

With the launch of the upgraded network, the name of the currency changed from Stellar to Lumen, a change intended to distinguish the currency from the Stellar network itself and Stellar.org, the nonprofit organization that funds the development of the network.

In recent months, the network has attracted partnerships from big names such as IBM and Stripe. With a market capitalization of approximately $8.5 billion as of February 1, 2018, Stellar Lumens has grown to be one of the most valuable digital currencies. In the past year, the currency has grown by 29,400%, making it one of the fastest growing altcoins.

Features
Stellar's inbuilt currency is based on blockchain technology and offers virtually all the features of a shared, distributed public ledger. Targeting individuals and enterprises, the platform facilitates low-cost money transfers across the globe between currencies in a manner almost similar to Ripple. Transactions on the network take 2 to 5 seconds on average.

Lumen serves two purposes. First, the currency has an anti-spam feature. Users on the network are charged a near zero fee of 0.00001 XLM for each transaction which acts as a protection against denial-of-service (DoS) attacks. In other words, Lumens function as security tokens that mitigate DoS attacks aimed at generating multiple transactions or consuming huge space in the ledger. Additionally, users are required to retain at least 20 XLM at any given time so as to guarantee account authenticity and ensure seamless transactions within the network.

Lumens also facilitates multi-currency transactions. The currency sometimes serves as a bridge between pairs of currencies between which a large direct market does not exist. This is only possible if there is a liquid market between the XLM and other currencies involved.

Stellar Lumens has the potential to revolutionize cross-border payments which can take days to clear through other channels. This long clearance time could soon be a thing of the past with companies like IBM partnering with the Stellar network and the currency could change how money is transferred across the globe, enhancing global transactions and fostering financial inclusion in developing countries. ∎

IOTA

IOTA is a new proof-of-work cryptocoin that facilitates machine-to-machine transactions without fees. Unlike most other cryptocurrencies, IOTA is not based on blockchain technology and operates on a system called Tangle, a blockless and scalable ledger. Since 2009, blockchain has been viewed by many as the ultimate step in revolutionizing financial transactions, but the arrival of IOTA into the cryptocurrency world has demonstrated that there are many more possible technologies to explore.

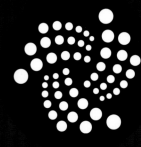

History

IOTA was created in 2015 by four German-based computer scientists. The first crowdfunding initiative raised over 1,300 coins. On June 13, 2017, IOTA launched its ICO on Bitfinex, and in the same year, SatoshiPay, a company that processes micro and nano transactions, abandoned Bitcoin in favor of IOTA, due to Bitcoin's rising transaction costs, raising IOTA's reputation and profile. IOTA also partnered with Refugees United (REFUNITE), a non-profit organization that unites refugees and missing persons with their loved ones, to incorporate IOTA technology into REFUNITE's operations.

Since 2017, several firms have embraced IOTA, including Microsoft, Samsung, CISCO, Volkswagen, and Huawei. As of January 31, 2018, IOTA was trading at about $2.33 per coin, with a market capitalization in excess of $6 billion, making IOTA one of the most valuable altcoins on the market.

Features

IOTA is capable of handling a large number of transactions per second with zero fees while simultaneously offering a stable infrastructure that involves no blocks or mining processes. Another distinction is the handling of consensus - while consensus is achieved via a competitive system on traditional blockchain platforms, IOTA allows all users to participate in consensus, creating a decentralized, self-regulating peer-to-peer network.

The key innovation that powers IOTA is the Tangle – a decentralized, scalable, and lightweight ledger platform that facilitates micro and nano transactions with zero fees. The potential for this system is enormous if it manages to reach widespread adoption, and the project is aimed at business-to-business (B2B) enterprises for this reason, ambitiously seeking to be the underlying protocol for the Internet of Things (IoT).

IOTA's masked messaging feature (MAM) enables nodes to communicate via the Tangle in a highly encrypted manner, allowing devices to exchange sensitive data with quantum-proof security. Similar to a radio, MAM enables multiple entities to share data by simply tuning in to their frequency.

Whereas IOTA is uniquely designed for the Internet of Things, the Tangle architecture can support other uses that require secure data transmission such as electronic voting. The application of IOTA in such areas is already being explored by many firms and scholars. With the advent of the Internet of Things, the significance of interoperability and resource sharing cannot be overemphasized. IOTA empowers businesses to explore new models by turning every technology into a service that can be traded in the open market on a real-time basis, without transaction fees - a worthwhile feature in the era of decentralized apps and the sharing economy. Many technological resources, from computer storage and computational power to WiFi bandwidth, drones, and appliances, remain idle or underutilized for most of the time. Through IOTA, companies and individuals can turn these resources into leasing services that work and earn money when not otherwise in use. ∎

Currency Code:
MIOTA

Launch Date:
2014

Market Cap:
$11,144M

Max. Supply:
2,779,530,283 MIOTA

Circulating Supply:
2,779,530,283 MIOTA

Consensus Mechanism:
DAG

Hashing Algorithm:
SHA-3

Block Time:
N/A

URL:
iota.org

Dash is Digital Cash.

A Self Governing, Self Funding Protocol.

DASH

A privacy-centric digital currency based on the Bitcoin software, Dash utilizes a second network tier of 'Masternodes' for additional functionality. Dash's mission is to deliver safe and reliable financial solutions to consumers and merchants in a decentralized manner and to provide a user-friendly and scalable, payment-focused currency.

History
Dash was initially released by Evan Duffield under the name 'XCoin' on January 18, 2014, with no pre-mine. On February 28, 2014, the cryptocurrency was renamed 'DarkCoin' and found increased popularity due to its anonymous payment technology. 'DarkCoin' was then changed to 'Dash' on March 28, 2014, in an effort to promote the cryptocurrency beyond the darknet.

An 'instamine' error in the code shortly after the launch meant that almost a quarter of the supply of Dash was mined instantly. Duffield attempted to re-launch Dash without the error but the community disapproved of it. A suggested airdrop of coins to increase distribution was also dismissed by the community, so development was continued with the erroneous coin distribution left in place.

In November 2017, an update to the Dash Core software introduced a new 2MB block size, with the actual implementation of the change occurring in December after miners and masternodes had upgraded. Duffield announced a plan to scale the currency using larger blocks, as opposed to off-chain scaling solutions, in an effort to keep all transactional data on the Dash blockchain. The plan would see scaling increase to a 45MB block size, allowing the network to handle up to 50 million users.

Features
Dash runs on an incentivized network of nodes and 'Masternodes'; a system pioneered by Dash. Anyone can run a node and support the network but a wallet with 1000 Dash or more can become a 'Masternode', that helps run Dash functions such as InstantSend and PrivateSend. They may also participate in the DAO (Decentralized Autonomous Organization) of Dash.

The DAO functions irrespective of outside control and decision-making is decentralized. This means that anyone can participate and make decisions within the framework of rules set out by the community. The Dash Treasury organizes monthly budget proposals that can be voted on by 'Masternodes' to produce value for Dash. This decentralized governance has facilitated quick decision-making for the project.

Dash features InstantSend technology, an innovation that allows Dash to be used in point-of-sale operations with payments being sent in approximately 1 second without being exposed to double-spending. Another Dash innovation, PrivateSend allows users to erase the history of received coins and therefore retain anonymity for their transactions.

This occurs by breaking down user transaction inputs into denominations of DASH, followed by a request being sent to a masternode to assist with input mixing. The transactional inputs of two other users are mixed by the masternode and sent back to their original users, with the new transactional history applied. ∎

Currency Code:
DASH

Launch Date:
2014

Market Cap:
$10,415M

Max. Supply:
18,900,000 DASH

Circulating Supply:
7,803,133 DASH

Consensus Mechanism:
PoSe (Proof of Service)

Hashing Algorithm:
X11

Block Time:
2.5 minutes avg.

URL:
dash.org

Currency Code:
XMR

Launch Date:
2014

Market Cap:
$7,417M

Max. Supply:
18,400,000 XMR

Circulating Supply:
15,572,528 XMR

Consensus Mechanism:
PoW

Hashing Algorithm:
CryptoNight

Block Time:
112 seconds avg.

URL:
monero.cc

MONERO

Monero is an open source and privacy-oriented cryptocurrency based on the CryptoNote protocol. One of the most popular privacy coins in the cryptocurrency market, it has a number of features that make it secure, private and untraceable.

History
Monero was announced to the public in April 2014 but in order to understand just how it came to be, we need to look at Bytecoin which was founded 2 years earlier in July 2012. In 2014, as Bytecoin continued to grow and interest gathered, reports began circulating that there had been a large pre-mine prior to its release to the public. This caused considerable disappointment with its users who desired a new and fairer distribution of the cryptocurrency.

Events led to a community member developing a fork of the CryptoNote blockchain. Assisted by others within the community, development work began and the result was BitMonero. However, the original BitMonero developer came under fire for poor communication and a lack of flexibility on key issues such as block time. Doubt set in as to whether BitMonero would be capable of succeeding Bytecoin under its current direction. This led to the community deciding on another hard fork and thus Monero was born.

Since its inception in 2014, Monero has grown steadily, with particularly large growth in market cap and transaction volume in 2017. This was helped by the introduction of privacy features such as the adoption of the Confidential Transactions algorithm in January 2017 and an improved version of Ring Signatures.

Features
Like other cryptocurrencies, Monero's transactions are securely recorded on the blockchain. The difference is that while others offer transparency, Monero focuses on protecting privacy. As such, transactions are always private for both the sender and recipient.

The sender's identity is protected through the use of ring signatures. When a transaction is sent, the sender's address is mixed with a group of other addresses, making it much more difficult to establish a link. This ensures that transaction outputs are untraceable, protecting the sender's identity and privacy. In terms of the recipient of a transaction, their identity is protected through the use of a stealth address. This is automatically generated and recorded as part of the transaction and serves to hide the receiving address.

Another advantage of Monero in terms of privacy is that it is fungible. This means that any single Monero can be substituted like for like with another. This is not the case with most other cryptocurrencies where everyone can see the various transactions and their trails within the blockchain. Because all data and transactions are private, the history of a particular Monero coin cannot be traced.

As Monero is based on the CryptoNote system, it uses a hashing algorithm called CryptoNight. CryptoNight was designed to offer a cryptocurrency system that was fairer; limiting the effect of mining pools and allowing for a more even distribution of the currency. So while Monero isn't ASIC-resistant, the cost of manufacturing ASICs for the currency would be so high that doing so would simply not be worth it. ∎

QTUM

A relatively new cryptocurrency, Qtum joined the crypto space in June 2017. Founded in China, and with a large team based all around the world, it has gained a considerable amount of interest from investors. The development of Qtum has become known for its transparency, with users updated with frequent posts on Facebook and Twitter, as well as many of the Chinese social media platforms, including a collaboration with Cfun.

History
After the ICO took place in April of 2017, 100 million tokens were made. 51% of these tokens were available to the public for purchasing, while the remaining 49% were distributed internally. In late November 2017, tokens were trading at $15.44 and a market capitalization of 1.14 billion dollars was achieved.

Features
Qtum is an open source technology which means that anyone can contribute to making advancements and optimizations throughout the network.

For the 49% of the tokens that have been allocated internally, 20% of the tokens are held by the founders, investors, and developers and the remaining 29% are reserved for the operational costs of the Qtum foundation with the intention that these funds will be distributed over the next 4 years. This includes; academic research, education, and marketing.

Highly influenced by both Bitcoin and Ethereum, Qtum can be considered to be a hybrid of the two, taking the best of both and combining them.

Qtum uses Bitcoin's blockchain technology coupled with intelligent and convenient smart contracts, generated by virtual machines. Their smart contracts have the capacity to provide users with terms and conditions that can be set between individuals to allocate payments in sophisticated ways – for example, a smart contract can pay an individual for every hour of work completed.

The smart contracts include formally verifiable translations of human-readable agreements to machine their smart contracts. As well as this, there are error-resilient specifications of their elements, terms, and conditions. Smart contracts can be created from mobile devices which makes this token incredibly user-friendly. This is an important feature since half of the internet's traffic is being generated by smartphones and tablets.

In preparation for mainstream adoption, the team has released a mobile-friendly wallet, allowing for the Qtum blockchain to be a part of everyday life transactions.

Qtum has the potential to become the biggest player in China's cryptocurrency world. With a strong presence on Chinese social media and a relatively low amount of competition with other cryptocurrencies due to the Chinese ICO ban, Qtum looks very promising. ∎

Currency Code:
QTUM

Launch Date:
2017

Market Cap:
$6,948M

Max. Supply:
100,000,000 QTUM

Circulating Supply:
73,789,331 QTUM

Consensus Mechanism:
PoS

Hashing Algorithm:
SHA-256

Block Time:
128 seconds

URL:
qtum.org

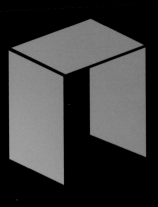

Currency Code:
XLM

Launch Date:
2014

Market Cap:
$6,809M

Max. Supply:
100,000,000 NEO

Circulating Supply:
65,000,000 NEO

Consensus Mechanism:
dBFT

Hashing Algorithm:
Scrypt

Block Time:
24 seconds

URL:
neo.org

NEO

A non-profit, community-based, smart economy platform, NEO uses block-chain technology and digital identities to digitize assets, and uses smart contracts for digital assets to be self-managed. NEO aims to make use of original technologies to create an infrastructure for the future economy.

History
NEO was created in 2014 by Onchain, a company based in Shanghai, China, that provides blockchain-based financial services. Da Hongfei, CEO of NEO and Onchain, maintains a distinction between the two entities. Onchain is financially backed by the Fosun group, a large financial entity in China while NEO is non-profit and community-supported. Originally named Antshares, NEO raised over $4.5 million during its fully-refundable ICO, the first of its kind.

In June 2017, Antshares completed the rebranding of the product in an effort to break into the global market and renamed the project 'NEO', inspired by the Greek word meaning newness, novelty, and youth. The rebranding was scheduled for the end of 2017, but the process was expedited due to securing a partnership with Chinese certificate authorities to develop Smart Contracts 2.0.

NEO's development is handled by two teams: the Shanghai development and management team, and the international community team known as 'City of Zion'. City of Zion is independent from the NEO core development team and produces products (such as the NEON wallet and NEOSCAN block explorer) and document translations for NEO.

Features
NEO utilizes three key concepts to construct their 'smart economy': Digital Assets, Digital Identity, and Smart Contracts. Digital assets are programmable assets that exist in the form of electronic data. When this data is stored on the blockchain, it becomes immutable, traceable and highly transparent. NEO allows for the trading of these assets on their platform, with assets registered on the blockchain protected by law. NEO features two forms of digital assets: global assets and contract assets. Global assets can be identified by all smart contracts and clients on the platform, while contract assets are stored privately within smart contracts and can only be accessed by compatible clients.

NEO handles digital identities with the PKI (Public Key Infrastructure) X.509 standard, the most widely accepted digital certificate issuance model. NEO will be compatible with facial, fingerprint, voice, SMS and other multi-factor authentication methods.

NEO Smart Contract 2.0 is the framework for developers to deliver smart contracts on the NEO platform. Contracts can be written in almost any high-level programming language, such as C#, VB.Net, F#, Java, and Kotlin. The NEO Virtual Machine (NeoVM) is a lightweight contract execution environment for smart contracts, closely resembling JVM and .NET Runtime environments. Additionally, the InteropService increases the utility of smart contracts, allowing them to access data outside the NeoVM, without compromising the stability of the NEO ecosystem. Increased scalability is possible as the smart contract is executed inside the NeoVM and communicates to the outside through an interactive service layer. The majority of upgrades to the smart contract can be achieved through the API of this layer. ∎

LISK

Lisk is a decentralized network, incorporating a cryptocurrency, a framework for users to build sidechains and develop their own blockchain applications, a unified blockchain service platform, a directory for applications, and a decentralized delegate marketplace, powered by a delegated proof-of-stake algorithm.

History

Lisk was created by two developers from the Crypti project and began as a fork from the Crypti blockchain. The developers announced their departure from Crypti, dissatisfied with the lack of progress within the project and with a desire to make the project open and public.

The team decided to use Javascript as the programming language due to its widespread usage, and larger companies such as Google and Microsoft actively developing its speed and security across a range of devices. In February 2016, an ICO was held to decide the initial distribution of LSK and to raise development funds. At the time Lisk was the second most crowdfunded ICO behind Ethereum. In May 2016, the Lisk main network went live and the LSK token became available for trading on major exchanges. By the end of 2016, community members began submitting proposals to become delegates on the network (the nodes responsible for forging new blocks and earning rewards).

In November 2017, the Lisk project partnered with design and brand strategy agencies in an effort to connect users from a variety of backgrounds and announced a rebranding to occur in early 2018.

Features

The Lisk App SDK is a framework for users to create sidechains for applications to be developed on. The sidechains are customizable, allowing for all specifications and parameters to be designated by the creator. The sidechains can use the Lisk native token (LSK) for transactions, or assign a custom token to the chain. Applications or services are then developed on top of the sidechain, which attaches to the Lisk mainchain.

Applications consist of four parts within the SDK framework: the consensus algorithm (the default being DPoS), sidechains (the immutable database), back-end (the application logic) and the front end (the application user interface). Applications are coded in Javascript, therefore there are a wide range of applications able to be developed that make use of the Lisk consensus protocol and networking algorithm. The decentralized application directory built into the Lisk platform allows users to search for applications that have registered on the main chain.

Lisk allows for the development of blockchain services; single-purpose applications that increase the functionality of the entire Lisk platform. As sidechains are attached to the main chain, existing services can be leveraged by other developers, enabling developers to focus on their core design and simultaneously expand the network and utilize the work of other sidechains. This results in an expanding ecosystem that promotes itself and provides an increasingly secure environment for developers.

The delegate marketplace allows application developers seeking to use the DPoS consensus method to rent a delegate for a recurring fee. If an application developer requires the API from another blockchain, delegates can promote their support for the third party application (e.g. Bitcoin blockchain) and provide developers instant access to the relevant data. ∎

Currency Code:
LSK

Launch Date:
2016

Market Cap:
$4,058M

Max. Supply:
Unlimited

Circulating Supply:
116,739,772 LSK

Consensus Mechanism:
DPoS

Hashing Algorithm:
DPoS

Block Time:
10 seconds

URL:
lisk.io

Currency Code:
ETC

Launch Date:
2016

Market Cap:
$3,986M

Max. Supply:
Unlimited

Circulating Supply:
99,947,153 ETC

Consensus Mechanism:
PoW

Hashing Algorithm:
Ethash

Block Time:
15 seconds avg.

URL:
ethereumclassic.github.io

ETHEREUM CLASSIC

Forked from Ethereum in 2016, Ethereum Classic is a public, open source blockchain-based, distributed computing platform. One of its key features inherited from its parent blockchain is the ability to create smart contracts.

History
Ethereum was conceived in 2013 after a failure to implement scripting language in Bitcoin, and the first tokens were sold in 2014. In 2015 an experimental release of the Ethereum distributed computing platform was released. In 2016, the decentralized autonomous organization which crowdfunded the project through smart contracts on the Ethereum network was hacked, which resulted in a soft fork (and the creation of Ethereum Classic) so that the community could recover the stolen coins.

Features
The main feature of Ethereum Classic is the Ethereum Virtual Machine and its ability to perform smart contracts. The Ethereum Virtual Machine is a distributed computing platform, which is able to run code through its network. Users are able to code smart contracts and upload them to the blockchain, to be stored and executed on the network.

Smart contracts are a way for contracts to be programmed into the blockchain and are based on if/then logic. An example of smart contract use is for crowdfunding startups. A smart contract could be programmed to hold coins in a wallet for a certain period of time - if the crowdfunding goal is reached, then the coins are released to the start-up and they would be successfully funded. However, if the time limit for the crowdfunding is reached and the wallet hasn't reached the crowdfunding goal, the smart contract can reverse the transactions and return the coins back to the funders. Another application for smart contracts is to secure a voting system. Smart contracts can determine the prerequisites needed (for example a unique registered ID) before a person can vote, and once votes are placed and registered on the blockchain, they can not be changed. It would be easy to verify the results and the validity of the data, and no authority would be able to change the results unless consented by a majority of the network (eg. a fork).

The Ethereum Classic community has strong beliefs regarding the use of the blockchain. They believe that the network should be decentralized and immutable, meaning that no authority is able to dictate the development or control the network that Ethereum Classic operates on. Therefore, the coin is developed publicly and any changes to the network require community agreement.

Ethereum Classic's philosophy of immutability was the basis for the disagreement of the soft fork, as the Ethereum Classic community believed that once a transaction had been written on the blockchain, it should be final. The idea behind this philosophy is that 'code is law'. Once a smart contract has been uploaded to the blockchain, the results should be completely determined by the terms of the contract and should not be able to be reversed. This emphasizes the importance of contracts and the finality of agreements, and it prevents parties from being disadvantaged through human error or failure to fulfill the agreement. ■

NANO

Nano is a minerless cryptocurrency with no transaction fee that works upon a unique development of the blockchain known as a 'block lattice'. With improved latency, a novel scalability solution, energy efficiency, and true decentralization, Nano aims to deliver on what most altcoins have failed to adequately achieve. In the teams own words: "Nano is designed to be a scalable, instant transactions and zero fees by design cryptocurrency."

History
Nano started out as RaiBlocks and is the brainchild of Colin LeMahieu who wrote the first RaiBlocks paper in December 2014 and began the beta implementation shortly afterward.

In October 2017, RaiBlocks' captcha-based faucet distribution system came to an end after 2 years. November saw the QR Code standardized, the desktop wallet updated and the alpha test of the mobile wallet.

In January 2018, Raiblocks announced its name change and rebranding to Nano. According to the Core Team, they wanted *"a name that represented the simplicity and speed of the project, and Nano does just that."*

Features
Perhaps the most notable thing about Nano is its block lattice structure which means that each account has its own blockchain, with each block containing a single transaction. This personal blockchain cannot be changed by anyone else and is controlled by the account's private key. When funds are sent, two blocks are created: one send block on the sender's personal blockchain and one receive block on the receiver's blockchain. The receiver then 'pockets' any outstanding funds by signing the receive block with their own private key so that the transaction may be added to their personal blockchain.

Effectively, the only thing needed for a successful transaction is the user's cryptographic signature on the send and receive blocks. When the node syncs, it scans through the ledger to ensure that the signatures are authentic and the transaction is confirmed. In order to avoid double spend attacks and conflicting transactions, the confirmation system uses 'representatives' which are special nodes in the system, always online and run by trusted individuals, that act as voting proxies for each account. In these cases, a so-called 'balance-weighted vote' is used to reach consensus - the weight of a representative's vote depending on how many XRB are linked to it.

Seeing as each Nano account maintains its own blockchain, there is no need for miners to verify transactions in the system. As well as doing away with the tendency towards mining becoming centralized over time, this also solves the highly polemic energy concerns that have been plaguing the likes of Bitcoin and others in recent months. It also means that the system is safe from mining attacks and allows for truly feeless transactions no matter what volume of transactions are being made.

The Nano team motto is *"doing one thing and doing it well"*, and considering the fact that they have managed to develop a trustless, low-latency, infinitely scalable cryptocurrency with no fees and instantaneous, secure transactions, it would only be fair to conclude that, at least until now, they have managed to live up to it. ∎

Currency Code:
XRB

Launch Date:
2014

Market Cap:
$3,738M

Max. Supply:
133,248,290 XRB

Circulating Supply:
133,248,289 XRB

Consensus Mechanism:
PoW / PoS

Hashing Algorithm:
Scrypt

Block Time:
Instant

URL:
nano.org

Currency Code:
BCN

Launch Date:
2014

Market Cap:
$2,942M

Max. Supply:
184,470,000,000 BCN

Circulating Supply:
183,253,534,612 BCN

Consensus Mechanism:
PoW

Hashing Algorithm:
CryptoNight

Block Time:
2 minutes

URL:
bytecoin.org

BYTECOIN

A privacy-focused cryptocurrency with open source development and decentralized governance, Bytecoin is the first cryptocurrency to be based on the popular CryptoNote algorithm and provides smoothed block rewards, difficulty adjustments, and ASIC resistance to encourage the participation of network users.

History
Launched in July 2012, Bytecoin was the first cryptocurrency designed to be used by the CryptoNote algorithm, providing complete anonymity for its users and paving the way for other anonymity-based currencies. Since its inception, over 20 different cryptocurrencies have been created as a fork from Bytecoin, the most notable being Monero.

Bytecoin had a turbulent inauguration with accusations of an unannounced premine of around 80% of the coin supply and a forged whitepaper to make it appear that it was a fair release with every miner allowed access at the same time. A lack of development and further issues causing unfair mining led to Bytecoin experiencing stagnant growth until 2017, when it received a resurgence in popularity.

In 2017, Bytecoin began a proof of concept aimed at bringing untraceable tokens to the platform in preparation for the increase in ICOs that are expected in 2018. The intended updates require multiple changes to the Bytecoin core, with a beta version to be released at the beginning of 2018.

Some of Bytecoin's blockchain contains extra information that is not directly related to money transfers such as the geographical coordinates of universities as well as quotes from several authors, such as science fiction writer, William Gibson.

Features
Bytecoin's CryptoNote PoW algorithm differs from other cryptocurrencies by taking advantage of CPU architecture, making it relatively more efficient to mine with a CPU instead of a GPU. This allows for a wider range of devices to participate in mining the currency and supporting the network.

Bytecoin makes use of ring signature technology to ensure anonymity. This process uses multiple public keys for a transaction but prevents the individual making the transaction from being identified. In addition to using multiple public keys, Bytecoin makes use of one-time addresses so transaction histories of public addresses are hidden.

The network is almost instantaneous and includes zero fees with transactions being conducted by the users of Bytecoin who are rewarded by the network. The users processing the transactions have no access to the information of the sender, receiver or the amount of money being transferred. ∎

VERGE

Verge is a privacy-centric cryptocurrency, aimed at providing true anonymity for users. According to the Verge project, one of the challenges of Bitcoin is the centralization of businesses using the Bitcoin ecosystem. Verge was created to allow all users involved in a transaction to remain anonymous, fulfilling the original ideals of cryptocurrency with integrated privacy networks such as TOR and i2p.

History

Verge was launched in late 2014 under the name 'DogecoinDark'. The project was announced on the bitcointalk.org forums by developer 'Dogedarkdev', who was seeking to create an accessible coin focused on anonymity and decentralization.

DogecoinDark was named after Dogecoin, a currency created in 2013 primarily as a joke that has experienced widespread popularity in the cryptocurrency community. However, when the creator of Dogecoin left his project, DogecoinDark realized that they would need to distance themselves from the Dogecoin brand so that the community and new users would recognize DogecoinDark as a serious currency. In February 2016, DogecoinDark rebranded to Verge, a change that was only cosmetic in nature. In January 2018, Verge released the full version of their Wraith Protocol, one of the long-awaited and key features of the currency that would allow users to switch between transparent and hidden transactions.

Features

The Verge network is integrated with two IP obfuscation services: Tor (The Onion Router) protocol, which enables anonymized access across the Internet; and, i2P (The Invisible Internet Project), a service designed to be a *"network within the internet"*, with traffic contained within the i2P network. Verge transactions can be made without the user having to set up the Tor or i2P networks separately on their computer.

Traditionally, a blockchain will feature either a public ledger (transactions are visible and linked to a public address) or a private ledger (transactional data is hidden and cannot be viewed). Wraith Protocol, a technology developed by the Verge team, allows users to switch between private and public ledgers on the Verge blockchain. Combined with Tor integration hiding the IP addresses of users, Wraith Protocol means that participating users' addresses cannot be identified and the amount of a transaction cannot be seen as it is not recorded on the public ledger. However, transparency via the public ledger is still possible for merchants and users who need to maintain a transactional record.

Verge features an encrypted peer-to-peer instant messaging system known as Visp. Messages using the system are encrypted using the AES-256-CBC algorithm and distributed between nodes to prevent the recipients of messages being inferred by third-party traffic analysis. Messages are distributed via the Verge P2P network and are stored for 48 hours on each network node. Verge makes use of an Electrum-based wallet with transactions completed via Simple Payment Verification. This technique allows for approximately 5 second transaction times by verifying that a transaction is included in a block without the need to download an entire block, only the block headers, which are significantly smaller than full blocks. Additionally, the Electrum wallet allows for multi-signature support, which can be enabled to require more than one key to authorize a transaction. ∎

Currency Code:
XVG

Launch Date:
2014

Market Cap:
$2,665M

Max. Supply:
16,555,000,000 XVG

Circulating Supply:
14,509,005,149 XVG

Consensus Mechanism:
PoW

Hashing Algorithm:
Scrypt, X17, Lyra2rev2, myr-groestl, blake2s

Block Time:
30 seconds

URL:
vergecurrency.com

Currency Code:
ZEC

Launch Date:
2016

Market Cap:
$2,447M

Max. Supply:
21,000,000 ZEC

Circulating Supply:
3,002,432 ZEC

Consensus Mechanism:
PoW

Hashing Algorithm:
Equihash

Block Time:
2.5 minutes

URL:
vergecurrency.com

ZCASH

A decentralized, open source cryptocurrency, Zcash uses advanced cryptography in order to provide strong privacy protections for its users. It is based upon the Zerocoin protocols proposed by Matthew D. Green, a professor at the Johns Hopkins University, who remains a team member. Zcash is led by the Zerocoin Electric Coin Company, known commonly as the Zcash Company.

History

Zcash is based upon the Zerocoin protocols first proposed in 2013 by Prof. Matthew D. Green, along with three graduate students - Ian Miers, Christina Garman and Aviel D. Rubin from the Department of Computer Science at Johns Hopkins University in Baltimore.

Their work then led to a collaboration with other cryptographers to create the Zerocash protocol, which in turn was developed into the Zcash cryptocurrency, released in 2016. In March 2017 the Zcash Foundation was created to guide the evolution of Zcash.

Features

Zcash has been developed using peer-reviewed cryptography research and utilizes an open source platform based on the Bitcoin Core codebase.

It has a fixed total supply of 21 million coins like Bitcoin, of which, 20% of those created in the first 4 years are allocated to investors, developers, and the Zcash Foundation.

Zcash users are able to make their transactions in two ways - one of them, like many other coins, is published on a public blockchain and is said to be 'transparent' - anonymous yet accessible on the public ledger. The other method is said to be 'shielded' and uses a special privacy feature called a zero-knowledge proof to conceal all information regarding the sender, the receiver, and the amount of the transaction.

A zero-knowledge proof is a method by which one user proves to another user that a given statement is true, without communicating any other information whatsoever, other than the fact that it is true or not. Zcash, however, uses a novel form of zero-knowledge proof known as a zk-SNARK which stands for Zero-Knowledge Succinct Non-Interactive Argument of Knowledge — a protocol developed by the Zcash team and based on recent breakthroughs in cryptography. With these protocols, Zcash offers its users the option of 'selective disclosure' allowing for transactions to be auditable if required but with disclosure under the control of the user. One reason given for this is that it gives users the choice to comply with authorities for tax regulation purposes or for questions of money laundering.

Mining Zcash is accomplished using an asymmetric proof-of-work algorithm called Equihash that requires high RAM requirements so as to discourage ASIC development.

Although the official Zcash wallet has been built for Linux, community members have since created an adapted version of it for both Mac OSX and Windows.

Zcash is also supported by the hardware wallets; Trezor and Ledger. All development and maintenance of the Zcash protocol and platform is now undertaken by the Zcash Foundation, a non-profit entity, launched in March 2017, to further the interests of Zcash users and the community in general. ∎

BITSHARES

Bitshares is a Decentralized Autonomous Company (DAC) that offers both tokens that are backed by assets such as USD, Bitcoin, or gold, and also a cryptocurrency exchange in which to use the tokens. The value of tokens is maintained through the use of Smart Coins. The aim of the project is to create a trust-less ecosystem for online trading and business.

History
The idea of Bitshares was conceived in 2013 and the trading platform was launched in July 2014. The first Bitshares (known as ProtoShares) were mined in November 2013 and in December 2013 the developers optimized the mining method into a proof-of-stake derivative (called delegated proof-of-stake or DPoS) in order to make mining more appealing to solo miners. In 2015, Bitshares 2.0 was launched under the name 'Graphene'.

Features
Bitshare has a very high-performance network, capable of processing over 100,000 transactions per second. This is the base speed, and developers aim to optimize the network so that the transaction time is even faster.

The Bitshares Decentralized Asset Exchange (DEX) is designed to allow users to trade, knowing that their assets are secure. As the exchange is decentralized, users are much less vulnerable to having their assets stolen, or the exchange being closed down for any reason. Decentralization means that no one entity owns the exchange or has authority to access account information and funds. It also means that as long as the network is being maintained by multiple parties, (no majority attack on the network) the exchange will remain resistant to being shut down or taken control of by third parties.

The Bitshares network has many components, acting as different parts of the Distributed Autonomous Company. Witnesses collect transactions into blocks and broadcast the blocks in return for shares. The Bitshares Committee component allows shareholders to vote on the conditions of the network, for example - on fees, block sizing, and development donations. Developers can contribute to the network and be paid for it by publishing their ideas on the blockchain and having shareholders vote on the idea. Therefore the company is able to continue developing without a centralized owner or decision-maker, and business decisions are completely determined by the shareholders.

Bitshares has also introduced the use of Smart Coins, a type of cryptocurrency in which the value of the coin is tied to the value of another asset, such as the US dollar or gold. The value of the asset is determined by calculating an average from several price feeds, (agreed upon by the shareholders) which gives users greater confidence that the value of their investment is secure. Using Smart Coins, users can trade non-cryptocurrency assets on the Bitshares platform, such as gold, allowing for a broader market. Users are also able to create their own Smart Coins, for example - a company may wish to create a tradeable Smart Coin based on their share price, or to use as a reward token for their business. Smart Coins such as BitUSD may be used by merchants and customers in place of USD with both parties being confident in the value of their exchange. ∎

Currency Code:
BTS

Launch Date:
2014

Market Cap:
$2,152M

Max. Supply:
3,600,570,502 BTS

Circulating Supply:
2,606,769,375 BTS

Consensus Mechanism:
DPoS

Hashing Algorithm:
SHA-512

Block Time:
3 seconds

URL:
bitshares.org

Currency Code:
DOGE

Launch Date:
2013

Market Cap:
$1,713M

Max. Supply:
Unlimited

Circulating Supply:
112,662,483,414 DOGE

Consensus Mechanism:
PoW

Hashing Algorithm:
Scrypt

Block Time:
60 seconds

URL:
dogecoin.com

DOGECOIN

Initially introduced as a "joke currency" on December 6, 2013, Dogecoin is a decentralized, peer-to-peer cryptocurrency and features, as its logo, an image of a dog taken from the 'Doge' internet meme. Its primary focus is facilitating the sending of money online and aims to become "the internet currency".

History

Dogecoin was created by a programmer known as Billy Marcus, a native of Portland, Oregon, and was officially launched on December 6, 2013. His idea was to make a digital coin that would enjoy a larger demographic spread than Bitcoin as well as create a certain distance from the controversies surrounding Bitcoin and other altcoins. Dogecoin was based initially on Luckycoin and used a randomized reward for mining, however, in March 2014, this was changed to a static block reward. Dogecoin began with 100 billion coins, released into circulation in mid-2015, with an extra 5.256 billion scheduled to be mined annually. The initial 100 billion coins had already been mined by June 30, 2015.

On December 19, 2013, the value of Dogecoin rose by almost 300 percent within 72 hours, to $0.00094 from $0.00026, with billions of the coin transacted daily. This milestone was made possible due to the hard stance the Chinese government had taken against Bitcoin and other cryptocurrencies at the time. However, just after three days of enjoying this boom, Dogecoin's value depreciated by 80% following excessive mining of the coins. By 2016, the open market value of 4,400 Dogecoins was equivalent to 1 USD.

Features

Dogecoin's main distinguishing feature is its use as an internet tipping system, where users of social media award Dogecoin tips to other members as compensation for noteworthy or interesting content they offer.

Dogecoin makes use of the Scrypt technology in its proof-of-work algorithm which means that SHA-256 mining equipment cannot be used and that dedicated mining devices are complicated to create. It has a faster transaction and confirmation time than many other altcoins out there and boasts of being 10 times faster than Bitcoin. For comparison, the current confirmation time of Bitcoin is 10 minutes while Dogecoin is only 60 seconds. Moreover, Dogecoin charges 50 times lower transaction fees than Bitcoin which means that Dogecoin is likely to play a major role in cryptocurrency exchanges and online transactions.

In addition, Dogecoin has lots of coins in circulation and is more user-friendly when it comes to micro-transactions. Its ongoing low rate of inflation also means that Dogecoin will not need to charge additional or expensive transaction fees to stay in business.

Another benefit is that Dogecoin enjoys relative security since hackers and crypto criminals are not too attracted to the currency because of its low inflation rate compared to other altcoins.

Mining is relatively easier and cheaper with Dogecoin compared, for example, to the cost of mining a Bitcoin. This has the capacity to make miners of Dogecoin richer in the long run when the value of the coin eventually appreciates further. By then, putting input and output side by side would mean that more money would be gained by those who have successfully mined the coin at a cheaper rate. ■

STRATIS

Founded in 2016, Stratis is a platform that enables development of blockchain based decentralized apps without the required overheads of a large distributed network. Using C# and the Microsoft .NET framework, developers are able to take advantage of the cloud computing abilities of the Stratis network.

History

Stratis was developed by the Stratis Group, with the aim of providing a platform on which clients may create their own private blockchain solutions. It uses the blockchain to perform cloud computing functions, and apps can be developed in C# and the Microsoft .NET framework. The Stratis Group also provides a consultancy service to assist businesses in using the platform. The first ICOs for Stratis were launched in early 2018.

The Stratis academy was introduced in 2017 to train people in the technology and contribute to an open source platform and is expected to be open to the public sometime in the second quarter of 2018. The academy has been created as a response to the current high demand for skilled blockchain developers from a wide range of industries and aims to assist in their training and education.

Features

Stratis allows developers to completely customize their apps without compromising security, by creating Private Chains. Developers can customize the block size and block times, control transactions and inflation and so on, for each Private Chain. This means that individual Private Chains can be optimized for each individual application. These Private Chains take advantage of the cloud computing benefits of the Stratis blockchain and enable developers to use the network without having to create their own. Developers are able to pay only for what they need through the ability to customize their Private Chains.

The Stratis platform will also allow developers to host decentralized applications over the Ethereum network and the Stratis Group aims to provide a consultancy service so customers are able to focus on app development without worrying about infrastructure. Customers are not limited to only using the Stratis blockchain for their app development, as the Stratis Group aims to provide consulting services for app provisioning over other networks such as Bitcoin, Ethereum, Bitshares, and LISK.

Stratis also allows organizations to create tokens that are pegged to a fiat value not affected by the volatility of the market. For example, if a company requires a transfer of value from one department to another, it can simply transfer the tokens, have the blockchain verify the legitimacy of the transaction, and then release the funds on the other end.

Stratis offers both a platform for developers to create apps and utilize cloud computing infrastructure, while also providing a consultancy service to clients interested in using the network.

The compatibility of their service with other coins also allows developers to utilize their consultancy services without depending on the Stratis network. The ability to create Private Chains enables developers to specify their needs, and easily customize their Private chain to suit the app that requires it. ∎

Currency Code:
STRAT

Launch Date:
2016

Market Cap:
$1,651M

Max. Supply:
N/A

Circulating Supply:
98,690,852 STRAT

Consensus Mechanism:
PoW / PoS

Hashing Algorithm:
X13

Block Time:
60 seconds

URL:
stratisplatform.com

ARDOR

Ardor is a scalable blockchain-as-a-service platform, based on Nxt proof-of-stake technology, and developed by Jelurida. Its unique parent-child chain architecture allows companies to build their products and services using unique child chains with pre-programmed smart contracts, and cross chain transaction functionality, all while relying on the security provided by the parent Ardor chain.

Currency Code:
ARDR

Launch Date:
2018

Market Cap:
$1,691M

Max. Supply:
998,999,495 ARDR

Circulating Supply:
998,999,495 ARDR

Consensus Mechanism:
PoS

Hashing Algorithm:
SHA-256

Block Time:
60 seconds

URL:
ardorplatform.org

History

Ardor was announced in May 2016, as 'Nxt 2.0'. It was intended to be a disruptive product built on to the original Nxt platform by maintaining the core features of the Nxt network that had been developed over the previous two and a half years, as well as adding an innovative architecture concept to the blockchain sector as well.

In Q1, 2017, the Ardor testnet was released to users to allow for security, safety and load testing of the network over a period of six months. On November 24, 2017, Ardor released their final testnet, as well as the Ardor source code for review under a temporary license. Coincidentally, the project also celebrated the four year anniversary of the Nxt project. Shortly afterwards, on January 1, 2018, the Ardor blockchain was officially released to the public.

Features

Ardor holds all the functionality of Nxt, but is a blockchain-as-a-service offering, enabling a new business to 'spin up' their blockchain infrastructure with minimal time and effort, and almost instantly gain access to a robust feature set with no need for additional hardware or software acquisitions.

There are two distinct parts to the Ardor platform - the parent chain and child chains. The parent chain is used to secure and process the transactions of all child chains built on Ardor. Child chains are blockchains connected to the Ardor parent chain created for various businesses, each with specific features and applications.

As Ardor is the successor to Nxt, child chains on the Ardor network make use of the entire feature set provided on the Nxt platform. These include (but are not limited to) - aliases, coin shuffling, data cloud services, a marketplace, and a monetary system. Upon creation of the child chain, users can determine which features they wish to include. Additional features can also be added after the deployment of the child chain.

Child chains also operate with native tokens, enabling them to act as separate entities. A designated account on the child chain collects the fees from transactions that are then used to pay the processing fees to the Ardor main chain, incentivizing the main chain to maintain security for the child chain. Child chain issuers can choose to pay those fees themselves, thus offering zero fee transactions to their users, who do not even have to know that they are using blockchain technology.

Normally, as blockchains record more transactions, the file size increases, forcing users to download growing blockchains before they can use them. Ardor avoids this blockchain 'bloat' of sequential data storage by allowing the child chains to perform transactions imperative to their chain while security is handled by the small, lightweight Ardor parent chain. Scheduled 'pruning' of the child chain removes dated transactions that are not relevant to the current status of the child chain. Pruned data can be stored separately on Archival Nodes that are connected to but not part of the blockchain.

With these innovations, Ardor hopes to create a blockchain platform that is open to everyone, including governments and established international fintech companies, enterprise-level and local businesses, as well as individuals. ∎

ARDOR, THE FIRST BLOCKCHAIN-AS-A-SERVICE OFFERING

The Ardor parent chain is a light blockchain that secures all of the child chains and processes their transactions following a proof-of-stake consensus.

Ardor Parent Chain
The Ardor parent chain uses the ARDR Token

THE ARDOR PARENT CHAIN

Multiple Child Chains
Every child chain uses its own token (ie. Ignis uses the IGNIS token, Ardorgate uses the AEUR token, etc...)

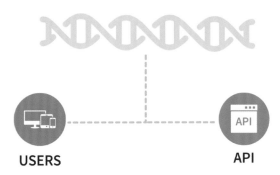

USERS

API

ARDOR CHILD CHAINS

Businesses and organizations can easily have their own private or public blockchain with the Ardor Blockchain Platform. Child chains on the Ardor Platform will be able to use all features currently seen in Nxt such as phasing transactions, decentralized voting, and trading, as well as cross chain transactions on the Ardor child chain network.

The first child chain of Ardor is the Ignis child chain. IGNIS tokens are used for its operation. In a nutshell, Ignis is the only child chain on the Ardor platform that is guaranteed to be permissionless and to support all available features. It will have all of the features that Nxt currently has.

Currency Code:
WAVES

Launch Date:
2016

Market Cap:
$1,292M

Max. Supply:
100,000,000 WAVES

Circulating Supply:
100,000,000 WAVES

Consensus Mechanism:
LPoS

Hashing Algorithm:
LPoS

Block Time:
60 seconds

URL:
wavesplatform.com

WAVES

Waves is an open source, peer-to-peer, blockchain platform, that allows users to launch their own cryptocurrency tokens. In a similar way to Ethereum, Waves allows users to create tokens using smart contracts and includes this functionality in its software and wallet. On the Waves platform, users can create, transfer and exchange blockchain tokens and pay transaction fees in WAVES tokens.

History

Waves was founded in 2016 by Sasha Ivanov, a Russian physicist who had previously founded the instant cryptocurrency exchange, Coinomat.com, the first fiat blockchain token, coinoUSD, as well as the first tradeable cryptocurrency index, CoinoIndex.com. Ivanov created Waves to address a number of issues that were preventing the wider adoption of blockchain technology, including speed, scalability and user experience. Its development was funded by a crowdsale in May 2016 and raised 30,000 BTC, which was at the time, the second largest crowdfunded blockchain project in history.

Waves was officially launched in November 2016, as a decentralized network, and featured token creation facilities which allowed developers to build their own blockchain-based applications. Waves launched its Bitcoin gateway in March 2017, allowing users to hold and transfer Bitcoin tokens on the Waves network.

Features

When Waves was founded in 2016, its inventor Sasha Ivanov wanted to reinvent entrepreneurship across the world using a shared infrastructure. His vision was to create an exchange for digital assets whilst also providing a crowdfunding solution. Waves aims to be a KYC and AML (Know Your Customer and Anti-Money Laundering) platform and intends to build partnerships with banks and financial institutions to provide gateways for fiat currencies to be deposited and withdrawn from. Waves is taking a pro-regulation stance on blockchain technology and in 2017, announced a partnership with Deloitte aimed at clarifying and shaping blockchain crowdfunding regulations. Waves' mission is to launch fiat currency gateways allowing users to trade their WAVES across various exchanges. These fiat gateways allow users to exchange any token issued on the Waves platform for 'real money', which can then be deposited in a bank with all transactions between cryptocurrency and fiat recorded on its blockchain.

Waves offers users the chance to store and release Waves tokens on a decentralized exchange via a Google Chrome extension, or by installing its wallet on WavesWallet.io. Waves offers a clean, accessible UX and an easy to use Chrome and mobile app with no requirement to download blockchain. Waves also allows businesses to create their own tokens and digital currency on its blockchain, pay for goods and services, and even crowdfund. Additionally, companies can use their created tokens for discounts, loyalty programs or even voting. To date, approximately 5,000 tokens have been launched on the platform. Waves is a proof-of-stake platform as opposed to the proof-of-work consensus model adopted by many others. This means that users are rewarded based on the commission from transactions which enables higher transaction volumes and fast confirmation times (up to 1,000 txs per second). Waves is also able to offer its users low fees with each transaction costing just 0.001 WAVES. ■

HSHARE

Hypercash, also known as HCash is a decentralized and distributed ledger system which bridges the gap between blockchain and blockless systems of digital currency. It has been designed to enable the exchange of value and information between blockchains and digital currency platforms, using a highly secure and authenticated channel.

History

Hcash was launched in June 2017. The Initial Coin Offering was spread over 15 days and each offering was sold almost immediately. In September 2017, the network was upgraded to a hybrid proof-of-work/proof-of-stake mining mechanism. Although HCash began development using a traditional blockchain, it plans to be able to operate on its own blockchain mainchain in 2018. It is currently listed on 21 exchanges.

Features

The aim of Hcash is to create a hive system where both blockchain and Directed Acyclic Graph (DAG) based cryptocurrencies can be easily exchanged. HCash is able to access all these different types of decentralized databases and transfer information and value between them. This is done by creating sidechains that work on both blockchain and DAG-based currencies, which can then be easily transferred and exchanged back into other paired currencies using HCash tokens.

HCash works with both public and private addresses to provide users with the option of transferring currency openly or privately. The public addresses are easily visible on the HCash blockchain and DAG records, while the private addresses are encrypted and masked, similar to other private cryptocurrencies such as Zcash or Byteball's Blackball.

A hybrid proof-of-stake/proof-of-work algorithm is used to mine HCash and to secure the network. The proof-of-stake system is used for making decisions as to the direction of the network with users able to vote on the protocol updates and upgrades through their staked coins. Once the votes have been collected they are written into the HCash blockchain. Proof-of-work is used as a security precaution as the algorithm has been proven to be an effective method of securing the integrity of any network.

HCash is also designed from the very beginning to be Quantum Resistant. One of the biggest concerns with current encryption methods is that they will become obsolete once quantum computing is fully developed and implemented. With current technology, most common encryption algorithms would take over 10 quintillion years to decipher, but only 6 months for a quantum computer. Using advanced encryption techniques, HCash is designed to prevent this problem from its inception by using a stronger quantum-resistant algorithm to create a future-proofed technology.

Decisions on the development and direction of HCash are all made through the Decentralized Autonomous Organization (DAO). The DAO is an open organization that allows all users in the community to participate in the decision-making and direction of the company. Any user of HCash can suggest changes which the community can then vote upon. 5% of all HCash is donated to the organization for any development or operational costs, such as auditing. ∎

Currency Code:
HSR

Launch Date:
2017

Market Cap:
$1,083M

Max. Supply:
84,000,000 HSR

Circulating Supply:
42,466,304 HSR

Consensus Mechanism:
PoW / PoS

Hashing Algorithm:
Hybrid PoW / PoS

Block Time:
60 seconds

URL:
h.cash

Currency Code:
DGB

Launch Date:
2014

Market Cap:
$1,263M

Max Supply:
21,000,000,000 DGB

Circulating Supply:
9,756,552,000 DGB

Consensus Mechanism:
PoW / PoS

Hashing Algorithm:
Sha256, Scrypt, Groestl,
Skein, Qubit

Block Time:
15 seconds

URL:
digibyte.io

DIGIBYTE

DigiByte is a rapidly growing, open source, decentralized payment network inspired by Bitcoin. It runs on the world's longest blockchain, composed of some 5 million blocks with a 15-second block time. It also has the most decentralized mineable blockchain in the market with over 100,000 nodes.

History
DigiByte was created in 2013 by programmer and entrepreneur, Jared Tate, and officially launched at the beginning of 2014 with its first block mined on January 10. Hashed into its genesis block was a headline from USA Today: *"Target: Data stolen from up to 110M customers"*, to highlight the importance of security in digital transactions.

In February 2014, the DigiShield fork was activated to increase security and protect against multi-pools that mine large numbers of DGB at a low difficulty. Since their implementation, the DigiShield protocols have been used by more than 25 other altcoins to protect them from fraudulent mining and malicious attacks, and a sudden influx or decrease of hashing power.

In September 2014, the MultiAlgo fork was activated which allowed for multi-algorithm mining. This led to more people being able to access DigiByte mining pools, creating a more decentralized blockchain and allowing for coins to reach those who were unable to mine on its earlier, single-algorithm Scrypt protocols.

December 2014 saw the implementation of the MultiShield hard fork which combined the Digishield and MultiAlgo protocols to allow them to be run across all five mining pools.

The following year, in December 2015, block time was reduced by 50% to 15 seconds and new block propagation code was added with the implementation of the DigiSpeed hard fork.

In April 2017, DigiByte implemented the DigiSync soft fork, becoming the second major cryptocurrency to implement Segregated Witness (SegWit).

Features
Since DigiByte is made up of decentralized nodes, any computer, mobile phone or server connected to its network automatically becomes a new node that assists in transaction relays. In addition, DigiByte uses 5 mining algorithms spanning some 100,000 nodes, compared with Bitcoin's 10,000 nodes, which increases both security and decentralization. DigiByte is 40 times faster and 5 times more secure and scalable than Bitcoin. It currently handles 560 transactions per second and with a block size that doubles every two years, DigiByte will be able to process 280,000 transactions per second by 2035. As for speed, while it takes Bitcoin about 10 minutes to confirm a transaction, DigiByte takes just 15 seconds.

Security, in particular, is an area where DigiByte has focused much of its attention. Transactions are encrypted, immutable and authenticated, with the individual's identity highly protected. The DGB has often been referred to as a 'digital asset', as each unit serves as a finite, transferrable, adaptive and secure 'digital byte' of data that cannot be destroyed and that may contain money, IOT data, photos, videos, music, messaging or documents. DigiByte is therefore able to perform multiple functions at any given time.

A significant recent development has seen DigiByte added to Ledger Nano S and Blue, allowing users to store their DigiBytes in a hardware wallet. ∎

DigiByte FOUNDATION

The DigiByte Foundation is a non-profit organization dedicated to supporting the DigiByte global blockchain through three primary pillars of education, outreach, and development.

Education
The Foundation will provide official learning material for developers, investors and anyone interested in the DigiByte Ecosystem.

Outreach
The Foundation will continue to reach out to potential partners, organizations and governments to further increase global adoption of the DigiByte Blockchain.

Development
The Foundation will oversee development and support to future-proof DigiByte applications and the core DigiByte protocol.

DigiByte's ultimate vision is to become, in the words of its founders, "a decentralized payment network used by millions of people across the planet to quickly and easily buy and sell goods and services over the internet, in-store, or person-to-person with little to no fees."

You can donate to the DigiByte Foundation by sending DGB to the following address:
DFVsFBiKuaL5HM9NWZgdHTQecLNit6tX5Y

digibytefoundation.org

Currency Code:
KMD

Launch Date:
2013

Market Cap:
$1,030M

Max. Supply:
Unlimited

Circulating Supply:
103,914,359 KMD

Consensus Mechanism:
dPoW

Hashing Algorithm:
Equihash

Block Time:
60 seconds

URL:
komodoplatform.com

KOMODO

The Komodo project focuses on empowering users with independence, security, and privacy through blockchain technology and provides entrepreneurs with a platform to launch independent blockchain solutions. Traders can also use Komodo's decentralized exchange, AtomicDEX (formerly called BarterDEX), in combination with Komodo's privacy services to privately trade among an ever-growing list of popular blockchain coins.

History
Komodo was launched in September 2016, as the first fork from the Zcash blockchain. Originally started as a privacy coin, Komodo used the open source code from Zcash, specifically their 'Zero-Knowledge Proofs' as the basis of their project.

Komodo steered towards becoming an ecosystem for blockchains; by empowering entrepreneurs in the blockchain space and allowing for a system of synergy between developers instead of seeking to solve any particular issue. In September 2017, Komodo announced its first ecosystem partner, Monaize - an e-banking platform that is to be the first ever decentralized ICO.

Features
Komodo focuses on providing independence, security, and privacy to two types of users: the blockchain entrepreneur and the average cryptocurrency investor.

The foundational pillar of the Komodo ecosystem is security. Komodo provides a unique and innovative form of security that uses the delayed proof-of-work (dPoW) protocol. dPoW functions by automatically making compressed records of the user's blockchain data and notarizing this information to the Bitcoin network. In the event that the user's blockchain is attacked, the Komodo framework can allow them to automatically rebuild their entire network based on the most recent record inserted into the Bitcoin blockchain. Therefore, to destroy the user's blockchain, an attacker would have to also destroy the Bitcoin network.

Another of Komodo's technologies is a method of trading cryptocurrencies, called AtomicDEX (formerly known as BarterDEX) which is essentially a kind of decentralized exchange. AtomicDEX relies on an underlying concept called the 'atomic swap' which is a direct exchange of cryptocurrencies between two users, removing all forms of middlemen, vouchers, and escrow services. AtomicDEX serves both the investor and the blockchain entrepreneur. For the investor, they can trade cryptocurrencies without having to pass through a centralized exchange. They also do not have to use an escrow service, voucher, nor even an intermediary coin. Furthermore, there is no registration process or withdrawal limits. Komodo is the first platform to offer decentralized ICOs (dICO). They also provide marketing channels, consulting services and allow for ICOs to secure crowdfunding via the Komodo exchange. DICO's built on the platform do not require a trusted third-party and can expect low fees as each asset chain is an independent blockchain secured by dPoW allowing for all dICO transaction fees to be paid with the dICO coin.

For the entrepreneur, Komodo's AtomicDEX enables the release of new blockchain products to the world without middleman involvement. Furthermore, many developers who have previously built other blockchain projects outside of the Komodo ecosystem can easily feature their coin on AtomicDEX. Komodo allows users to make their funds private. This allows the investor to trade on AtomicDEX with privacy, and it also allows the entrepreneur to crowdsource funds with an audience that may prefer privacy. ∎

TRADE CRYPTOCURRENCIES WITH
ATOMIC SWAPS & ZERO-KNOWLEDGE PRIVACY

LAUNCH YOUR OWN BLOCKCHAIN

DPOW SECURITY

ZERO-KNOWLEDGE TRANSACTIONS

PEGGED ASSETS

DEX CAPABILITY

ULTIMATE PRIVACY TOOL

PEERCHAINS SCALABILITY

DECENTRALIZED CROWDFUNDING

MICROPAYMENT CHANNELS

BLOCKCHAIN DATABASE

KOMODO SCONTRACTS

KOMODO API

WHAT NEXT?

The Komodo platform allows investors and entrepreneurs to take full advantage of open source blockchain technology. With Bitcoin-level security, a decentralized Initial Coin Offering platform, zero-knowledge privacy, and an atomic-swap powered decentralized exchange, everyone can find ample opportunities to innovate and prosper.

KOMODO

FOR BUSINESS DEVELOPERS THE DECENTRALIZED INITIAL COIN OFFERING

HOW TO LAUNCH A NEW INDEPENDENT BLOCKCHAIN ON KOMODO

STEP 1
LAUNCH EMPTY CLONE

The entrepreneur commands the Komodo software to launch an empty clone of the KMD main ware to launch an empty clone of the KMD main chain. This clone natively integrates with the Komodo ecosystem, but is itself a fully independent blockchain.

STEP 2
ACTIVATE dPOW

To protect this new indepedent blockchain, the entrepreneur activates Komodo's dPoW security system. This instructs Komodo's decentralized 'notary nodes' to begin monitoring the entrepreneur's blockchain. The notary nodes will record its history to the strongest PoW network (Bitcoin). The entrepreneur's endeavor now has maximum security.

STEP 3
CUSTOMIZE YOUR RULES

The entrepreneur now programs into this new independent blockchain any rules that they desire. So long as they do not interfere with the basic Komodo framework, the sky is the limit, and their project natively integrates with the rest of Komodo.

STEP 4
ADD TO EXCHANGE

With their independent blockchain now prepared for public release, the entrepreneur turns to Komodo's decentralized exchange, AtomicDEX.

STEP 5
LIST ON ATOMICDEX

Because AtomicDEX is decentralized and powered by atomic swaps, there is no approval process required to feature a coin. The user can simply market when it will be available and then use AtomicDEX's listing capabilities to make the coin supply available for sale.

STEP 6
RELEASED TO PUBLIC

The entrepreneur's audience can purchase the new blockchain coin immediatley on AtomicDEX. Also, through Komodo's privacy technology, the audience can participate within their right to privacy.

STEP 7
INSTANT TRADE MARKET

The immediacy of AtomicDEX allows the entrepreneur to instantly establish a trading market for their project. Furthermore, as AtomicDEX is decentralized, there is no fear of being delisted.

STEP 8
FREEDOM TO MOVE

If the entrepreneur's blockchain ever grows so large they no longer need Komodo's dPoW security, the entrepreneur can leave the Komodo ecosystem at will. Unlike other blockchain platforms, the entrepreneur can take their entire blockchain product with them wherever they go.

KOMODO™

FOR INVESTORS

REASONS TO HOLD KMD

THE CENTRE OF THE KOMODO ECOSYSTEM
KMD is the most integral currency in the Komodo ecosystem. With every new technology built, Komodo seeks to tie its usefulness to KMD

RECEIVE 5% ANNUAL REWARDS
Any wallet address that has at least 10KMD automatically receives an annual 5% reward.

COLLECT 5% KMD REWARDS IN JUST ONE CLICK

CLAIM NOW

MAIN FORM OF PAYMENT
KMD is the main form of payment necessary for dPoW security.

BUILT-IN TRADING FEATURES
KMD has built-in privacy features, allowing users to anonymize their funds for purchases, crowd sourcing, and trading on AtomicDEX.

KMD'S LIQUIDITY ENHANCED BY ATOMICDEX
All fees paid on AtomicDEX are transferred back into KMD, increasing liquidity for KMD and all other coins.

KMD IS THE FUEL FOR THE FUTURE
KMD will also be the fuel for the future language-agnostic smart-contract technology, which is currently in development.

FOR TRADERS WHO TRADE ON ATOMICDEX

TRADERS CAN TRADE PRIVATELY

STEP 1

DETERMINE HOW MUCH AND PURCHASE KMD
The trader first determines how much currency value they want to have available for trading. The trader then purchases the appropriate amount of KMD.

STEP 2

ZERO-KNOWLEDGE PRIVACY
KMD's native zero-knowledge privacy features allows the trader to completely break the trail of their cryptocurrency transaction history.

STEP 3

TRADE KMD FOR ANY OTHER COINS VIA ATOMICDEX
The trader then uses AtomicDEX to trade their KMD for any available coin. Popular coins for trading include BTC, BCC, LTC, DOGE, VTC, PIVX, DASH, STRAT, SUPERNET, ZEC and dozens more.

STEP 4

MAINTAIN TRADING HISTORY PRIVACY
When the trader desires to spend their coin, but also wishes to maintain privacy over their trading history, they can then use KMD again.

STEP 5

TRADE ONCE MORE VIA ATOMICDEX
The trader uses AtomicDEX to trade their current holdings for KMD once more. They perform KMD's privacy-creation process, again, thus eliminating any trail to their trading history.

STEP 6

TRADE BACK TO DESIRED COINS
With their history-less KMD, they exchange back for their desired coins on Atomic-DEX. They can now spend this currency in any manner they choose, without revealing their private history

Currency Code:
STEEM

Launch Date:
2014

Market Cap:
$1,028M

Max. Supply:
Unlimited

Circulating Supply:
249,294,000 STEEM

Consensus Mechanism:
PoW

Hashing Algorithm:
SHA-256

Block Time:
1-3 seconds

URL:
steem.io

STEEM

Steem is a cryptocurrency using blockchain technology, designed for the blogging and social networking website Steemit.com. Users on the Steemit platform are rewarded by community members in Steem tokens for creating posts that are deemed interesting and valuable by the community. The tokens can also be awarded for activity in the form of sharing comments or posts.

History

Steemit.com was created in 2016 by a team of developers based in New York and in 2017 the Steemit.com platform reached some 171,000 users. There are a total of 263,431,886 Steem tokens that are mineable and as of December 2017, 246,457,292 tokens have already been mined, using proof-of-work (POW) protocols. Upon the induction of Steem, no coins were pre-mined. All of the mining took place after the coin was officially announced on Bitcointalk.org.

Features

One of the most appealing things about Steem is that users can get started on the Steemit.com platform and start making money almost immediately, with no sign-up fees. After a few clicks and the confirmation of the account, users are ready to start earning tokens. Users are also able to have their own profile which gives them the freedom to have an avatar, cover image and the capability of building a following. Once an account has been created, users can buy tokens on exchanges or begin to earn them by providing posts that are deemed valuable by the community. Essentially, users exchange the currency of positive emotions for money, by providing engaging content. A custom Google search add-on is used for browsing the site.

Anything informative, intriguing, funny or entertaining may be enough for people to send the creator of the content micro-donations. Posts can be in the form of quotes, phrases, anecdotes, photos, videos, songs, memes, and so on, with Steem urging their users to be creative about the content shared.

It is worth being mindful of the fact that accounts created cannot be deactivated or deleted, as the account, along with its usage history, is forever stored within the blockchain.

As well as earning tokens for their posts, users can pay in tokens to promote their posts within the platform. This serves as an alternative form of paid advertising, as the more views a post receives, the more profits there are to be made by the user.

A mobile Steem wallet is currently available, making the currency more usable and accessible to the public and offering an added incentive to investors.

On Steemit, unlike other content creating websites, people are motivated to behave more consciously with the incentives to write and share well thought-out content helping to nurture a more thoughtful community. Steemit has a well-established intellectual community, many of whom were early adopters of cryptocurrencies. Through this kind of social structure, trends can be dictated by what people really want. Steemit can be hugely beneficial for writers, artists, and content creators to get in early on the platform and start building a following since the tiny donations received now could be worth significantly more in the future as the currency gains more adopters. ■

ELECTRONEUM

Launched in late 2017, Electroneum is a cryptocurrency designed around mobile use. The team behind Electroneum have already launched an app for both IOS and Android markets, where users can mine the coin through a gaming experience. Electroneum aims to be used by the mobile market, with a heavy focus on the integration of micropayments through mobile devices.

History

Electroneum first began development in 2015, and its ICO was launched in 2017. It was originally called 'Electron', however, it was rebranded after it was discovered that there was another competing cryptocurrency with the same name. The Electroneum development team is based in the United Kingdom, and their prime directive is to create a currency that is easily used by the mobile market.

Features

Electroneum's main goal is the widespread adoption of the coin as a currency. With this in mind, the developers have focused on making the coin easy to use and simple to understand. For example, the high market cap of 21 billion coins is designed to help users understand the value of the currency better. The team believes that the value of the tokens will be easier to understand for mass adoption; the value '20 tokens' being easier to deal with and calculate than '0.00000020 tokens'.

The CryptoNote algorithm that is used by Monero is also used in Electroneum, allowing them to utilize the same anonymization features of Monero, which means that users can be assured that their ingoing and outgoing payments are private and untraceable.

Electroneum has further developed the algorithm so that users who try to create multiple mixed transactions with the same private key can be linked, which prevents any problems with double spending. This means that users are protected from attacks from scammers on the network. CryptoNote also prevents blockchain analysis, as every transaction is sent to a different temporary address so that no transactions can be linked or identified.

Additional security is also implemented in Electroneum through their wallet, which includes an option to create an unhackable offline wallet. The design is focused on allowing new users of cryptocurrency to easily store their money in a secure manner, with no requirement for technical expertise.

One of the ways that the Electroneum team is introducing the cryptocurrency into the mass market is through mobile mining. A mining app has been released on both the iOS and Android platforms that turns the mining experience into a game. Coin distribution on the app is based on the value of viral marketing. The app is designed to introduce users to the concepts of the cryptocurrency and stimulate the growth of the Electroneum ecosystem. The developers of Electroneum believe that there is a great benefit in a currency being used as a transfer of value between games, and mobile mining is a pivotal part of their strategy for widespread adoption of their coin.

Finally, the Electroneum team has created an API for third-party developers to easily integrate payment options into their apps to further aid in the adoption and use of the coin as a currency. ■

Currency Code:
ETN

Launch Date:
2017

Market Cap:
$918M

Max. Supply:
21,000,000,000 ETN

Circulating Supply:
5,861,686,924 ETN

Consensus Mechanism:
PoW

Hashing Algorithm:
CryptoNote

Block Time:
59 seconds

URL:
electroneum.com

REDDCOIN IS THE SOCIAL CURRENCY THAT ENRICHES PEOPLE'S SOCIAL LIVES AND MAKES DIGITAL CURRENCY EASY FOR THE GENERAL PUBLIC. REDDCOIN ACHIEVES THIS BY INTEGRATING A DIGITAL CURRENCY PLATFORM SEAMLESSLY WITH ALL MAJOR SOCIAL NETWORKS TO MAKE THE PROCESS OF SENDING AND RECEIVING MONEY FUN AND REWARDING FOR EVERYONE.

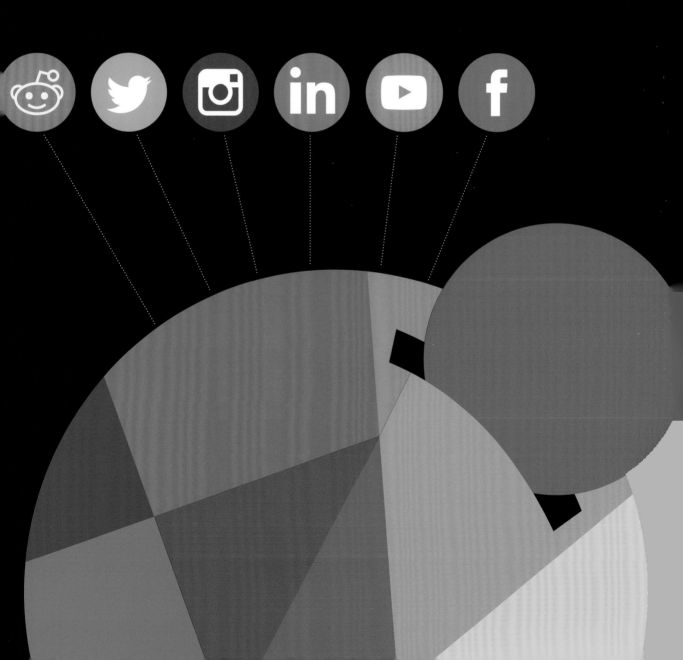

REDDCOIN

ReddCoin is a decentralized, peer-to-peer cryptocurrency aimed at enriching people's social lives; to be used for humanitarian aims and positive social change. The vision for its team is for Reddcoin to become the coin people use to 'tip' people seamlessly over social media.

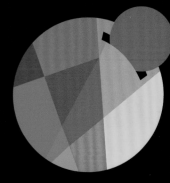

History

Reddcoin was announced in January 2014 as Scrypt proof-of-work' (PoW) currency via an initial public coin offering on Bitcointalk.org. This took place with the aim of becoming a cryptocurrency specially designed for integration with social media. During its first 6 months, coins were mined using a proof-of-work protocol although now, Reddcoin is no longer directly mineable. Reddcoin's white-paper was written by their lead developer Larry Ren in early 2014. It was originally using a proof-of-work (PoW) algorithm but in August 2014 they changed it to the proof-of-stake-velocity' algorithm (PoSV).

Features

Reddcoin is an open-source, peer-to-peer currency that is derived from Litecoin's source code. The team's objective is to build a button or plugin that will allow for higher levels of implementation among users on such websites as Facebook, Twitter, LinkedIn and many more. Reddcoin encourages microdonations, users on Reddit.com tip community members for sharing appreciated posts or comments.

Perhaps its most distinguishing feature is that it makes use of a proof-of-stake-velocity (PoSV) algorithm. Proof-of-stake is an innovative technology which requires only a small amount of energy and computational power when coming to a consensus among users. Since the implementation of proof-of-stake-velocity, users are able to earn more Reddcoins by regularly staking and maintaining their wallet online at all times. Due to these proof-of-stake-velocity protocols, Reddcoin users take part in 'minting' as opposed to mining. By utilizing their online wallets to help the network establish consensus, they are rewarded with interest. As already mentioned, this process involves a lowered expenditure of processing power and energy compared to traditional mining, making Reddcoin more eco-friendly. Boasting a 60 second block time, it is exceptionally fast at processing transactions and currently there is no transaction fee for senders or receivers.

Reddcoin rewards the user who makes more transactions instead of being an 'investor' that holds coins, and greater interest and dividends are awarded when coins are circulated more frequently. Members also get more power over the protocols based on the merit of how many tokens they own and how much they send to others. People who hold a digital wallet allow for the network to be maintained by taking part in the verification of transactions. Newly received coins generate more interest for the user, working as an incentive for users to circulate the coins.

Another innovation is the Redd-ID which allows users to have their public keys associated with a username. This means that instead of sharing a long and complex code in order to make a transaction, as with other cryptocurrencies, the only thing needed is for users to input their unique ID. This will allow for easier integration into websites and social media sites that already work on the principle of user IDs. ∎

Currency Code:
RDD

Launch Date:
2014

Market Cap:
$817M

Max. Supply:
27,500,000,000 RDD

Circulating Supply:
28,716,347,981 RDD

Consensus Mechanism:
PoSV

Hashing Algorithm:
Scrypt

Block Time:
60 seconds

URL:
reddcoin.com

Currency Code:
ARK

Launch Date:
2017

Market Cap:
$767M

Max. Supply:
125,000,000 ARK

Circulating Supply:
97,981,284 ARK

Consensus Mechanism:
DPoS

Hashing Algorithm:
SHA-256

Block Time:
8 seconds

URL:
ark.io

ARK

Ark is a decentralized, open source cryptocurrency, that is intended for mass adoption. With a block time of 8 seconds, Ark is one of the fastest cryptocurrencies on the market. At present, the Ark Crew consists of 17 core team members who aim to create an ecosystem of connected chains by acting as a mediator, that allows cross-chain communication. This bridging technology has the potential to be utilized as a means for transferring information, functions and even coins, across different chains.

History
Ark came online at 1900 UTC on March 21, 2017. Since then it has been listed on 12 different exchanges. It was created by a diverse, and decentralized team of 27 members coming from 11 different countries.

The framework of ARK was shaped, and influenced by 3 other cryptocurrencies: Lisk, Bitshares, and Crypti, all which make use of the DPoS consensus algorithm. It is interesting to note that Francois-Xavier Thoorens, a co-founder and head of development at Ark, was once a core developer at Lisk.

Features
The Ark platform was designed and intended for making the technology of the blockchain conveniently accessible to the everyday user. It is a decentralized ecosystem that is proposed for mass consumer adoption. The Ark Crew focuses on spotlighting two crucial fields of development – a core technology which is both fast and secure, as well as providing services that are genuinely practical for the average user. Ark has an interesting feature called Smart Bridging which gives it the ability to adapt to market needs, furthermore adding an amount of flexibility to the platform. Smart Bridging is, in essence, the act of linking together other blockchains which each have a serviceable use case.

These Smart Bridges allow the Ark platform to delegate functions and tasks to other bridged blockchains. With this technology, the Ark Crew is capable of developing a merged network of various blockchains, with Bitcoin, Ethereum, and Lisk among the first chains to be bridged. Ark utilizes a consensus algorithm called Delegated proof-of-stake (DPoS) which was made known by Bitshares.

The algorithm was designed with the intention of eliminating the issues which are faced by the proof-of-work (PoW) system. Such issues include the centralization of computer processing power and the needless waste of energy.

The ARK DPoS system also implements a newly adapted voting procedure, as well as the integration of several upgrades over the previous DPoS system. Ark also provides users with the option of sending transactions anonymously.

In conclusion, with an ambitious roadmap, an experienced team, and a flexible platform, Ark is well on their way to becoming a scalable cryptocurrency, able to be adopted by the masses. ∎

DECRED

An open source, self-funding cryptocurrency, Decred prioritizes decentralized self-governance and utilizes the world's first, user-activated, on-chain consensus voting system to determine decision-making outcomes. It runs on a hybridized proof-of-work/proof-of-stake (PoW/PoS) consensus system that aims to create a balance between miners and voters while giving all stakeholders voting power in regards to decisions that affect the Decred ecosystem.

History

Although the beginnings of Decred are somewhat obscure, what we do know is that in April 2013, an anonymous programmer by the name of tacotime responded to a thread on Bitcointalk titled: *"Want to make an altcoin that actually changes something?"* Four days later, tacotime started a new thread and began working alongside another anonymous individual, _ingsoc, who later approached Company Zero's CEO Jake Yocom-Piatt and presented him with their concept. A partnership between them was born and the initial developments of the new coin began with the name, Decred, an abbreviation of 'decentralized credits'.

Decred officially launched its mainnet on February 8, 2016, and published the 'Decred Constitution', outlining its rules regarding 'Principles', 'Blockchain Governance', 'Project Governance', and 'Funding'. Decred was initially funded by C0 (Company Zero) and from the pockets of individual developers. Interestingly enough, no one received free coins and even developers had to purchase the coins at a rate of $0.49 per coin or in exchange for their work, charged at the same rate.

Features

Decred's primary aim is to develop an autonomous, self-running and self-funding cryptocurrency in which all of its stakeholders play a role in the decision-making process. To achieve this, it primarily relies upon an innovative hybrid proof-of-work/proof-of-stake (PoW/PoS) consensus voting system as well as a censorship-resistant, blockchain-anchored platform for public proposals which allows for any of its users to make suggestions. In order to do this, proposals are submitted to the Decred Assembly, a group of vetted users who have been voted into the position. Once a new improvement has been developed and tested, it is added to an updated version of the source code as 'dormant code' and users update to the new version in order to show their support for it. When 95% of the past 1000 blocks have been mined with the updated code and 75% of verifying votes on the previous 2016 blocks contain the updated code, then voting formally begins. Voting lasts around 28 days (8064 blocks), and includes both miners and stakers voting either 'yes', 'no' or abstaining. Any proposal requires at least a 75% majority vote in order to be implemented, at which point the dormant code becomes active immediately.

Another interesting feature is Decred's separation of transaction signatures from the rest of the transaction data, something similar to the SegWit protocol, which provides immutable transaction hashes as well as allowing for transactions to be signed off-chain. Transactions also come with an optional expiry date, when, if activated, prevents them from being included in the blockchain after a certain block height has been reached, and ensures they are automatically canceled in the event of confirmation delays or other factors.

Along with such things as cross-platform wallets, Lighting Network smart contract capability and cross-chain atomic swaps, Decred has much to offer anyone looking to return to cryptocurrency's original guiding principles. ∎

Currency Code:
DCR

Launch Date:
2015

Market Cap:
$752M

Max. Supply:
21,000,000 DCR

Circulating Supply:
6,507,595 DCR

Consensus Mechanism:
Hybrid PoW/PoS

Hashing Algorithm:
BLAKE

Block Time:
5 minutes

URL:
decred.org

Currency Code:
SIA

Launch Date:
2014

Market Cap:
$740M

Max. Supply:
Unlimited

Circulating Supply:
32,447,344,872 SC

Consensus Mechanism:
PoW

Hashing Algorithm:
BLACKE

Block Time:
10 minutes

URL:
sia.tech

SIACOIN

Siacoin makes use of the same technological principles behind Bitcoin but uses them instead as a means of providing cloud storage for users in a decentralized and publicly auditable way. Sia's technology also enables users to earn money by renting out their free hard drive space.

History
Sia was created by Luke Champine and David Vorick who originally worked for Nebulous Inc, a VC-funded startup based in Boston.

The idea was for Siacoin was conceived in 2013 and by June 2014 the project received support from angel investors. By November 2014, the first white-paper was published, however, Siacoin was not officially launched until June 2015.

By July, Sia made its way onto the exchanges, including Poloniex, YUNBI, Bitsquare, and ShapeShift. In January 2017, additions to the structures were made, allowing for a speed boost in upload and download times.

Features
The project's aim is to compete with existing cloud storage solutions by allowing the disassembly of files which are spread across the network and saved on storage space rented by its users. One of the key advantages Sia has over traditional cloud storage is that files can only be opened by the user, whereas other centralized options are also accessible using the corporation's master keys.

Siacoin is concerned with privacy and works by separating files into thousands of pieces so that the user's files are distributed over many different hard drives. The only person able to access the complete file is the owner of the private keys which are protected by encryption.

Cloud storage capacity is acquired simply by buying Siacoins, costing approximately $2 for one terabyte of space, which is significantly cheaper than the other options available.

One of the main benefits of Sia is that all of the unused hard drive space from around the world can be put to use at a relatively low cost, however, there is still some question as to whether the service can keep up with the speeds of other cloud storage providers as it is a more complicated process to transfer data from thousands of computers so as to reassemble a single file.

Although Siacoin is still in its early stages, it shows much promise in allowing users to securely store sensitive information, remotely, in a way that is inaccessible to outside users or hackers. ∎

NEXUS

Nexus was released in early 2015 and is a mineable coin that uses block-chain technology. It is arguably the most quantum resistant cryptocurrency at this stage and is run as a not-for-profit project. Their most pioneering project yet, currently underway, is the creation of a private satellite network to ensure their users' uninterrupted connectivity, even in the event of power cuts and internet failures.

History

Nexus was founded by Colin Cantrell, a software engineer who originally sought anonymity by using the name Videlicet and only chose to reveal his true identity in September 2015. Initially, Nexus was named Coinshield (CSD) and was created with the intention of improving upon Bitcoins earlier foundations. The first CSD block was mined on September 24, 2014, and on October 23, 2014 the hashing (GPU) channel was launched to function as a second proof channel. On January 24, 2015, it was listed on the Bittrex Exchange.

Features

Nexus specializes in ensuring that their coins are fast, secure, scalable and accessible. As a means of preparing for potential future risks, the Nexus team have taken advantage of multiple technologies to ensure that their coins are resistant to hacks from quantum computers. Nexus makes use of a more sophisticated form of encryption, using 571-bit private keys compared to Bitcoin's 256-bit version and due to this increased encryption, Nexus is more resistant than other cryptocurrencies to attacks by quantum computers. The author of the white paper is also a physicist which gives Nexus users a certain confidence that the team understands what is required for a coin to be quantum resistant.

Since the induction of Nexus, their software team has made several key adaptations that ultimately will make the coin more user-friendly and scalable for many more years to come. It takes the network approximately 50 seconds to reach a consensus and transactions are managed in terms of their importance in order to create a faster and more efficient system.

There is also a system in place for reversible transactions, so conditions can be set for a scenario where, for instance, if a transaction is taking more than 30 minutes to take place, your tokens can be refunded to you automatically; a feature that most other cryptocurrencies lack. Another problem this coin will solve is the issue of accidentally paying the wrong person. Nexus is soon to feature a two-way digital signature requirement so that when coins are sent, the receiver must confirm the transaction for it to be completed. Coins are mined using proof-of-stake (PoS) rather than proof-of-work (PoW) so as to increase energy efficiency and for every new coin mined, a portion is sent to the developers as well certain exchanges.

The Nexus team is currently building a Three Dimensional Chain (3DC) also known as a Multi-Dimensional Chain (MDC) set to further increase security, decentralization and resource utilization compared to traditional blockchains. One of the team's most ambitious plans is to build and launch a decentralized network of satellites so as to keep the Nexus platform up and running at all times, allowing all users equal access whether in 1st or 3rd world countries. The satellites are to begin launching in 2018 and count on the collaboration of Colin Cantrell's father Jim, a founding member of the SpaceX team and the current CEO of Vector Space. ∎

Currency Code:
NXS

Launch Date:
2015

Market Cap:
$670M

Max. Supply:
55,519,477 NXS

Circulating Supply:
54,857,684 NXS

Consensus Mechanism:
nPOS

Hashing Algorithm:
SHA3

Block Time:
2.5 minutes

URL:
nexusearth.com

THE XP ECOSYSTEM
A NEW APPROACH TO AN EXPERIENCE BASED ECONOMY

XP FOUNDATION

FOUNDATION MOTHERNODE
INCOME: RECEIVES A PERCENTAGE OF STAKE REWARDS FOR DEVELOPMENT
100% AUDITABLE
ESTABLISHES DEVNODES, SALESNODES, AND GEONODES AS NEEDED
MOVING 90-DAY COIN BURN

SUPERNODE
1,000,000,000
ANNUAL RETURN = 1 BILLION (UNVERIFIED FIGURE??)

NODE COST: 1 BILLION
TARGET MARKET: INVESTORS
LOCKING: ONE WEEK DELAY TO BREAK NODE
100% COIN BURN ON PURCHASE

UPGRADE THE ICE CREAM SHOP OWNER CONVERTS THEIR MASTERNODE TO A SUPERNODE

100% "BURN" ON PURCHASE
A TBD PORTION OF STAKE REWARDS

MASTERNODE
50,000,000
ANNUAL RETURN = 25M (UNVERIFIED FIGURE??)

NODE COST: 50 MILLION
TARGET MARKET: INVESTORS
LOCKING: NONE

UPGRADE THE ICE CREAM SHOP OWNER CONVERTS THEIR WALLET TO A MASTERNODE

A TBD PORTION OF STAKE REWARDS

REGULAR NODE
<50,000,000
ANNUAL RETURN = TBD (UNVERIFIED FIGURE??)

NODE COST: NO STARTING COST
TARGET MARKET: END USERS
LOCKING: NONE

DEPOSIT THE ICE CREAM SHOP OWNER STAKES THIS PAYMENT IN THEIR CORE WALLET

DEVNODE
50,000,000
STAKE RATE = TBD (UNVERIFIED FIGURE??)

NODE COST: FREE FOR VERIFIED DEVELOPERS
TARGET MARKET: DEVELOPERS
LOCKING: PERMANENTLY LOCKED
CAN ONLY BE ACCESSED THROUGH IN-GAME API
100% COIN BURN ON ESTABLISHMENT
100% COIN BURN FOR COINS NOT USED IN 10 DAYS

DEVELOPERS CREATE GAMES AND APPS USING THE XP API, WHICH WILL ALLOW THEM TO DISTRIBUTE REWARDS IN-GAME

USERS CAN THEN SPEND IN-GAME ON FREEMIUM ITEMS OR TRANSFER TO THEIR PERSONAL WALLET TO USE IN THE BROADER XP ECONOMY

SALESNODE
50,000,000
STAKE RATE = TBD (UNVERIFIED FIGURE??)

NODE COST: FREE FOR VERIFIED RETAILERS
TARGET MARKET: RETAILERS
LOCKING: PERMANENTLY LOCKED
100% COIN BURN ON ESTABLISHMENT
100% COIN BURN FOR COINS NOT USED IN 10 DAYS

MERCHANTS OF ANY TYPE USE XP TO INCENTIVIZE PURCHASES OR TO THANK GUESTS

XP IS CREATED AND GIVEN TO CUSTOMERS WHO CAN THEN SPEND IN RETAIL LOCATIONS OR IN THE BROADER XP ECONOMY

NOTE: RETAILERS COULD USE EITHER SALESNODES OR GEONODES, DEPENDING ON THEIR BUSINESS MODEL

GEONODE
ZERO
NO RETURN - RAINS (UNVERIFIED FIGURE??)

NODE COST: FREE FOR NOTABLE LOCATIONS
TARGET MARKET: END USERS
LOCKING: PERMANENTLY LOCKED
COIN BURN: REACHES A PREDETERMINED MAXIMUM AND XST SECURES THE NETWORK

XP ENTHUSIASTS AT NOTABLE LOCATIONS CAN ESTABLISH AN "XP STOP" WHICH WILL RAIN COINS TO ALL LOCATION WALLETS NEARBY

IDEAS:
- CONCERT
- MONUMENT
- SCHOOLS
- MUSEUMS
- PARKS
- GYMS
- EVENTS

MT. EVEREST

BLOCKCHAIN BASED ADVERTISING CAN BE USED TO ADVERTISE LOCAL FEATURES DIRECTLY TO THE XP MOBILE WALLET, ALERTING THEM TO LOCATIONS TO SPEND THEIR XP NEARBY OR ONLINE

THE XP ECONOMY

RAIN A USER RECEIVES A RAIN AT THE FAIR

START

SPEND THEY BUY COFFEE

SPEND AGAIN THE COFFEE SHOP GIVES A REWARD THAT SOMEONE SPENDS ON ICE CREAM

Cake Shop
ICE CREAM
GRAND OPENING
CORN DOGS

Discover Experience Points (XP)
Incentive Rewards & Digital Currency

EXPERIENCE POINTS

XP is a cryptocurrency based on the concept of 'experience points'. The basic concept is to provide users with an incentive reward when completing real-world actions such as, participating in a discussion, visiting a restaurant, or going to a certain location. XP aims to create an economy based on experiences with a cryptocurrency where people can gain real-world rewards for achieving goals - just like in a game.

History

The concept of gaining experience points to level-up originally came from the roleplaying game 'Dungeons and Dragons' when it was released in 1977. Since then, it has been widely used in games as a measure of progress. In the past few years, the concept of 'gamification of life' has become more popular. People are creating their own 'ledgers' (or using apps) to collect experience points based on activities that they do every day (for example, exercising, reading, working), incentivizing themselves by treating life like a game. XP aims to become the next development of this idea by using cryptocurrency principles to create real-world rewards for real-life experiences. The XP wallet was released in December 2017.

Features

XP aims to achieve its goals using their 'XP Pentanode System'. Instead of using just one specialized node for network security and verification of transactions, the developers of XP have separated the network into five specialized nodes.

Masternodes are designed for investors and create approximately 2800 XP per hour, regardless of how much XP the node is holding. A Masternode costs 50 million XP to purchase, and expected returns are just less than 50% annually.

Supernodes create a significantly larger amount of XP (around 2 billion XP annually) but are much more expensive, at the cost of 1 billion XP. The original 1 billion XP cost of the node is 'burnt', meaning that they are removed from the XP ecosystem. The high cost of setup and high return, in combination with the burning of the initial deposit, are designed to incentivize serious contributors to the XP network while protecting inflation.

Salesnodes are designed for merchants, and while the function is similar to a Masternode, the biggest difference is that the node cannot be broken up or sold, and the stake rewards can only be used as promotions. If a merchant decides to no longer use the XP network, the remaining XP on the node is burned.

Devnodes are free for developers and are designed to help create growth in the XP economy. XP generated can only be distributed through the XPlay API - they can only be distributed to wallets as a reward in a gaming system. In order to prevent inflation, XP that have not been distributed within a 10 day period are burned.

Geonodes provide XP to users when they visit participating locations, for example - retail shops, concerts, or museums. These are designed to help boost the XP economy by giving users a way to gain currency through promotions.

The XP Foundation Mothernode exists to create and control growth in the XP network by creating non-investor nodes and burning unused tokens. Overall, XP aims to create a system with controls for inflation and security, where users are incentivized through promotions provided by retailers. ■

Currency Code:
XP

Launch Date:
2017

Market Cap:
$729M

Max. Supply:
N/A

Circulating Supply:
210,175,479,355 XP

Consensus Mechanism:
Hybrid PoW / PoS

Hashing Algorithm:
SHA256 / Scrypt

Block Time:
60 seconds

URL:
xpcoin.io

PIVX

Private Instant Verified Transaction, or PIVX, is an open source currency created from a combination of Bitcoin and Dash protocols. The creators of PIVX envisioned a community-based currency of value with privacy features and fast transaction times. The development of PIVX is very heavily community-based, with an open invitation for contributors to add to the project rather than restricting innovation through rules or hierarchy within the community.

History
PIVX was originally called Darknet (DNET) and launched in January 2016. DNET was rebranded to PIVX in January 2017. DNET was originally a proof-of-work based coin and mined coins using this method until August 2016, when it was then switched over to proof-of-stake. In 2018, PIVX plans to introduce wallet upgrades, website upgrades, a decentralized exchange, a redesign to its voting system, upgrades to its mining protocol, and security upgrades that focus on increasing privacy and anonymity.

Features
The main features that PIVX focuses on are privacy and anonymity. While most cryptocurrencies use addresses that are not linked to a person's identity, a third-party could trace a series of transactions from certain addresses to link these back to a specific user.

This can cause problems even if the user is using the currency for legitimate uses, for example, the coins that the user previously received may have been used for illegal purposes, before being linked to the user. In order to address this issue, PIVX uses the Zerocoin protocol, creating a second coin on the network called zPIV. zPIV uses the Zerocoin protocol to mix coins on the network so that there are no links between the sender and receiver. The balance of zPIV wallets are also masked so that no parties can determine the value of any wallets. As the encryption keys used in zPIV are generated entirely from the protocol with no developer input, all parties can be assured of the anonymity provided by zPIV.

PIVX uses proof-of-stake in order to secure the network and generate currency. Security is maintained through many nodes holding PIVX tokens. PIVX uses a Seesaw Reward Balance System in order to balance out the staking rewards between master nodes and staking nodes. When there are more master nodes than staking nodes, then more rewards are given to staking nodes, and vice versa. This system is designed to discourage users from creating too many master nodes which increases risks as staking becomes more centralized. It also increases the liquidity of PIVX as an asset.

In 2018, PIVX plans to add two more anonymity measures. The Dandelion Protocol Integration will be able to make user's IP addresses untraceable through creating a series of layers. The first layer, called the 'stem phase', relays the user's connection through a series of hops, similar to using a network of virtual private networks.

In the 'fluff' phase, the connection is broadcast symmetrically and simultaneously to a series of nodes. These two layers of relays make it difficult for anyone to trace the original source of the transaction. The second measure is to integrate the use of I2P (Invisible Internet Project) into the network. I2P is a peer-to-peer network for anonymization, similar to the TOR network. ∎

Currency Code:
PIVX

Launch Date:
2014

Market Cap:
$652M

Max. Supply:
Unlimited

Circulating Supply:
55,290,249 PIVX

Consensus Mechanism:
PoS

Hashing Algorithm:
Quark

Block Time:
60 seconds

URL:
pivx.org

FACTOM

An open source record-keeping system on the blockchain, Factom functions as a verification and validation layer for businesses and aims to create, design and build products that make the world more transparent and honest.

History

In January 2014, co-founders Paul Snow and David Johnston began collaborating on an idea regarding distributed identity, which led to the invention of Factom. Factom was created to address certain issues with the Bitcoin blockchain that had been identified by the team, such as — high transaction costs, and not being able to handle large transaction volumes.

The first code made was published on GitHub in June 2014, with the project originally named 'Notary Chains'. By November of the same year, the white-paper had been released and exactly one year after collaboration began, Factom version 0.1 was released. An ICO was held for Factom at the end of March 2015 and raised 2,278 BTC ($1.1m at the time). On September 1, 2015, the genesis block for Factom was born and the network went live to early adopters and beta users. The Universal Declaration of Human Rights in 443 different translations was the first item to be anchored and secured to the Bitcoin blockchain.

March 2017 saw the launch of the first commercial project, Factom Harmony, built to store and create permanent mortgage records. Peter Kirby, the former CEO of Factom, said *"The Harmony solution... was fundamentally missing from the industry."* It was the first practical deployment of blockchain technology in the mortgage industry.

Features

Factom works by separating the data layer (notarizations) from the value layer of a blockchain (the method of transferring value). By allowing users to notarize data and anchor it to the blockchain of Bitcoin, immutability is attained for relevant data. The Factom data layer is only accessible to verified users, with all information kept separately and entry granted on an individual basis.

Factom is built on 'hash technology'. This cryptographic function transforms data into a fixed alphanumeric string. These collected hashes are created by Factom users and then anchored to the Bitcoin blockchain. The network resolves the following types of proof for records created on the Factom platform - Proof of Existence, Proof of Process and Proof of Audit.

Proof of Existence occurs when a user allows Factom to create a hash for the data, which is then anchored to the Bitcoin blockchain, proving its time of creation and existence. Proof of Process is the grouping of all entries in a chain, allowing their order and process to be examined and therefore their validity to be confirmed. Lastly, as any document is anchored to the Bitcoin blockchain, it can be produced at any time, providing Proof of Audit.

Factom Harmony provides a single platform that removes the cost of document assembly and storage in the mortgage industry. It enables organizations to coordinate compliance audits and interact with loan documents and data across multiple sources. By securing data to the blockchain, documentation errors are reduced, thereby ensuring compliance for successful audits, and creating a permanent and authentic record of final loan documents. ∎

Currency Code:
FCT

Launch Date:
2014

Market Cap:
$581M

Max. Supply:
N/A

Circulating Supply:
8,745,102 ETN

Consensus Mechanism:
PoS

Hashing Algorithm:
SHA-256

Block Time:
10 minutes

URL:
factom.com

Currency Code:
NXT

Launch Date:
2013

Market Cap:
$562M

Max Supply:
1,000,000,000 NXT

Circulating Supply:
998,999,942 NXT

Consensus Mechanism:
PoS

Hashing Algorithm:
SHA-256

Block Time:
60 seconds

URL:
nxtplatform.org

NXT

Nxt is a blockchain technology available for public and private use, with a five-year development history, proven stability, a large community, and a well established proof-of-stake model. Developed by Jelurida, it offers a multiple core-level feature-set such as a Decentralized Asset Exchange, Marketplace, Voting system, Alias system, Phased Transactions, Shuffling, and Data storage.

History

The Nxt project was announced by an anonymous developer, known as 'BCNext', on the bitcointalk.org forums in September 2013. The developer asked for donations from the community which would be used to determine the initial distribution spread of NXT coins. On November 18, 2013, fundraising ended with approximately 21 BTC donated. The genesis block was created six days later and the full supply of one billion NXT coins was distributed to the 73 donors. In March 2014, the full source code was released to the public.

In October 2016, a Dutch company Jelurida was incorporated by the core-developers of Nxt to protect intellectual property and on January 1, 2018, Jelurida launched the Ardor public blockchain platform.

Features

The Nxt Asset Exchange (AE) is Nxt's decentralized trading engine, providing users with a platform to trade assets and eliminate the need for trusted third-parties. Nxt Assets can be issued by any user for a wide variety of data, such as - financial instruments, public and private records, semi-private records, physical asset keys, and intangibles. The Monetary System allows users to design and issue customized cryptocurrencies, using the Nxt blockchain to secure them. Several parameters can be set, for example, users can issue crowdfunding coins, which are only released to the buyers if a set funding goal is met. If goals aren't met, the buyers' funds are returned to their accounts.

With the Nxt Voting System, users can create polls with one question and up to 100 answers. Filters can also be set to ensure only certain Nxt accounts are eligible to vote in polls, such as a minimum required balance of NXT, or other assets. Nxt's fully decentralized Marketplace enables direct peer-to-peer trading. For example, users can list products, search for products, buy directly on the blockchain, send digital goods encrypted over the blockchain or leave private or public feedback after receiving a product.

Nxt's messaging feature enables users to send small amounts of open or encrypted data (Arbitrary Messages) on the blockchain. The term 'message' is a loose one as any data can be stored on the blockchain. Encrypted messages can have a shared key which allows them to be shared with third-party accounts. The Nxt Data Cloud can be seen as an extension of unencrypted messages, with searchable metadata fields for the uploaded documents and files.

Nxt Aliasing allows one piece of text to be substituted for another, so easy to remember keywords or key phrases can be used to represent other things such as website URLs, ipv6 addresses, account numbers, email addresses, product SKU codes, and more.

The Nxt Phased Transaction feature makes 'programmable' transactions possible. Users can set multiple conditions (up to 10) before a transaction is executed. It extends the definition of multisig to include many more functions, for example, shareholders can vote to release transactions. When applied to an account, it can limit use to only submit phased transactions as an additional level of security, so even if the controlled account's passphrase (or private key) is compromised, the assets are still safe. Finally, Nxt Plugins enable third-party software developers to add functionality to the Nxt Client that runs locally. ∎

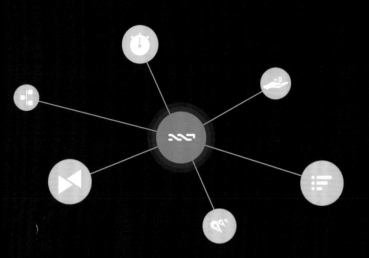

Nxt is a pioneer in many aspects, one of which being its out-of-the-box features or functionalities. Often Nxt will work without any particular installation, configuration or modification. Many in-demand features are available to new users by default, with no additional fees, or configuration requirements.

"The focus of Nxt is to allow anybody to start using blockchain technology with the Nxt Creation Kit, as well as enabling enterprises and organizations to build their public or private blockchains without the need of hiring or learning different languages because it is built in the reliable and well known Java programming language."

PUBLIC AND PRIVATE BLOCKCHAIN, FOR ALL NEEDS.

Nxt pushes on as a viable solution capable of achieving the same functionality found in Ethereum, with a five-year development history, proven stability, massive community, and well established proof-of-stake model.

If a company wants to keep the blockchain public, the Nxt creation kit is the place to start. It helps to clone the Nxt blockchain, create the genesis block and start experimenting with it. The JPL (Jelurida Public License) that asks you to drop 10% of your tokens to the NXT holders.

If a company needs a private blockchain, they can license the technology directly from Jelurida.

If a new or existing company is building a blockchain-based business approach, there is a good chance the Nxt feature set will cover a significant amount, if not all, of the functionalities needed. If there is still customization required, chances are it will be minimal given the existing platform. This means more resources available for marketing, and other critical core expenses.

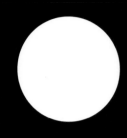

Currency Code:
GBYTE

Launch Date:
2014

Market Cap:
$542M

Max. Supply:
,000,000 GBYTE

Circulating Supply:
645,222 GBYTE

Consensus Mechanism:
DAG

Hashing Algorithm:
N/A

Block Time:
N/A

URL:
byteball.org

BYTEBALL BYTES

Byteball is a decentralized storage system that enables users to store information which can be used for verification, title ownership, contractual agreements, or as a currency. Users pay to store their information onto the Byteball system by spending Bytes, at a rate of 1 Byte to 1 byte of storage. Other types of currencies can be issued by users through the Byteball system and these can be used to represent assets such as shares, or ownership of assets. Byteball allows users to easily create and use conditional payment systems with an integrated chat system that allows users to process payments through direct peer-to-peer chat, or through chatbot systems.

History
Byteball was first announced in September 2016 and became immediately available on 5 exchanges. It was released with almost complete functionality in order to make the system immediately usable. Further improvements added functionality and bug fixes. Byteball is distributed according to how many Bytes and Bitcoin users hold. The first distribution was in December 2016, with 9 distributions since. The next free distribution is scheduled for March 2018.

Features:
Byteball does not use a blockchain. Instead, it uses a Directed Acyclic Graph (DAG) algorithm to form and store a chain of transactions. There is no mining or use of other algorithms that are common to other cryptocurrencies, such as proof-of-work or proof-of-stake. Byteball uses a Main Chain to define the order of transactions and trusted users called Witnesses, in order to establish consensus within the network.

Transactions made on the network must contain previous transactions, as the network relies on the order of transactions to ensure that double spending attacks do not occur. When double spending occurs, the network uses the earliest transaction in the network, and discards the subsequent transaction, deeming it fraudulent. Witnesses in the network are real users who are deemed as trustworthy by others. Their role is to help maintain network integrity by monitoring double spend attempts, as well as validate the correct transactions when there are any complications.

Peer-to-peer conditional payments are enabled in Byteball. Users can set conditions in which payments are made when they are sent. For example, a user can set a condition in which payment is to be made upon receiving another payment, and if not, the transaction is to be reversed within a certain time limit. Alternatively, users can set payments on condition that they are signed by certain parties. There is a lot of flexibility in the way that users can define smart contracts using the Byteball wallet, and the system is designed so that the smart contracts are easily read and understood. All of this is done through the Bytecoin network without any need for an intermediary party.

Oracles are trusted users who can post and verify real-world events. This can be used to create smart contracts that are applicable to the real world. For example, users can bet on sports events, make payments conditional on market values, or even ensure their payments are canceled if there are large fluctuations in the markets before certain conditions are met.

All of these transactions can be done through the Byteball wallet, as well as through a text messaging platform within the wallet. ■

MONACOIN

An open source, decentralized cryptocurrency, Monacoin was forked from Litecoin and officially launched in Japan in January 2014. One of the key features that gives it an edge over its parent is its block time of just 1.5 minutes, compared to Litecoin's 2.5 minutes.

History

Monacoin was launched in 2014 in Japan, its name taken from 'Mona' a cat-like ASCII art character used on the bulletin board "2channel". It was initially based upon Litecoin, which was then perceived to be Bitcoin's ideal successor. After its release, Monacoin went through some periods of price volatility before eventually settling down, with local media playing an active role in boosting its popularity by using the narrative *"like Bitcoin, but made in Japan"* and vigorously promoting it.

Monacoin soared in popularity when official bodies in Japan designated it to be a cryptocurrency for both online and offline transactions. Since then, Zaif (an online exchange) has installed several 'Smart ATMs' across the country to enable investors to buy and sell the coin.

Zaif has also built an online shop with a physical store that allows both Bitcoin and Monacoin payments. With over 500,000 customers making use of their online shop monthly, Zaif has succeeded in taking Monacoin to the doorsteps of the buyers and has also increased the acceptability of the cryptocoin.

Monacoin is considered by many to be the Japanese national cryptocoin because it is now being accepted in virtually every area of their day-to-day society – from restaurants to fuelling stations and department stores – most places where goods and services are traded are now accepting Monacoin.

Features

Monacoin has a number of unique features that make it easily distinguishable from other altcoins. One of these is its lightning network implementation. This has been designed to increase transaction speeds, making almost instant payment possible and also enhancing cross-blockchain transactions. Its confirmation time is only 1.5 minutes — currently 7 times faster than Bitcoin. With the activation of SegWit, Monacoin can be likened to a hybrid combination of Ripple, Ethereum, and Dash.

Another feature to note is that the coin is designed to resist centralization – the inclusion of the Lyra2REv2 algorithm is intended to make the development of custom mining hardware and multipool mining impossible, thereby making sure that validation of transactions occurs through a widely distributed network.

In addition, Monacoins can easily be exchanged for Japanese Yen on Japanese exchanges, unlike many other altcoins where one has to first buy Bitcoin in order to acquire them.

The final feature to consider is that Monacoin has legal backing from the Japanese government. This makes it possible for the digital coin to be used with freedom and peace of mind, without any form of harassment from central regulatory authorities. ∎

Currency Code:
MONA

Launch Date:
2014

Market Cap:
$487M

Max. Supply:
105,120,000 MONA

Circulating Supply:
56,544,552 MONA

Consensus Mechanism:
PoW

Hashing Algorithm:
Lyra2REv2

Block Time:
90 seconds

URL:
monacoin.org

Currency Code:
XZC

Launch Date:
2013

Market Cap:
$430M

Max Supply:
21,000,000 XZC

Circulating Supply:
8,935,681 XZC

Consensus Mechanism:
PoW

Hashing Algorithm:
Lyra2z

Block Time:
10 Minutes

URL:
zcoin.io

ZCOIN

Zcoin is a decentralized, open source cryptocurrency whose mission is to increase individual liberty by guaranteeing financial privacy and freedom of commerce. Zcoin is based on the Zerocoin protocol - originally created in 2013 as an extension to run on top of Bitcoin and uses 'zero-knowledge cryptographic proofs' to wipe the links between transactions.

History

Zcoin is the first fully functional implementation of Zerocoin, a cryptocurrency that was first proposed by Matthew D. Green, a professor at the Johns Hopkins University, along with two graduate students - Ian Miers and Christina Garman. It was initially conceived as an extension to the Bitcoin protocol that would add true cryptographic anonymity to Bitcoin transactions. The testnet software was publicly released on December 19, 2015, with the name, Moneta, before being changed to Zcoin for its official release on September 28, 2016, by Poramin Insom, who was also the founder of Vertcoin.

Features

Zcoin is a proof-of-work cryptocurrency that uses the same mining method and halving cycle as Bitcoin (4 years) but a different hashing algorithm - Lyra2z. They are moving towards implementing MTP (Merkle Tree Proofs), designed to be ASIC-proof, as well as discourage botnets through the high use of memory.

Zcoin's greatest achievements have been in the area of anonymity and privacy. Bitcoin and other altcoins before it have aimed to improve the anonymity of their transactions by using transaction mixers or ring signatures. These are methods that either mix transactions with others to hide their origins and destinations or, in the case of a ring signature, require the endorsed digital signature of someone in a selected user group. The problem with these methods is that their score is very low on the traceability set - a measure of a coin's privacy. This is because of certain inherent limitations due to the number of transactions per cycle and the block size. So while they demonstrate a traceability set rating typically less than ten per transaction, Zcoin has managed to increase this to the order of many thousands, thanks to their system of zero-knowledge cryptographic proofs. This is basically a method by which one user proves to another user that a given statement is true, without communicating any other information whatsoever, other than the fact that it is true or not.

The other problem that is solved by this system is due to the inability to perform a topological analysis of the transaction history. There are multiple research papers that demonstrate how a topological analysis can identify the owners of supposedly anonymous wallets by comparing a separate network like Facebook with the transaction history of a cryptocurrency's blockchain. With Zcoin, this chain of transactional history simply does not exist. There is literally nothing that can be analyzed.

Zcoin seems to have even taken a step further than this in their drive towards perfect privacy. Although zero-knowledge setups provide a great deal of anonymity, they still utilize what is known as a 'trusted setup'. This basically means that at some point, someone needs to be trusted to generate the initial parameters before destroying them. In order to improve on this situation, Zcoin has implemented the Sigma protocol which does away with the need for a trusted setup in the first place. ∎

Zero-Knowledge cryptographic proofs

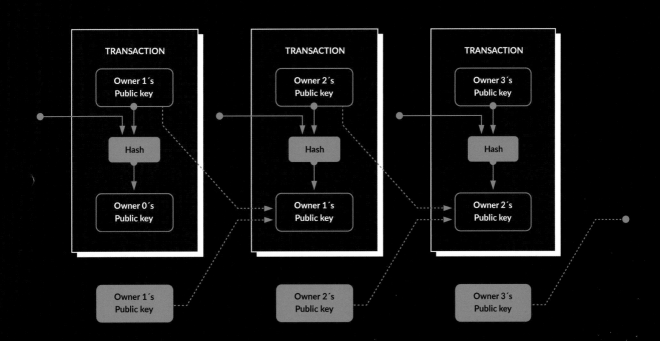

In Bitcoin, all transactions are broadcasted on a public ledger. Research has shown that external information, such as publicly announced addresses, can be used to link identities and organizations to transactions. The default reuse of bitcoin addresses exacerbates this problem.

Furthermore, the same type of mechanism used to break privacy in social networks, such as the analysis of social network topology, can be used to break privacy in the Bitcoin network.

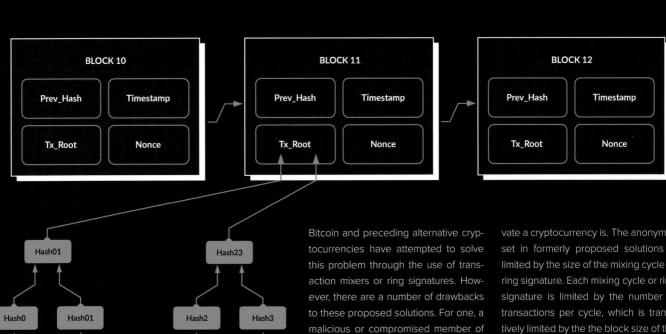

Bitcoin and preceding alternative cryptocurrencies have attempted to solve this problem through the use of transaction mixers or ring signatures. However, there are a number of drawbacks to these proposed solutions. For one, a malicious or compromised member of a mixer or ring signature can break privacy. Furthermore, the anonymity set is a key metric to understanding how pri-

vate a cryptocurrency is. The anonymity set in formerly proposed solutions limited by the size of the mixing cycle ring signature. Each mixing cycle or ring signature is limited by the number transactions per cycle, which is transtively limited by the the block size of the cryptocurrency. Thus, the anonymity se in previous attempts at privacy tends only be a few hundred transactions

Currency Code:
SYS

Launch Date:
2014

Market Cap:
$443M

Max. Supply:
888,000,000 SYS

Circulating Supply:
530,070,629 SYS

Consensus Mechanism:
PoW

Hashing Algorithm:
SHA-256

Block Time:
60 seconds

URL:
syscoin.org

SYSCOIN

Syscoin is a database, based on a blockchain, that has the ability to be used as a store of information, with tokens traded as a currency. The database is used to create a marketplace in which users can buy and sell items using the cryptocurrency. Syscoin uses a Dark Gravity Wave algorithm for mining and has an 888 million maximum coin limit. Miner rewards increase as network traffic increases, and this is done without increasing transaction fees. Smart contracts are enabled for Syscoin, and aliases are used in place of addresses for sending and receiving currency.

History

The idea of Syscoin was conceived in 2014 in a white-paper which detailed how the project would create a decentralized ecosystem for a marketplace, smart contracts, data storage, and document certification.

The code was originally based on Litecoin, and the Initial Coin Offering was in August 2014. During the Initial Coin Offering, one of the partners in the company allegedly stole 750 BTC which resulted in a legal case being filed against the partner. In 2016, the Blockchain Foundry was released, which allowed the development of merchant platforms on the Syscoin platform.

In September 2017, BlockMarket Desktop was released, allowing the use of multiple types of cryptocurrencies on the blockchain-based marketplaces. BlockMarket Web, a web-based version of the marketplace is planned for release in 2018, which will eliminate the need for users to install software to access their wallets or the marketplace.

Features

Syscoin uses the Dark Gravity Wave algorithm for mining. This algorithm adjusts the difficulty of each individual block, depending on data gained through mining previous blocks, in order to ensure that block issuing times are consistent, regardless of fluctuations in hash power.

This results in optimized transaction times and better resistance to hard fork or majority attacks on the network. Changing the difficulty for every block may open up the network for a 'Time Warp Attack' in which a majority attack with varying timestamps may take over the network during a low difficulty block, however, the Dark Gravity Wave algorithm overcomes this problem by combining different average block difficulties.

Smart contracts are enabled on Syscoin, however, these are different to the Turing-complete smart contracts that are available on Ethereum. The smart contracts on Syscoin were developed with a focus on being backward compatible with the Bitcoin protocol, and are designed to be able to be used to create e-commerce solutions.

Syscoin uses an alias identity system, which makes it easier for users to send and receive currency using their own designed aliases, as opposed to a cryptographically generated wallet address. This means that users can send and receive currency from an easily recognizable address, for example, an email address. The aliases are signed through the blockchain so that security is not compromised.

In order to incentivize miners consistently, Syscoin automatically increases block mining rewards as the network traffic increases. This ensures that miners are adequately rewarded for their contribution to the network while maintaining consistent transaction fees for users. ∎

GAME CREDITS

A cryptocurrency designed for use in gaming, Game Credits provides fast, secure, and private transactions and has been developed by a company with the same name. Game Credits (company) has brought out a number of products to be used with their currency, such as a gaming store, a Massive Multiplayer Online RPG, and a game creation engine. The aim of the company is to move the gaming industry towards blockchain technology in order to create a more secure and integrated system for value exchange.

History

Game Credits was launched in 2017, and in the same year released a community forum, a gaming store, a wallet, a Massively Multiplayer Online RPG for mobile platforms, a game creation engine, as well as a mobile gaming platform for in-game purchases. In the future, Game Credits aims to create a platform for competitive esports, a cryptocurrency exchange, and a community-based charity organization.

Features

Game Credits aims to bring value to the game industry by providing a fast, semi-anonymous, and fraud-resistant method of value transfer. It aims to benefit developers by introducing a faster, cheaper, and more direct method of receiving payments. Gamers also benefit as they can purchase items without the restrictions and privacy issues of using a credit card. All of this is integrated into their gaming platforms.

The Game Credits network is able to process tens of millions of transactions simultaneously. Relying on the blockchain to confirm valid payments means that developers can be confident that fraudulent transactions (through credit card chargebacks, for example) are no longer an issue. Developers are also able to receive their payment with minimal delay and take advantage of the use of Game Credits to avoid payment processing fees through credit cards, banks, or other content distributors.

The development platforms that Game Credits have created enable developers to easily integrate the cryptocurrency into their games for the purchase of in-game items. Gamers are able to buy items directly without having to use a credit card, which empowers the consumer as they are able to define their own spend limits and use the same currency across all games. Current restrictions mean that currency is usually limited to a single game ecosystem, but with Game Credits this restriction would be lifted and customers can use their currency across all games developed with the Game Credits platforms.

Some of Game Credits innovations are:
Game Credits - a community called GNation in order to connect developers and gamers. GPlay - Game Credits' gaming store, providing developers with a high payout per sale (90%), and providing gamers with a portal to spend Game Credits to buy games. PixelWars - a Massive Multiplayer Online RPG for mobile platforms which uses Game Credits as its in-game currency. AppMarka and MobileGo - tools designed for developers to integrate the use of Game Credits within their games. GExchange, Game Credit's own cryptocurrency exchange, has no scheduled launch date, however, when released, it will allow users to trade in fiat and other cryptocurrencies. ∎

Currency Code:
GAME

Launch Date:
2017

Market Cap:
$316M

Max. Supply:
84,000,000 GAME

Circulating Supply:
64,355,352 GAME

Consensus Mechanism:
PoW

Hashing Algorithm:
Scrypt

Block Time:
90 seconds

URL:
gamecredits.com

Currency Code:
CT

aunch Date:
015

larket Cap:
310M

lax.Supply:
000,000,000 ACT

irculating Supply:
00,000,000 ACT

onsensus Mechanism:
DPoS

lashing Algorithm:
HA-512

lock Time:
 seconds

JRL:
chain.com

ACHAIN

Achain is a public blockchain platform allowing users to issue tokens, create smart contracts, develop applications and implement their own blockchain, with priority placed on security, stability, and extensibility. The Achain project is aiming to build a global blockchain network that facilitates the exchange of information and value transactions.

History
Achain was developed by the Achain Foundation, a Singapore based non-profit organization, co-constructed and co-maintained by the Achain community. Initially known as 'Thinkyoung Blockchain', the project was initiated in May 2014 and was officially commercialized in July 2015. The first Virtual Machine on the platform, based on a LUA smart contract, was developed in mid-2016, with the network upgrading to the smart contract sandbox mechanism in August 2016.

At the end of June 2017, Thinkyoung Blockchain rebranded as Achain, with the technical white-paper released to the public and tools for smart contract development being released shortly after. The Achain ICO commenced on July 7, 2017, raising 2189.05 BTC and 10436.34 ETH and was concluded in 61 seconds. The Achain main network was launched on July 22, 2017, and within two months, four separate dApps had been developed and initiated on the Achain network.

In late November 2017, the Achain team announced its forking theory, signifying their intended move from the Singularity milestone to the implementation of the Galaxy milestone, and encouraging the mutual agreement of participating blockchains.

Features
The Achain network is being developed in three stages: 'Singularity' – the modular smart contract network and sandbox, 'Galaxy' – the forking network, and 'Cosmos' – the event-driven interconnected network.

Singularity is the first stage of development to enhance the Achain network's stability and security. Smart contracts and digital assets can be created by developers, with sandbox simulations available, to automatically test and monitor the environment where the newly created smart contracts operate, ensuring that the contracts run securely within the Achain network.

According to Achain, forking in the blockchain ecosystem is a method of evolution, with different characteristics of each fork being required for different applications. The Galaxy milestone will allow users to fork multiple new blockchains off a currently existing blockchain, such as Bitcoin, with the Achain network being the initial network. Achain will split into multiple sub-chains that will meet the needs of different applications, by integrating the features of other blockchains. Users can create personalized networks with the advantages of multiple blockchains, in a low-cost and user-friendly environment.

Cosmos, the final milestone of the project, will be an interconnected network that uses BaaS (blockchain-as-a-service). BaaS and VEP (Value Exchange Protocol) will unify the main chain and sub-chains, and additionally allow for the connectivity of non-blockchain information to the network. The Achain network will be able to access offline data (e.g. from public or enterprise databases) while the VEP will receive the information and execute smart contracts based on the data received. ∎

SKYCOIN

A third generation cryptocurrency developed on its own blockchain, Skycoin was created in order to address many of Bitcoin's technical shortcomings. One of these shortcomings Skycoin aims to improve upon is blockchain centralization, whereby all blockchain transactions are controlled by just a few mining pools. Skycoin will address this problem via a protocol that builds trust between users, community members, the network, and nodes.

History

The Skycoin project is an ongoing, open source blockchain project launched in 2012. Initiated as a collaborative effort between multiple interdependent groups, the project seeks to implement Satoshi Nakamoto's original idea of a fully decentralized cryptocurrency. As Bitcoin came to be controlled by three mining pools, instead, Skycoin has embarked on creating a consensus algorithm (Obelisk) to achieve total decentralization.

Phase 1 of the project primarily focused on research and experimentation, establishing the technical boundaries of the platform. Phase 2 commenced in early July 2017, focusing on the development of a vast ecosystem of applications aimed at solving complex real-world problems. Phase 3 is planned to start in the second quarter of 2018 and will focus on large-scale adoption of the platform.

Features

Skycoin comprises six core elements: Aether (a store replication protocol), CXO (an immutable object system), BlockDB (blockchain storage), CX (a Turing application language), Skycoin (the secure, anonymous transaction token that powers the platform), and Skywire (Skycoin's networking standard). Developers can build applications on the platform and create an ecosystem that integrates features like VPN applications, messaging, and social media.

Skywire is an important pillar of the Skycoin project which the Skycoin team ambitiously refer to as "the next internet" – a network aiming to redefine privacy protocols in the future. Inspired by net neutrality and peer-to-peer technology, Skywire aims to render the role of conventional internet service providers obsolete. The network's privacy protocol proposes to place the internet under the control of the users and usher in a new era of internet privacy.

The Skycoin project is not just a blockchain project, but a platform that supports a network of applications and services. It emphasizes usability, simplicity, fairness, speed, privacy, and security. Privacy and security are particularly critical features of the Skycoin project. Through the CoinJoin protocol, the platform mixes transactions from multiple wallets to enhance privacy and anonymity. The network guarantees stronger security since it is not dependent on miners and is 51% attack proof.

Ultimately, Skycoin aims to be the foundation for internet decentralization. The tech world has long desired a more open, distributed, secure, internet, and Skycoin is taking steps to accomplish that. With its focus on long-term network growth, it is clear why developers are claiming that their project could help shape the future of the internet, taking digital contracts, communication, and identity infrastructure to a whole new level. ∎

Currency Code:
SKY

Launch Date:
2014

Market Cap:
$306M

Max. Supply:
100,000,000 SKY

Circulating Supply:
6,925,739 SKY

Consensus Mechanism:
Obelisk

Hashing Algorithm:
N/A

Block Time:
10 seconds

URL:
skycoin.net

Currency Code:
BTX

Launch Date:
2017

Market Cap:
$287M

Max. Supply:
21,000,000 BTX

Circulating Supply:
10,624,902 BTX

Consensus Mechanism:
PoW / PoS

Hashing Algorithm:
Timetravel10

Block Time:
2.5 minutes

URL:
bitcore.cc

BITCORE

Bitcore is a hybrid fork cryptocurrency that combines SegWit, Core 0.15 and Bloom with the latest Bitcoin crypto technology. It features a 10 MB block size, fast 2.5 minute block times with an extremely small blockchain currently less than 400 MB. It also uses the GPU-mining algorithm, Timetravel10 as well as the Diff64_15 difficulty algorithm.

History
Bitcore was created on April 28, 2017, by the same team of developers behind Bitsend (BSD). Bitcore is one of the first cryptocurrencies to utilize the hybrid fork method which consists of creating an empty blockchain rather than copying the full blockchain up until the moment of the fork.

On November 2, 2017, at block 463619 of the Bitcoin blockchain, a snapshot was taken and in the following weeks some 5 million transactions were made in order to fill the public keys of the new Bitcore blockchain.

From November 2, the time of the snapshot, holders of Bitcoin had until October 30 to claim their Bitcore at a ratio of 0.5 BTX : 1.0 BTC. The claiming took each user's security into consideration and ensured that their private keys were not unduly exposed to the public, which is one major concern Bitcore intended to address.

Bitcore has since risen in value from under $2 USD per coin to the current worth of over $20 per coin. It also currently enjoys a market capitalization to the tune of over $280 million.

Features
Bitcore has several features and advantages worthy of note. One of them is that it has 10 MB blocks that can scale to 20 MB with SegWit enabled, thereby making it possible for the network to handle up to 17.6 billion transactions annually. To give this some perspective; at this rate, Bitcore is able to handle all the transactions that Bitcoin can handle in a year, in just three days. In addition, Bitcore has a transaction speed that few can rival, with the capacity to confirm transactions in a matter of seconds.

Its difficulty algorithm known as the Diff64_15 is also something completely new and unique to Bitcore and guarantees that no more than 15 percent change in difficulty occurs within a period of 64 blocks. This has systematically eliminated the block time problems synonymous with Bitcoin Cash.

Bitcore's maximum total supply is 21 million coins and the ASIC resistant Timetravel10 algorithm is required for mining them. Apart from that, the block time for Bitcore is just 2.5 minutes and its mining reward is 3.125 BTX which matches the halving schedule of Bitcoin.

Another advantage Bitcore has is its extremely small blockchain of under 400 MB. This makes it feasible for even tablets and cell phones to store and run the blockchain. ∎

BITCORE BTX: THE FAST PAYMENT SOLUTION

Comparison Chart (19th of January 2018)	Bitcoin (BTC)	Bitcore (BTX)	Bitcoin Gold (BTG)	BitcoinCash (BCH)
Max. Supply	21 Mil.	21 Mil.	21 Mil.	21 Mil.
Distribution	mining	mining, claiming, airdrops	mining, claiming	mining, claiming
Mining Algorithm	sha256 (ASIC)	timetravel10 (GPU)	equihash (GPU)	sha256 (ASIC)
Blocktime	10 minutes	2.5 minutes	10 minutes	10 minutes
Max. Blocksize (segwit)	1 MB (2 – 4 MB)	10 MB (20 MB)	1 MB (2 – 4 MB)	8 MB
Blockchain Size	~152 GB	~500 MB	~163 GB	~158 GB
Difficulty Algorithm	standard BTC: 400%, 2 weeks	smooth Diff64_15: 15%, 3 hours	moving average over 30 blocks	standard BTC: 400%, 2 weeks + EDA
Max. TX / Day	~1.2 Million	~48 Million	~1.2 Million	~4.8 Million
Segwit	yes	yes	yes	no
Replay Protection	not necessary	not necessary	yes	yes
Established Since	2009	April 2017	October 2017	August 2017
Circulating Supply	16 812 000	10 760 000	16 773 000	16 920 000
Current Market Cap.	$195 259 Mil. USD	$310 Mil. USD	$4 500 Mil. USD	$30 126 Mil. USD
Price / coin	~ $12 000 USD	~ $28 USD	~ $220 USD	~ $1800 USD

Comparison chart against the original Bitcoin and the three most prominent Bitcoin forks to date.

BITCORE BTX - THE FUTURE IS NOW

REGISTER YOUR BTX ADDRESS TO RECEIVE 5% AIRDROP EVERY MONDAY!

www.bitcore.cc

Currency Code:
VTC

Launch Date:
2014

Market Cap:
$301M

Max. Supply:
84,000,000 VTC

Circulating Supply:
42,373,053 VTC

Consensus Mechanism:
PoW

Hashing Algorithm:
Lyra2REv2

Block Time:
120 seconds

URL:
vertcoin.org

VERTCOIN

An ASIC resistant, peer-to-peer cryptocurrency and software project, Vertcoin aims to return to the original vision of cryptocurrency by becoming "the people's coin" - a decentralized system owned by its users. Featuring Stealth Address technology and proof-of-work, ASIC resistant protocols, Vertcoin is committed to ensuring that mining remains decentralized and transaction fees remain low.

History

Vertcoin was created by James Lovejoy when he was still in high school and released to the world on January 8, 2014, via a GitHub user. Lovejoy had been programming since the age of 10 and is now an undergraduate researcher at MIT's Digital Currency Initiative, working on decentralized monetary policy. On July 1, the Vertcoin wallet was released, supporting Stealth Address transactions and giving greater anonymity to users' transactions.

December 2014 and August 2015 saw two separate Vertcoin forks due to threats of centralization; the first as a defense against Scrypt-Adaptive-N capable ASIC mining technology, and the second as a means to avoid the majority control of the Vertcoin network's hashing power by a botnet.

On May 7, 2017, the SegWit protocols were adopted, resulting in an increase in block size limit as well as allowing for the implementation of second-layer solutions for further development. In December 2017, Vertcoin's prize per block was reduced by half, from 50 to 25 coins. This halving takes place in order to stabilize the value of Vertcoins and is planned to take place every 4 years until all of its 84 million coins have been released.

Features

Vertcoin's development team consists of around 10 full-time personnel that work closely with an open source community of volunteers around the world. Their main focus is to safeguard decentralized mining so as to *"ensure the long-term security and fair distribution of the currency."*

To this ends, Vertcoin has established what is known as the 'Adaptive N-Factor' to the Scrypt algorithm. What this does is determine exactly how much memory is needed to calculate the hashing functions. The N-Factor then increases over time in order to discourage the use of specialized mining hardware and instead, encourage the wider distribution of the verification task among individual users. Vertcoin is currently developing a '1-Click' miner to further facilitate the mining of their coins for home users, the idea being that *"building a strong network requires more miners."*

The SegWit protocol, implemented by Vertcoin in May 2017 included Lighting Network technology for scalable, instant transactions. This technology moves a large portion of the burden of transactions off the blockchain for faster processing and leads to a considerable increase in the network's capacity. Another benefit of the Lighting Network technology is something known as 'atomic cross-chain trading'. This is, in effect, a software layer that crosses blockchains and allows for the smooth, decentralized exchange of cryptocurrencies from within the Vertcoin wallet.

Although some have criticized Vertcoin for their lack of a marketing strategy, for a coin with no premine, ICO or airdrop, the past year has seen an incredible 20,000% increase in value and a growing, loyal, community. One might conclude that in the world of cryptocurrencies, it pays to have principles and stick to them. ∎

BLOCKNET

Blocknet is a blockchain-agnostic, decentralized Platform-as-a-Service. It is a peer-to-peer infrastructure for inter-blockchain services, that is designed to enable a tokenized ecosystem between multiple cryptocurrencies.

History

Blocknet was launched in October 2014 by Dan Metcalf of XCurrency to try and solve the issue of XCurrency's small user base and to improve the interoperability of cryptocurrencies. Although Blocknet was initiated by XCurrency, it is not the core coin. Instead, the Blocknet Foundation was created to spread decision-making across all participating coins, giving equal weight to each of the members of the board.

The Blocknet Foundation and its open-ended communication helped to curate viable cryptocurrencies for the "internet of blockchains", which would be connected by Blocknet. The goal was to identify and realize the potential of inter-operable cryptocurrencies as well as ensure that supported coins were contributing to the blockchain ecosystem, as opposed to taking advantage of the new technology for purely monetary gain.

In 2017, Blocknet established a design partnership with VSA Partners to deliver its decentralized exchange application. This partnership will expand upon the UI (user interface) for the technological backend, allowing for the realization of a major feature of the Blocknet.

Features

Blocknet aims to create an "internet of blockchains," positioned to enable the frictionless monetization of APIs, and in doing so, empowering blockchain technology by converting its thousands of isolated chains into a token ecosystem.

It is founded upon the open-source communication protocol between different blockchains known as XBridge. XBridge allows interoperability between projects, providing users with the benefits of a multi-chain ecosystem that plays to the strengths of each cryptocurrency. Xbridge is open source and is implemented in every Blocknet-enabled app, giving dApps interoperability, mobility, and modularity.

Blocknet features a decentralized exchange that provides a gateway for fiat currencies and allows for the buying and selling of supported cryptocurrencies, without the need for an intermediary. The exchange supports over 30 cryptocurrencies for trading and is one of the key components of the Blocknet, allowing for the monetization of different blockchain services by removing the friction and high costs of traditional payment networks.

These systems work synergistically to enable multi-blockchain services to be delivered to devices that contain only a single blockchain. This ensures that device and network resources are conserved while allowing for flexibility, mobility, and scalability for the user. ■

Currency Code:
NLG

Launch Date:
2014

Market Cap:
$263M

Max. Supply:
10,000,000 BLOCK

Circulating Supply:
4,959,879 BLOCK

Consensus Mechanism:
PoS

Hashing Algorithm:
N/A

Block Time:
90 seconds

URL:
blocknet.co

Currency Code:
BBAY

Launch Date:
2014

Market Cap:
$260M

Max. Supply:
N/A

Circulating Supply:
1,008,859,402 BBAY

Consensus Mechanism:
PoS

Hashing Algorithm:
SHA-512

Block Time:
64 seconds

URL:
bitbay.net

BITBAY

BitBay is a cryptocurrency and free software platform that includes the world's first, fully-functional, decentralized marketplace. Using innovative technology such as Unbreakable Smart Contracts, a Double Deposit Escrow (DDE) system, and a wallet replete with novel security features, BitBay allows users to buy and sell goods and services securely and anonymously, without the need for middlemen.

History
BitBay was created in Poland in 2014 with the initial goal, according to Sylwester Suszek, the current CEO, of creating *"a professional and intuitive trading platform for buying and selling Bitcoins and Litecoins."* Suszek had previously been involved with the founding of two successful companies in the financial sector, as well as an earlier Bitcoin exchange.

In 2015, an updated version of the platform was launched with several improvements, such as the inclusion of the first professional trading tools, the addition of new cryptocurrencies, as well as general improvements in user-friendliness. This coincided with a move towards international expansion, with a second office opening in Amsterdam, and an increase in the team from 14 to 31 members.

At the beginning of 2016, the team started work on BitBay 3.0, an updated version of their platform that went online at the end of 2017, and included general improvements to the design, speed, and overall user experience.

Features
Although it's easy for any cryptocurrency to start out decentralized, it's considerably harder to keep it that way. Over time, mining centralizes power into the hands of the miners with the greatest hashing power, and a bloated blockchain allows only dedicated nodes with sufficient storage space to participate. To avoid these inherent problems, BitBay has chosen to use a proof-of-stake protocol, more specifically PoS3, over proof-of-work, and whilst some other cryptocoins have blockchains larger than 130GB, BitBay has managed to keep their blockchain size under 1GB after 3 years, allowing for larger numbers of nodes to engage and maintain decentralization.

A problem many potential investors have with cryptocurrencies, that BitBay is aiming to overcome, is price volatility. Using David Zimbeck's revolutionary 'rolling peg' technology, BitBay offers its users the added bonus of what they call 'user value protection' (UVP). Normally, if a cryptocoin is bought at $100 and then loses 10% of its value, the investor is left with $90. If, however, the same scenario happens when purchasing BAY, the 10% loss will be frozen or 'pegged' and released back to the user when the value rises again. They can still go ahead and sell their coins for the $90 they are now worth but in addition, they will have the remaining $10 of BAY on hold, to be retrieved at a later date − a far more attractive option to investors.

For added security, BitBay utilizes a number of features that are innovative and unique, the most important being; cold staking, steganography, and anti-keylogger protection. Cold staking takes advantage of multisig protocols and the ability to create joint accounts. It makes it possible to use two computers for storage and/or staking, with one key on each computer. For a hacker to be successful against this system, they would have to find both computers, hack them, find the pictures with the keys, (perhaps hidden among thousands of pictures) as well as crack the passwords on both computers. And with anti-keylogger activated, they could not even rely on using keylogger malware to help with that.

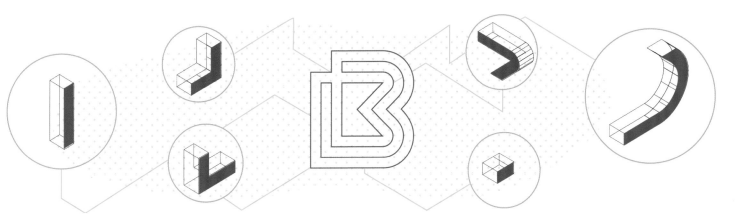

BitBay is the world's first fully-functional decentralized marketplace. Using innovative technology, BitBay enables you to buy and sell goods and services securely and anonymously, without the need for middlemen.

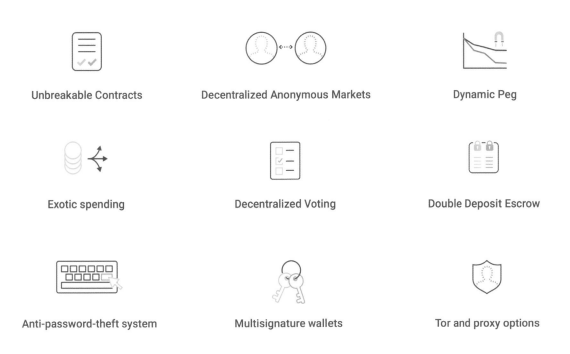

Unbreakable Contracts

Decentralized Anonymous Markets

Dynamic Peg

Exotic spending

Decentralized Voting

Double Deposit Escrow

Anti-password-theft system

Multisignature wallets

Tor and proxy options

Not surprisingly, BitBay confidently claims to have the most secure wallet crypto has ever seen. BitBay has focused much of its attention on 'cutting out the middleman', and one important feature that enables them to do this is what they call Double Deposit Escrow (DDE). In this system, the buyer and seller deposit an agreed amount into an escrow account and once the transaction has been completed successfully, both parties can release the collateral being held in the temporary address. If, however, something goes wrong, then the parties involved must resolve their differences in order to have their deposit returned to them. This system helps to guarantee the involvement of only genuine buyers and sellers as there is nothing to be gained from any intentional wrongdoing. BitBay certainly has a great deal to offer; it is a cryptocoin, a secure software platform, a decentralized marketplace, an exchange — it even offers its users a credit card linked to their account that can be used to make purchases or withdraw cash from ATM machines.

In a world where innovation is king, BitBay certainly looks to have its sights firmly set on the crown. ■

Currency Code:
NAV

Launch Date:
2014

Market Cap:
$255M

Max. Supply:
57,000,000 NAV

Circulating Supply:
62,267,897 NAV

Consensus Mechanism:
PoS

Hashing Algorithm:
X13

Block Time:
30 seconds

URL:
navcoin.org

NAVCOIN

An open source, decentralized cryptocurrency based on the Bitcoin blockchain, Nav Coin uses a proof-of-stake (PoS) algorithm that allows users to earn 5% interest on their investment. Nav Coin combines Bitcoin's technology and its own NavTech system to offer fully anonymous and fully decentralized cryptocurrency transactions.

History

Nav Coin was launched in July 2014, under the leadership of New Zealand developer Craig McGregor, with the aim of enhancing the privacy and anonymity of cryptocurrency transactions. Originally known as Summercoin, the network was rebranded to Navajocoin before finally settling on the name Nav Coin shortly afterwards.

Though Nav Coin started as a proof-of-work (PoW) coin, it later switched to the proof-of-stake (PoS) algorithm. Nav Coin has been a constant presence on the major cryptocurrency exchanges and has become one of the best performing cryptocurrencies over time. As of January 26, 2018, Nav Coin was valued at approximately $161.2 million in market capitalization.

Features

The Nav Coin wallet is easy to use and comes with a user-friendly setup guide that provides the user with all information required to load the blockchain and conduct transactions. Nav Coin is based on the Bitcoin Core, and in addition to the benefits Bitcoin offers, Nav Coin offers faster transaction speeds, lower transaction costs, an active development team, and optional anonymous transactions. The anonymity provided by Nav Coin is one of the features that sets it apart from Bitcoin as well as many others.

NavTech, a combination of the Bitcoin blockchain and the 'Subchain', scrambles and randomizes Nav Coin transactions, making them unidentifiable. The connection between the sender and the receiver, together with their IP address and tracking information, is wiped out completely and guarantees a heightened level of privacy and security. Towards the end of 2017, the Subchain and Nav Coin were merged into a single multi-chain wallet, encompassing an open network of nodes. The new wallet allowed developers to rebuild the blockchain and refactor the entire Subchain.

Nav Coin is fully decentralized, and the NavTech system allows servers to operate in trusted private clusters, enabling anyone to install their own server and earn income from it. Another benefit of Nav Coin is that users can earn up to 5% per annum on the amount in their wallet by enabling 'staking mode' in their wallet. This way, Nav Coin guarantees profitability with relatively little computational work – the PoS algorithm is such that even a 5V Raspberry Pi can be used to mine Nav Coin.

Nav Coin's unique features make it easy for people without much knowledge of the cryptocurrency world to purchase and trade the currency safely. It's usability, increased anonymity, and full decentralization are features that continue to contribute to its success and potential to reach greater heights in the future. ∎

NEBLIO

Neblio is an enterprise-grade blockchain solution for storing information and distributed applications. The Neblio platform aims to provide decentralized applications through their blockchain using a variety of already popular and established programming languages, in order to ease companies into the adoption of using blockchain technology. Deploying nodes and applications is designed to be a simple process through using their APIs and tools.

History
The idea of Neblio was introduced in early 2017 as the developers identified the need for simple enterprise-grade solutions that utilized blockchain technology. Current implementations of blockchain technology were complicated and the Neblio team aimed to simplify the process for developers, in order to create more widespread adoption of the blockchain.

The first version of Neblio was deployed in Q3 2017, with the introduction of a wallet and a token pre-sale. In Q4 2017, staking wallets were introduced, where users can hold Neblio tokens and increase the value of their holdings. The team aims to release their development platforms and APIs in early 2018, and their goal is to have industry-wide adoption by 2019.

Features
Neblio uses a proof-of-stake algorithm, which allows users to receive rewards after keeping tokens in their wallet for over 24 hours. This method allows the network to remain secure, as wallets that are staked are actively checking that transactions made on the network are valid. Rewards are given to random wallets every 2 minutes, and the more tokens that are staked in a single wallet, the more chance that wallet has of receiving a reward.

Staking rewards require wallets to be open and actively participating, which incentivizes users to continue contributing to the network. Using proof-of-stake also reduces the amount of energy used by the network, saving users the high energy costs currently incurred by networks which use proof-of-work based algorithms. It also allows people to use their own personal computers to gain rewards, rather than needing to invest in a mining rig, as proof-of-stake mining uses very little of the computer's resources. This makes Neblio more accessible for many users.

Neblio's APIs are designed with simplicity in mind. Developers are able to use 8 existing programming languages to develop applications to be distributed on the Neblio blockchain. The goal is to ease existing developers into blockchain development without the need for the developers to fully understand the workings of blockchain technology. There are two layers to Neblio's APIs; the first being the development APIs which allow applications to be developed, and the second is Neblio's RESTful API layer, which allows developers to access information stored on the blockchain through raw HTTP requests. This allows developers to easily access information stored on the Neblio blockchain through centralized applications, in order to widen the possibilities for development using the platform.

The Neblio Business Service team will provide a consulting service in order to help developers create applications using their blockchain. Neblio Business Services will guide companies through every stage of development, including node deployment, private blockchain development, and the use of their API to develop decentralized applications. ∎

Currency Code:
NEBL

Launch Date:
2017

Market Cap:
$245M

Max. Supply:
13,472,663 NEBL

Circulating Supply:
12,699,849 NEBL

Consensus Mechanism:
PoS

Hashing Algorithm:
N/A

Block Time:
120 seconds

URL:
nebl.io

Currency Code:
UBIQ

Launch Date:
2017

Market Cap:
$233M

Max. Supply:
50,000,000 UBIQ

Circulating Supply:
39,058,362 UBIQ

Consensus Mechanism:
PoS

Hashing Algorithm:
Ethash

Block Time:
88 seconds

URL:
ubiqsmart.com

UBIQ

A decentralized, peer-to-peer platform, Ubiq enables the creation and application of smart contracts and decentralized applications (dApps). It functions as a large distributed ledger and supercomputer built on an improved Ethereum codebase, allowing developers to create automated solutions to tasks normally carried out by third-party intermediaries. Ubiq also provides a value token (UBQ) which can be traded on cryptocurrency exchanges and used to pay for transaction fees and services on the Ubiq net.

History

UBQ was originally generated by transferring the value of a 3-year old token Jumbucks (JBS) onto a blockchain with Ethereum functionality. Ubiq was forked out of Ethereum 1.5.8 and subsequently launched in January 2017. It has since received a large amount of praise for being a superior solution to Ethereum in the implementation of a range of different processes. To date, UBQ is the only Ethereum-type cryptocurrency that has had assets built on top of it.

UBQ started with a supply of 36,451,770 units in January 2017 and increases by 8 UBQ per block. In order to control inflation, the developers have ensured that the reward decreases by 1 UBQ per year, eventually decreasing to 1 UBQ per block in 8 years' time.

As of December 2017, the market capitalization of UBQ was approximately $95 million. Ubiq Technologies Inc. was founded by a development team who have been heavily involved in the cryptocurrency space working as contractors or advisors to a number of blockchain projects. The team has solid experience in building blockchain-backed services and have managed to integrate their technology with a number of financial platforms.

Due to a number of hard forks planned for Ethereum's future, any business that wants to put their applications onto an Ethereum Virtual Machine will be subject to a number of updates and the instability that is associated with blockchain hard forks.

Features

Because Ubiq forked out of Ethereum, its network can host an Ethereum Virtual Machine which integrates a decentralized Turing-Complete Virtual Machine enabling the creation of smart contracts and tokens. As such, Ubiq provides Ethereum Virtual Machine functionality in a blockchain that is completely separate from that of Ethereum.

The UBQ tokens technical specifications feature the Dagger Hashimoto algorithm for proof-of-work, which features ASIC-resistance and light client verifiability. For desktop, Ubiq offers a fusion wallet which brings together a users' accounts, assets, and application in one secure interface. Ubiq also offers a browser-based wallet, Pyrus, enabling users to send Ubiq and any other ERC-20 Standard Tokens as well as generating and sending offline transactions.

Lastly, Ubiq offers a hardware wallet that can be connected by USB to any computer so that users can store their cryptocurrencies and digital payments securely offline. Ubiq's mission is essentially to improve on Ethereum's platform by creating a network that is stable, free of bugs and reliable to provide an enterprise-ready solution. Although Ethereum and Ubiq are similar, it may be this factor which ultimately drives Ubiq's popularity past that of Ethereum. ∎

BURST

Burst is a cryptocurrency that looks to solve a list of issues which challenge the vast majority of other cryptocurrencies. Such issues include the lack of true decentralization, high energy consumption, mining hierarchies, and unfair releases. Burst has dubbed themselves the green innovative cryptocurrency as it consumes only 1 kWh per transaction as opposed to Bitcoin which uses 400 kWh per transaction.

History
Burst was first made public as a network which forked from NXT on August 10, 2014, by the original developer who referred to himself with the pseudonym 'Burstcoin'. The true identity of Burstcoin still remains unknown to this very day. On August 11, 2014, the genesis block was released and the coin was inaugurated with no initial coin offering, crowd sale, or premine.

Roughly a year later, Burstcoin disappeared with no apparent reason or explanation. The disappearance led other community members to take over the development of the project as it was an open source project in the first place. On July 22, 2017, an attacker spammed the Burst network, splitting it into multiple forks and causing wallets to crash.

The attack rendered the network unstable for several days. On August 11, 2017, during the aftermath of the spam attack, a new team of developers called the Poc Consortium became formally recognized as the appointed successors of the Burst Reference Software.

Burst is unique in the fact that it was the first and only cryptocurrency to be secured by the proof-of-capacity algorithm. Burst was also the first to carry out working 'Turing complete' smart contracts in the form of Automated Transactions.

Features
The Burst Network is a lot less taxing on the environment as it uses the proof-of-capacity algorithm or PoC. PoC makes use of hard drives which consume less power, are inexpensive and more secure in comparison to the more power-intensive processing devices used by the proof-of-work algorithm.

Burst also allows for atomic cross-chain transactions which give users the ability to trade between two cryptocurrencies without the need of a third-party exchange.

Other features include a built-in asset exchange, a platform for smart contracts, a marketplace where users can buy and sell items over the blockchain, a user-friendly crowdfunding system, and a messaging system that allows for sending and receiving encrypted data over the Burst blockchain.

In the near future Burst will implement the Dymaxion, which was recently described in its own dedicated white-paper - a layer that combines different technologies such as Tangle, Lightning Network, PoC, Ring Signatures, and zk-SNARKs. The implementation of these combined technologies will allow for the Burst network to become a truly scalable, anonymous, and environmentally friendly cryptocurrency which can be used as a transaction system on a global scale. ∎

Currency Code:
BURST

Launch Date:
2017

Market Cap:
$196M

Max. Supply:
2,158,812,800 BURST

Circulating Supply:
1,800,339,818 BURST

Consensus Mechanism:
PoC

Hashing Algorithm:
Shabal256

Block Time:
4 minutes

URL:
burst-coin.org

FUNDING THE FUTURE WITH
THE FUTURE OF CURRENCY

EINSTEINIUM

Einsteinium is a non-profit digital currency based on the Bitcoin source code. It is a distributed, peer-to-peer currency designed to fund charitable causes and scientific research.

History

Einsteinium was launched in 2014 and was significantly redeveloped in early 2017. On March 1, 2017, the Einstein Foundation (EMC2) was officially launched in Montreal, Canada and registered in April as a non-profit organization - the first research-oriented non-profit organization in the crypto world. From 2014 to 2017, Einsteinium traded constantly at less than a 10th of a cent, but it registered a steady rise towards the end of 2017, reaching an all-time high of $2.77 in December.

Today, Einsteinium is one of the top 50 digital currencies, with a market capitalization of approximately $73.2 million as of February 2, 2018. The coin is traded on major coin exchanges such as Bittrex, Cryptopia, and Poloniex.

Features

Einsteinium is based on the proof-of-work (PoW) algorithm and will have a maximum supply of 245 million coins in total. The mining of Einsteinium occurs in epochs, each of which lasts about 25 days, and during which a total of 36,000 blocks are mined. At the end of each period, a new scientific research project is selected to receive funding from EMC2. Projects are selected by members of the Einsteinium community through voting. 2.5% of every block mined is donated to EMC2 for donations – 2% is donated to scientific research while 0.5% goes to faucets, donations, as well as marketing expenses.

There will be 730 epochs from which miners can be rewarded, and Einsteinium's model is designed in such a way that block rewards decrease as more epochs are completed. Over time, the amount of coins miners are awarded will decrease – for example, block rewards in the first two epochs were 1,024 Einsteinium tokens whereas in the last epoch, the reward will only be one Einsteinium token.

One wonders why miners would be interested in mining a coin whose rewards decline as the blockchain grows, and this can be explained with the Wormhole Event, which is a unique way through which Einsteinium contributes to the PoW model. The Wormhole Event is a random event that occurs in each epoch and lasts for 180 blocks. During this time, the standard epoch reward is substituted by a reward of 2,973 Einsteinium tokens. This lottery system serves as an incentive for miners and compensates for the decline in block rewards that occurs as the blockchain grows. Based on this approach, the Einsteinium network anticipates mining to be more rewarding in the future. Wormhole Events will become more lucrative as the value of EMC2 coins increases.

Einsteinium offers a core wallet for both Windows and Mac. Also, a mobile wallet for Android is available via Coinomi. The Einsteinium team plans to launch a web and mobile wallet in the near future.

Overall, Einsteinium is somewhat unique from most other digital currencies as it brings philanthropy, scientific research, and cryptocurrency technology together. In doing this, Einsteinium holds the possibility of furthering scientific research while at the same time increasing cryptocurrency adoption. ∎

Currency Code:
EMC2

Launch Date:
2014

Market Cap:
$193M

Max. Supply:
299,792,458 EMC2

Circulating Supply:
216,265,024 EMC2

Consensus Mechanism:
PoW

Hashing Algorithm:
Scrypt

Block Time:
60 seconds

URL:
emc2.foundation

Currency Code:
EMC

Launch Date:
2013

Market Cap:
$181M

Max Supply:
1,000,000,000 EMC

Circulating Supply:
41,163,155 EMC

Consensus Mechanism:
PoW / PoS

Hashing Algorithm:
SHA-256

Block Time:
10 minutes avg.

URL:
emercoin.com

EMERCOIN

Emercoin is a cryptosystem that combines a digital currency and a distributed ledger of arbitrary data. In this way, it can be used both as a cryptocurrency and as a basis for creating new distributed services for business and personal use. The two key drivers in Emercoin development are reliability and extensibility.

History

Emercoin was founded by Evgeny Shumilov and Oleg Khovayko. It was announced on December 8, 2013, and released to the public three days later with no pre-mine. Emercoin inherited its core code from Bitcoin, proof-of-stake mining from Peercoin, and Name-Value Storage from Namecoin, in an attempt to combine the key strengths of the best systems of the time.

In early January 2016, a partnership was announced and Emercoin began working alongside Microsoft Azure and its BaaS department (Blockchain as a Service). The partnership aimed to bring innovation to the field and develop scalable products for businesses seeking to implement blockchain technology. In March 2017, Emercoin completed its switch to a merged mining protocol to benefit miners and increase the security and trust levels of the network.

Additionally, in 2017, The Emercoin Consortium was created to collaborate and implement non-monetary services at companies in Russia using the Emer blockchain. EmerSchool is an initiative aimed at raising the awareness of Emercoin within the business community and teach developers to use the blockchain in their products.

Features

In most cryptosystems, miner votes are weighted using the proof-of-work mechanism, where 'work' refers to the computing capacity used for mining. PoW forces miners to keep investing in new hardware, inducing an 'arms race' among them. Proof-of-stake, in turn, relies on the number of coins already held by a miner, creating a calmer climate and favoring coin-holding over trading and innovation over exploitation. Although PoS was first introduced by Peercoin, Emercoin has increased its weight in consensus calculation to 80%.

Emercoin's Name-Value Storage is a simple yet powerful concept. In a nutshell, it allows you to store arbitrary data in the form of name-value pairs. This can be DNS routing, such as "dns:flibusta.lib→81.17.19.227", public keys, e.g. "ssh:emergator→AAAAB3...", or any other data that can be represented in such a way. The NVS concept was first used in Namecoin, where it was used to keep a ledger of domain names, however, Emercoin has taken it a step further, by allowing each node to work as a native DNS server and, most importantly, by enabling the storage of any kind of data. The strings defining the name and value in an NVS record can be of any format provided there is a parser to support them. Yet they are still just strings. This is in stark contrast to smart contracts, which can be used to write virtually anything, including malicious code. While it could be said that not using smart contracts limits experimentation, Emercoin's avoidance of them is intentional, instead, opting for a cryptosystem with industrial-class reliability rather than one that is experimental in nature due to a use of smart contract-based projects.

Some of the dozen decentralized technologies already enabled by Emercoin include - a distributed domain name system, public key infrastructure, CPC ad network, and free VoIP platform. These are just a few of a growing list of worthy features that are the result of Emercoin's open architecture and time-tested reliability. ∎

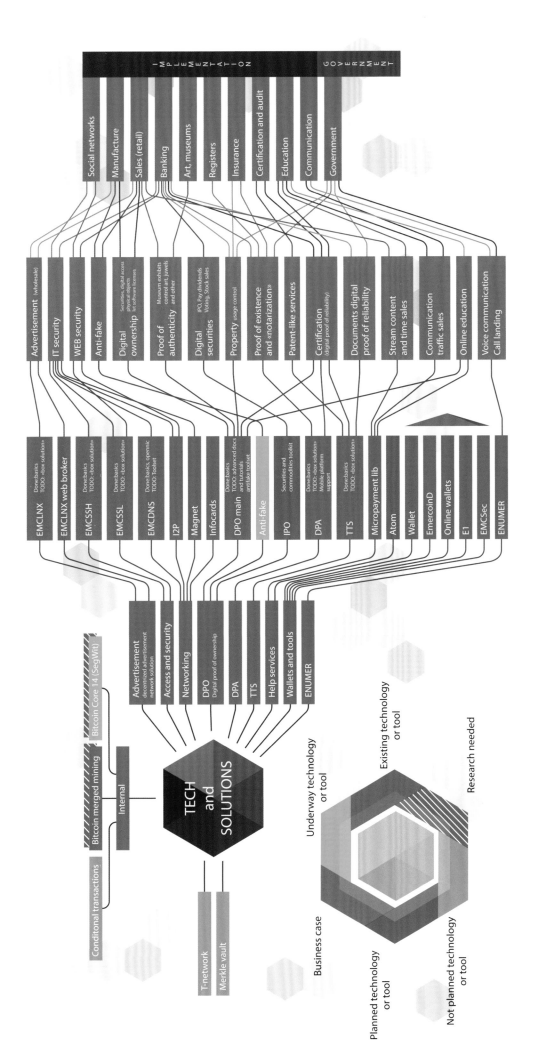

EMCNVS (Name Value Storage) allows for the safe storage of relevant ownership information via name->value pairs. These pairs are stored without imposing a narrow set of specializations and limitations allowing for universal adaptation by users.

EMCDPO (Digital Proof of Ownership) is a mechanism which excludes the possibility of fraud in payments, allowing simultaneous transfer of any type of digital asset. This allows for the setup of electronic trades and auctions without the need of third-party escrow services.

EMCLNX (Link the Exchange) is a peer-to-peer advertisement link exchange network based on a per-click payment model. EMCLNX contains 3 roles: the Buyer (the party advertising their website using EMCLNX), the Host (the website displaying the Buyer's EMCLNX advertisements and redirecting Visitors to the Buyer's website) and the Visitor (users who click on the advertisement). The Buyer pays the Host for each Visitor.

Emercoin Testnet allows users a space to create and test blockchain-enabled projects that makes use of the Emercoin platform. This private (or public) Testnet contains all the non-monetary properties of EMC so users can debug their project before full deployment on the Emercoin blockchain.

Currency Code:
PART

Launch Date:
2017

Market Cap:
$168M

Max. Supply:
8,816,675 PART

Circulating Supply:
7,820,675 PART

Consensus Mechanism:
PoS

Hashing Algorithm:
N/A

Block Time:
120 seconds

URL:
partcl.io

PARTICL

Particl is an open source, decentralized privacy platform built on the blockchain, on which users can utilize or create tools that respect their rights to privacy. Such tools currently include its native privacy coin (PART), a peer-to-peer (P2P) encrypted messaging system, a decentralized voting system, and a fully anonymous and trustless marketplace (MVP Q1 2018). All platform fees such as regular/private currency transactions, marketplace listing fees, and others, are paid in totality to PART staking nodes.

History
Particl is a relatively new project launched on July 17, 2017. It is supported by the Particl Foundation (Particl Stiftung), a non-profit Swiss foundation registered in Zug on July 4, 2017, with the help of Swiss law firm MME.

Particl Foundation's goal is to enable the organization and deployment of funding and logistics to ensure the safe development of the Particl project and vision. Particl Stiftung's foundation status provides legal protection and resources to the Particl project ensuring its sustainability and compliance to current and new regulations.

Features
Particl's decentralized privacy marketplace will be a P2P/blockchain hybrid eBay-style marketplace, self-governed by its community of stakers. It serves the purpose of letting people trade any goods and services in perfect anonymity and security using a decentralized and highly-scalable no-fee escrow system. Particl's privacy marketplace accepts almost any coin and stores its data (pictures, videos, digital files, etc) off-chain for increased scalability. Its privacy is assured at its core by using many of the platform-wide features that can also be used by any developer to create their own privacy dApp. These features include (but are not limited to) decentralized voting, governance, messaging, escrow smart contract, atomic swaps, as well as the CT privacy protocol, the SMSG decentralized storage network, and the Tor network.

Another major aspect of the Particl platform is that it is both currency- and protocol-agnostic. Currency-agnosticism means that it accepts almost any currency, making the platform usable by any crypto community. However, even though Particl accepts almost all currencies, they are converted into PART whenever the platform requires a currency transaction (regular, untraceable, marketplace or smart-contract) so that it can leverage its features (CT, RingCT, voting, etc).

Protocol-agnosticism, on the other hand, refers to the ability of the platform to use any protocol as its decentralized data storage (DSN) protocol. Technology moves at an exponential rate, and the very few protocols that survive the test of time are all designed with extensibility in mind. A protocol looking to be relevant on a long enough timeline should be both robust and flexible enough to easily allow any developer to securely expand it. The development of decentralized storage networks (SMSG, IPFS, DHTs, BitTorrent, etc) and blockchain solutions is still young and there aren't any clear 'winners' that meet all criteria, nor may there ever be, thus the protocol must accommodate for it. Having extensibility built at the core of the platform allows it to easily scale up and switch between any DSN without having to patch the project with fixes that compromise privacy or decentralization. ∎

Particl Desktop

Built on Electron and Angular, Particl Desktop is Particl's flagship application. It includes a powerful, open source HD Wallet that features multi-wallet support, cold staking, stealth addresses, public/private transaction selection and more.

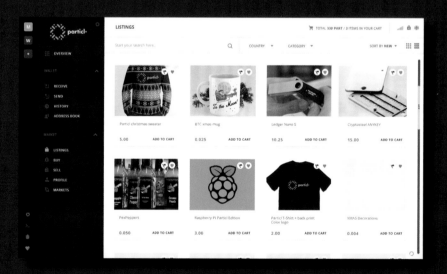

Particl Marketplace

Integrated into Particl Desktop is Particl's decentralized marketplace - a highly scalable and trustless solution for e-commerce. Built with privacy at its core, it uses several platform-wide features to deliver the full suite of tools required to shop and sell products and services online.

Security:
Bitcoin Core 0.15.1 Codebase
Being built on the latest Bitcoin codebase not only allows the Particl platform to benefit from both Bitcoin's stability and security, but it also enables developers to leverage and easily fork any product, service and technology development from the Bitcoin developer community. The latest Bitcoin Core codebase (0.15) also fixes a critical node-crashing bug disclosed at the 2017 Breaking Bitcoin conference.

Particl Proof-of-Stake:
Cold Staking & Quantum-Resistance
When a Particl block is staked from a cold staking node, the public key of the address on the staking node (which contains no coin) is broadcast to the network instead of the public key of the address which contains the funds. Because cold staking nodes are able to sign staked blocks on behalf of any wallet, hot or cold, cold stakers can effectively remain shielded from theoretical quantum computer attacks based on the reversal of a node's public key into a private key.

Privacy:
Confidential Transactions
This type of transaction uses the Confidential Transaction (CT) privacy protocol developed by Bitcoin Core developer Gregory Maxwell to keep the transferring amounts visible only to the transaction participants (and those they designate), while still guaranteeing the transaction's cryptographic integrity.

Currency Code:
ZEN

Launch Date:
2017

Market Cap:
$162M

Max. Supply:
21,000,000 ZEN

Circulating Supply:
2,943,784 ZEN

Consensus Mechanism:
PoW

Hashing Algorithm:
Equihash

Block Time:
2.5 minutes

URL:
zensystem.io

ZENCASH

A recently launched cryptocurrency platform, Zencash enables secure and private economic activity. It was derived from Bitcoin and aims to facilitate safe, off-grid communications, as well as resilient networking. The project ultimately intends to create a digital currency that allows individuals and businesses all over the world to conduct private transactions and private messaging anonymously.

History
Launched on May 30, 2017, as an advancement of the ZCash codebase, ZenCash is one of the newer currencies in the crypto market. Unlike other cryptocurrencies, ZenCash did not start off with an ICO or pre-mine. Instead, ZenCash was launched as a chain split from ZClassic, which in turn was a split from ZCash.

The ZCash codebase predominantly originated from Bitcoin, and the succession of forks has led to ZenCash being referred to as "the great-grandson of Bitcoin". In fact, ZenCash is essentially a newer version of Bitcoin with additional anonymity and privacy. Originally, ZCash's financing model involved taking a 20% stake in each ZEC (the currency's monetary unit). This was a controversial move, leading to the hard fork that created ZClassic.

In spite of its infancy, ZenCash has made tremendous progress. The coin is presently trading on Bittrex, with a market capitalization of $162.4 million at the time of writing.

Features
The ZenCash project is based on the proof-of-work (PoW) algorithm. This means that transactions must be confirmed on the blockchain and in exchange for verifying transactions, miners receive block rewards. For each block mining reward, 8.5% goes to development, operations, and marketing, while an additional 3.5% goes to node operators. This funding model is one of the features that makes ZenCash different from other cryptocurrencies. Ongoing funding enables the network to fund its growth.

ZenCash is designed as a fully encrypted network for sending and distributing money. According to the ZenCash website, it is the first TLS integration, which functions like an SSL cert for node encryption. With cryptographic techniques and zero-knowledge encryption, ZenCash offers anonymous peer-to-peer transactions. Zero-knowledge encryption means that transactions across the network are undecipherable, including the identities of the sender and the receiver as well as the amount transacted. This protects users against spamming, denial-of-service attacks, and other security vulnerabilities. ZenCash's efforts towards full anonymity has been touted as a critical feature to its success in the rapidly evolving crypto economy.

In addition to anonymity, ZenCash facilitates resilient networking. Secure nodes in the network enable users to develop and sustain a secure network for transacting ZEN and ZenCash wallets can connect to thousands of secure nodes all over the globe.

ZenCash also has features that allow users to include private messages along with their transactions to contextualize payments. With a distributed blockchain and encrypted transactions, the project has significant implications with respect to the right to privacy. ∎

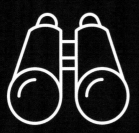

Designed for Long-Term Operation
21 million ZenCash cap - no premine, no ICO
Thousands of Secure Nodes in operation - 3.5% of mining reward
Treasury funds for development, support, marketing - 8.5% of mining reward
Secure Nodes provide a resilient, distributed network

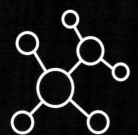

With a Focus on Research and Development
Partnered with Input Output Hong Kong (IOHK), a leading R&D company
Decentralized Autonomous Organization Treasury Study
Scalability Study
Network Stack Anonymization

 zencash **Treasury Model**

ZenCash Treasury Model is an inclusive, provably fair, and transparent economic system with incentives to participate.

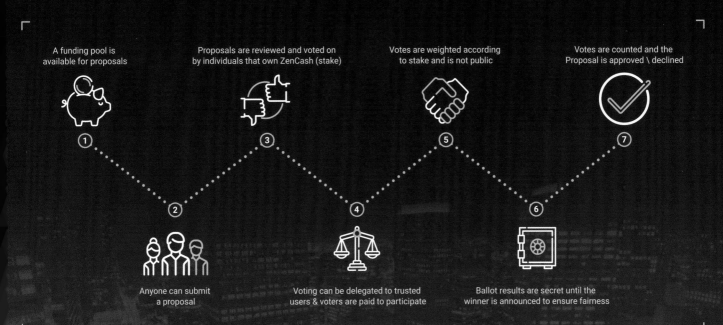

1. A funding pool is available for proposals
2. Anyone can submit a proposal
3. Proposals are reviewed and voted on by individuals that own ZenCash (stake)
4. Voting can be delegated to trusted users & voters are paid to participate
5. Votes are weighted according to stake and is not public
6. Ballot results are secret until the winner is announced to ensure fairness
7. Votes are counted and the Proposal is approved \ declined

DECENT

A decentralized, open source, encrypted, and secure content distribution platform, Decent aims to bring creative freedom to digital content producers by abolishing the need for third-party publishers with the use of the blockchain. The Decent platform is dedicated to freedom of speech and allows creatives, authors, bloggers, and publicists, along with their fans and followers, to publish all forms of content without the intervention or interference of intermediaries.

History

Decent was originally founded in March 2015 and then described in a white-paper by Matej Michalko and Josef Sevcik later that year. In 2016, they launched a fully-functional prototype of the Decent Network as well as an ICO. On March 10, 2017, Decent launched testnet #1 which they gave the name 'Caesar'. Two months later, they released version #2 of the testnet, this time, called 'Albert'. The official launch of the network came soon after in June of the same year.

Features

The Decent platform eliminates the ability for media manipulation as it has no involvement with any third-party and, unlike most platforms, there are no limits to what form of content can be posted as it excludes no one. This means that songs, books, source code, articles, videos, and or any form of digital content in any format is welcomed onto the Decent blockchain.

Decent is an autonomous decentralized application, (dApp) built for the publication of digital content on its own independent blockchain. This blockchain serves as the public distributed ledger for all the transactions that have occurred since the release of its genesis block.

Decent runs without any form of third-party intervention and is owned by no single individual or organization. Decent focuses on the elimination of political and geographical barriers, and due to its peer-to-peer nature, it cannot be blocked or censored by firewalls, as the content is released from multiple sources, making it practically impossible for any government or organization to deny user access. Decent is also an extremely stable and secure platform for storing content as it does not rely on any single server and has no central point of failure.

Decent has made it clear that they care very much about the fairness of their platform and have designed it so that every creator starts at the same level and can only build their reputation through the quality of their content and other users' engagement with it.

Decent also provides a spam-free mechanism which makes the pervasive publishing of content a lot more expensive for spammers, thus canceling out the rewards of spam posting.

Decent also promises to never take a percentage of the profits made by creators. The freedom which Decent provides ensures fairness and equality amongst digital content creators. ∎

Currency Code:
DCT

Launch Date:
2015

Market Cap:
$157M

Max. Supply:
51,306,089 DCT

Circulating Supply:
51,306,089 DCT

Consensus Mechanism:
dPoS

Hashing Algorithm:
N/A

Block Time:
5 seconds

URL:
decent.ch

COUNTERPARTY

CounterParty is an extensively tested, open source protocol, that uses the XCP token, and aims to provide functionality where Bitcoin cannot. Not only does CounterParty give users the opportunity to establish and trade any form of digital token, it also allows for new forms of innovation by broadening the functionality of Bitcoin. Counterparty does this by enabling anyone to create and execute their own smart contracts on the Bitcoin blockchain.

History

CounterParty was Launched in 2014 as an open source project, co-founded by Evan Wagner, Robby Dermody, and Adam Krellenstein. On January 2, 2014, they commenced a month-long proof-of-burn period in which 2,648,755 XCP tokens were created.

Counterparty ended the same year on a high note by announcing the board of directors and establishing the Counterparty Foundation; a non-profit organization dedicated to upholding the CounterParty project's development and growth.

Features

Essentially, CounterParty provides a series of financial tools built upon the Bitcoin blockchain, whose sole purpose is to add new functionalities with the help of the XCP token, making it, in many ways, comparable to the Ethereum platform. It is important to note that XCP is a non-mineable token, which is instead created by the process of 'burning' Bitcoins. Simply put, this is the act of sending Bitcoins to an address that has no private keys, rendering it unspendable.

With CounterParty, users can create their own smart contracts, and decentralized applications as well as their own custom tokens, which can be used in many ways. The official Counterparty website has the following list of potential uses:
"Tokens are being used today to conduct successful crowdfunding and voting, to monetize access to decentralized application (dApp) software features, to represent a product or personal brand, to act as a sort of 'blockchain domain name', as an authentication token, to represent digital goods, such as in-game cards, as a proxy for real-world goods or services (i.e. tokens exchangeable for paper, biofuel, etc), to act as a reward for providing valuable time or resources, as an educational service to explore the functioning of a blockchain, purely for fun."

Other features provided by CounterParty include a decentralized asset exchange or DEX, which eradicates gratuitous costs, time, and the need to trust in a third-party, as the tasks of the escrow agent and clearinghouse are dealt with by the CounterParty protocol on its own.

Currently, CounterParty is in the process of developing features that will allow the use of the lightning network, which will enable tokens to be transacted off-chain in a decentralized manner at rapid speeds.

CounterParty also provides numerous methods for decentralized voting, and the ability to create a multi-signature address, which requires a signature from more than one Bitcoin private key in order for funds to be transacted. Counterparty's stated mission is to bring added functionality to the Bitcoin blockchain and there is little doubt that they offer some interesting additions and features of their own. ∎

Currency Code:
XCP

Launch Date:
2014

Market Cap:
$155M

Max. Supply:
2,650,000,000 XCP

Circulating Supply:
2,617,419 XCP

Consensus Mechanism:
PoW

Hashing Algorithm:
SHA-256

Block Time:
10 minute

URL:
counterparty.io

Currency Code:
PPC

Launch Date:
2014

Market Cap:
$153M

Max. Supply:
23,225,991 PPC

Circulating Supply:
24,559,317 PPC

Consensus Mechanism:
PoW / PoS

Hashing Algorithm:
SHA-256

Block Time:
10 minutes

URL:
peercoin.net

PEERCOIN

Peercoin is the world's first proof-of-stake/proof-of-work hybrid coin. The Peercoin team is led by core developer 'Sunny King' and Scott Nadal whose mission is to create the fastest and most reliable coin, with low transaction fees. Many recent altcoins have been influenced by the design and technology behind Peercoin, with developers cloning the source code and then altering it, only to make their new coin less secure. The Peercoin team has placed a large amount of emphasis on ensuring that the foundations of the currency are secure so that Peercoin can remain relevant for many decades to come.

History
The Peercoin technology was announced on August 10, 2012, and was released on August 19. There were no pre-mined coins, and the source code was made public at the time of its release, giving everyone an equal opportunity to mine Peercoins from the very beginning.

The coin distribution was fair for all of its users, with the developers choosing to not receive a portion of the coins before its release, unlike most other coins.

In 2014 the coin had a relatively high degree of success, reaching a market cap of approximately 160 million with a pricing of about $8 per coin. From July 2014 to early 2017, the market cap remained under 25 million (about $1 per coin) before recovering, and as of January 2018, the coin has a total market cap of 190 million (about $8 per coin).

Features
Peercoin uses both the proof-of-stake and proof-of-work protocols. The proof-of-stake protocol is used to achieve consensus throughout the network, whereas proof-of-work is used for the continuous distribution of new coins. Contrary to Bitcoin's proof-of-work coin, where higher amounts of computational power are required in order to keep the network secure, coins are instead minted, which is cheaper and more energy efficient than the conventional proof-of-work approach. Another benefit to minting is that it can be done on almost any device.

Proof-of-stake minting is used for the production of coins and earns its users 1% annually. Coins can be minted 30 days after they are transferred and at 90 days and beyond the probability of higher earnings is maximized.

The more a user mints, the more their earnings will compound, which creates an incentive for users to hold on to their coins in order to create value. Coins are released at a steady inflation rate of 1 percent per year.

Technically, there is a limit of 2 billion coins although this is not expected to be reached in the foreseeable future. Transaction fees spent are burnt which creates the possibility of the currency having an overall deflationary effect over time (0.01 PPC per transaction is burnt). ∎

LBRY CREDITS

LBRY is a free, open, decentralized digital marketplace that aims to revolutionize how content is created and shared. Powered by blockchain technology, it is an online library where users can share and access music, games, videos, pictures, ebooks, articles, and other types of artistic content, using any internet-enabled device. The content sharing platform links content creators with content consumers directly, and consumers pay creators for access to content via LBRY credits.

History

LBRY was founded in 2015 by Jeremy Kauffman and Mike Vine together with Bitcoin. Jeremy and his co-founder wanted to develop a platform that would decentralize how content was shared and published on the internet. They envisioned a content sharing network, where content creators would be paid directly without traditional intermediaries.

The first trial of the platform was introduced to creators and fans on U.S. Independence Day (July 4, 2016) via invitation, with the date chosen to express an ideal of freedom and independence from centralized content sharing corporations. Following the Independence Day release, new users could join the platform via a referral system, and since May 2017, LBRY has been open for everyone.

Features

LBRY has been recognized as the first digital marketplace owned and controlled by market participants as opposed to a corporation or third party. It is an open marketplace for a broad array of digital products, including ebooks, movies, music, videos, and games.

Similar to the hypertext transfer protocol (HTTP), the domain name system (DNS), and other internet specifications, LBRY facilitates access to, and sharing of, digital content as a protocol, as opposed to a proprietary service. Users do not require special permission for access.

LBRY is different from other internet content sharing platforms in several major ways. Content publishers can charge a fee for access to their content. Published content is distributed and centralized, not limited to a single computer or network, meaning no one, including the LBRY team, can unilaterally block or remove content from the network – only the publisher can remove content, a feature which helps in building trust within the network.

This distinguishes LBRY from conventional publishing networks such as Amazon, Spotify, YouTube, and iTunes, where the intermediary has the power to change rules or remove controversial content. The other way in which LBRY differs from other digital publishing systems is that domain names are operated through a continuous auction, and domain names are allocated to publishers that value them the most. The auction is based on a digital currency called LBRY credits (LBC). LBC is a proof-of-work (PoW) currency, meaning that it can be mined using a GPU.

The invention of LBRY has certainly added value to content reproduction and sharing, taking advantage of blockchain technology to disrupt the paid content market, which is estimated to exceed $180 billion in value. LBRY is expected by many to capture a considerable portion of this market in the future. ∎

Currency Code:
LBC

Launch Date:
2014

Market Cap:
$141M

Max. Supply:
10,000,00,000 LBC

Circulating Supply:
128,620,180 LBC

Consensus Mechanism:
PoW

Hashing Algorithm:
SHA512 / SHA256 / RIPEMD

Block Time:
2.4 minutes

URL:
lbry.io

Currency Code:
RISE

Launch Date:
2016

Market Cap:
$138M

Max. Supply:
113,139,200 RISE

Circulating Supply:
113,139,200 RISE

Consensus Mechanism:
DPoS

Hashing Algorithm:
N/A

Block Time:
30 seconds

URL:
rise.vision

RISE

"RISE is an ecosystem for developers, businesses, tech startups, investors and device users." Powered by a secure delegated proof-of-stake Blockchain; Rise enables users to build Decentralized Applications (dApps) in a variety of programming languages using Drag and Drop development tools, create Smart Contracts as well as produce their own Side-chains/tokens.

History

Rise announced its project in April 2016 and attracted over 6000 participants raising 1700 BTC during the 6 week ICO period from May 10th to June 24th, 2016. Initial development of the project was outsourced to Don't Panic Consulting Inc. However, slow development times resulted in lost community support and the Rise team (currently led by Cormac Lucking (founder of CloakCoin), Steven Remington and Frank Thijssen) announced in February 2017 that Don't Panic was no longer working on Rise and that Lucking and Remington would oversee development.

This move triggered a panic in the community due to uncertainty in the platform and its future. The old coding team was soon replaced and the number of developers working on the Rise platform grew steadily.

Rise updated from the Lisk to Ark codebase after the development team transition in early 2017. This new codebase lacked the Dapp functionality and a web-wallet so a hybrid code was created with the lacking features adopted from the Shift project.

A successful 1:1 coinswap to the new mainnet network occurred from June 21 to July 19, 2017, and resurgence in popularity and confidence in the project followed after its initial development issues.

Features

Rise is powered by a DPoS algorithm, originally created by Bitshares, which lowers the costs of safeguarding and running the network and democratically allows users to decide on the 101 Delegates who are trusted with signing blocks on behalf of the network. The DPoS system features a 30-second block time and lowers forging rewards on a yearly basis. After the 6th year, there will be 1 Rise per block and the rate will not change, meaning that each of the 101 delegates will earn approx 28 Rise per day (technically forever).

Rise offers Software Development Kits (SDKs) for multiple programming languages, allowing developers to create applications that integrate Rise on Windows, Android, iOS, Linux and other operating systems. The Drag and Drop utility coupled with the variety of SDKs means that development on the Rise platform is accessible and open for developers with varying levels of experience.

Rise Blockchain Incubator is an initiative assisting blockchain startups get off the ground by using the Rise platform. The Incubator aims to develop ideas from concepts into viable business models. Startups built with the Rise Blockchain Incubator will see 20% of its issued tokens given back to Rise holders and 10% given back to the Rise development team. This process allows Rise to self-sustain as well as expand the network. ∎

RISE - THE USER FRIENDLY APPLICATION PLATFORM

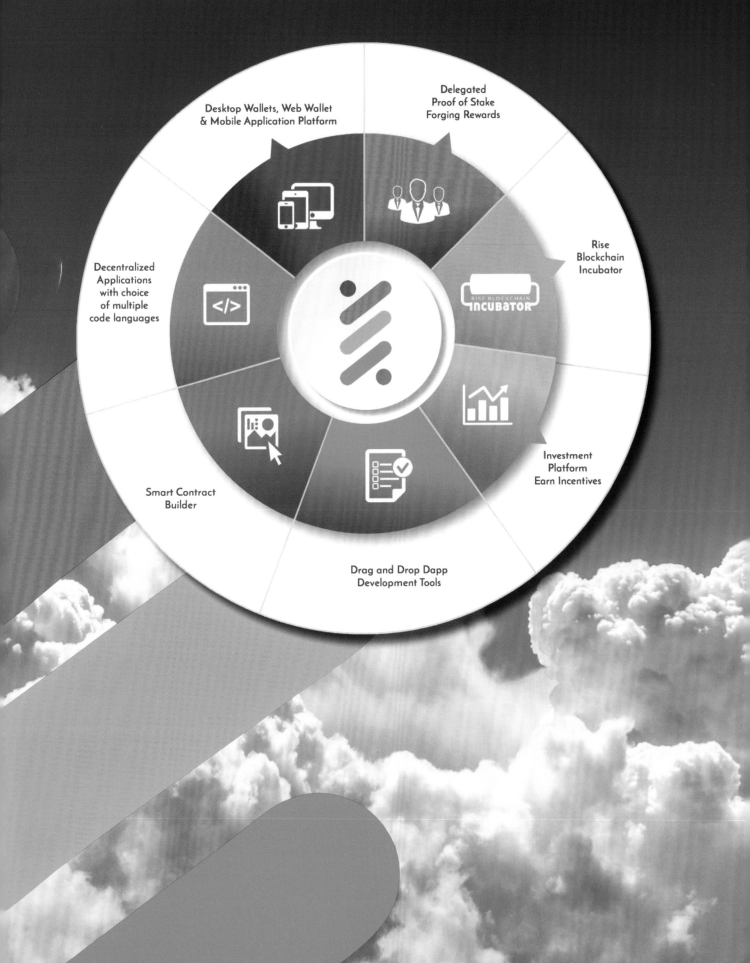

ASCH

A decentralized application platform developed using the JavaScript programming language, ASCH aims to reduce the skill threshold for developers looking to adopt blockchain technology by providing a series of SDK and APIs for use in a variety of different sectors. ASCH is based on the delegated proof-of-stake (DPoS) consensus algorithm, powered by the XAS token, and makes use of sidechains to host dApps, reducing blockchain bloat and allowing dApps to be flexible and personalized.

History

The ASCH program was initiated on January 1, 2016. In late June 2016, after internal testing, the first ASCH block was born and the blockchain was subjected to testing to ensure forking did not occur and security expectations were met. On July 13, 2016, ASCH released version 0.9.1 and the public beta began, with majority delegates allowed to participate in the 49 node testnet. Early August 2016, saw the DPoS consensus algorithm upgraded from version 0.5 to 1.0 to optimize bandwidth costs of the network, with the testnet seeing its peak network traffic cost reduced by more than half. After this upgrade, the ASCH mainnet was officially launched and the open source code base was released to the public on GitHub.

ASCH released multiple version updates and mainnet upgrades in 2017, as well as becoming members of multiple blockchain associations based in China. Additionally, CCTime, a news aggregation dApp, and Koumei Cottage (KMC), a forecasting market dApp, both adopted the ASCH platform for their releases.

Features

ASCH makes use of the JavaScript programming language for developers to create their dApps. It is popular, widely used and accessible for newer developers, resulting in dApp development being more similar to traditional web application coding.

ASCH provides a fully customizable sidechain system for hosting dApps that can be individually adapted with databases, consensus mechanisms, trading methods, and account architecture. DApps on sidechains are hosted by delegate nodes to avoid bloating of the ASCH mainchain. Owners of a dApp control a main node for their sidechain, which creates the consensus for a new block and validates the sidechain on the ASCH mainchain. Once a sidechain has been synced with the ASCH blockchain via its main node, further dApp blocks will validate through the mainchain, making it impossible to remove previous dApp blocks from the blockchain.

Developers can also replace the ASCH blockchain with Bitcoin as the ASCH API is the same, allowing sidechains to use both XAS and BTC as the currency of their dApp. DApp owners can also issue their own currency for the sidechain, however, these tokens cannot be directly transferred from one dApp to another.

The ASCH sandbox runs dApps within a closed virtual machine module of Node.js. The sandbox does not make use of APIs such as network communication, instead, running only the JavaScript code of the dApp. The sandbox restricts a program's activities under the security policy and prevents damage to the network. ∎

Currency Code:
XAS

Launch Date:
2016

Market Cap:
$137M

Max. Supply:
113,494,861 XAS

Circulating Supply:
91,700,324 XAS

Consensus Mechanism:
dPOS

Hashing Algorithm:
SHA2-256

Block Time:
10 seconds

URL:
asch.io

VIACOIN

Viacoin is an open source cryptocurrency project based upon the Bitcoin blockchain and integrating ClearingHouse - "a protocol that allows for asset issuance and peer-to-peer trading." Introduced publicly in mid-2014, this Scrypt based, proof-of-work coin integrates decentralized asset transaction on the blockchain while improving considerably on the speed of other cryptocoins.

History

Viacoin was released on July 18, 2014, with a presale over a period of 8 days, of 10 million coins at 6100 satoshis per coin. It was founded by BtcDrak, a known and prominent Bitcoin trader who later teamed up with Peter Todd, one of the main developers of Bitcoin Core. In the summer of 2016, a young programmer named Romano began working with them to deploy a Viacoin node on Azure. The news of this development caused a doubling of the price of the VIA in under 24 hours. Following more work by Romano and due to his willingness to invest and develop Viacoin, on September 9, 2016, BtcDrak formally entrusted the project to Romano and stepped down from his leadership role.

Since the Romano takeover, Viacoin has seen a number of improvements such as; the implementation of SegWit, Lightning Network, hardware wallet support, conditional payment, atomic swaps, as well as optimizations of memory, encryption, and storage.

Features

Viacoin has a total supply of 23 million coins and a mining reward that halves every six months. It is derived from the Bitcoin protocol and uses Scrypt Merged mining, also known as Auxiliary proof-of-work (AuxPoW), which enables transaction times 25 times faster than Bitcoin. Merged mining allows users to mine several Scrypt based coins simultaneously, resulting in a more secure blockchain, with almost no impact on the hash rate of either one.

Viacoin's decentralized contract platform, ClearingHouse, uses a protocol it calls the 'Blockchain Notary', which is basically a twofold system that allows for the cryptographic time-stamping of digital assets, as well as the ability to own and transfer them.

Just like coins, notaries are owned by a key and can be transferred, along with the digital rights, to a new owner's key. Clearwallet is the user interface that runs on ClearingHouse and currently offers users a decentralized environment for conducting contracts, an asset marketplace, a betting terminal and section for decentralized games, as well as a live chat box. For security purposes, the 12-word passphrase to unlock the wallet is only stored in the memory of the users' local device. Additionally, since the wallet is web-based, users can log in from anywhere using their personal passphrase.

Other Viacoin technical features include; activated SegWit and Lightning Network, an open source mining difficulty adjustment algorithm called Dark Gravity Wave (DGW) to address flaws in Kimoto's Gravity Well, as well as Versionbits, that allows for up to 29 soft fork changes to be implemented simultaneously.

It would seem, however, that Romano and his team are just getting started, with plans for 2018 including; smart contracts, a decentralized exchange of digital elements (coins, documents, images etc), the incorporation of Viacoin into GeneralByte ATM machines, as well as technical upgrades such as the Schnorr Signature and Merkel's Abstract Syntax Tree (MAST). ∎

Currency Code:
VIA

Launch Date:
2014

Market Cap:
$132M

Max. Supply:
23,000,000 VIA

Circulating Supply:
22,950,985 VIA

Consensus Mechanism:
PoW

Hashing Algorithm:
Scrypt

Block Time:
24 seconds

URL:
viacoin.org

Currency Code:
CLOAK

Launch Date:
2014

Market Cap:
$126M

Max Supply:
N/A

Circulating Supply:
5,053,693 CLOAK

Consensus Mechanism:
PoS - 6% p.a.

Hashing Algorithm:
x13

Block Time:
60 seconds

URL:
cloakcoin.com

CLOAKCOIN

CloakCoin is a truly anonymous cryptocurrency designed to facilitate private, secure, and untraceable, decentralized transfers, with the use of the Enigma transaction system. It is based on blockchain technology with certain additions, as well as a sophisticated off-blockchain coin-mixing system, making it impossible for third-parties to trace transactions between CloakCoin wallets.

History
CloakCoin was introduced in June 2014, to provide cryptocurrency users with a coin giving total privacy. However, due to a lack of development and it being the victim of a pump-and-dump scam, the project soon crashed and was abandoned by the original development team.

In October 2014, CloakCoin was taken over by community members and the project was re-imagined with only the name remaining in place.

After the source code was handed over, it was discovered that CloakCoin's user base had been misled and it was revealed that only 10% or so of the required coding for the project had actually been completed. The current development team then set out to develop the trustless, anonymous, transfer system that would form the backbone of the new Cloak project.

The first fully-functional wallet with its untraceable transaction system was released in March 2016. CloakCoin's open-source Enigma was released at the end of 2017, signaling a significant step in the development process of the platform.

Features
CloakCoin's focus on privacy, anonymity, and security led to the development of the Enigma transaction system — the platform that CloakCoin rests upon. Enigma allows CloakCoins to be sent anonymously while avoiding the need to trust other nodes not to steal funds or leak sensitive information. Users with any amount of Cloak in their wallet can assist in cloaking transactions, with higher returns expected over those who are only staking coins. This helps increase decentralization as there are no masternodes on the system.

CloakShield allows users to send Cloak to one or more recipients by creating an encryption channel for secure communication between users when 'Cloaking Mode' is enabled. It provides nodes with protection from snoopers (intruders between nodes) and imposters. Users request assistance in a cloaked transaction from elected Enigma nodes who are rewarded for successful cloaked transactions.

Staked coins on the network offer a 6% interest rate per annum and users are also eligible to share a network fee if they elect to support Enigma transactions. While transactions are taking place, no intermediate or third-parties are involved. Therefore, the coins are always safe and secure, and the sender can be guaranteed that the coins he sent will reach the recipient. There is currently a total supply of approx. 5.1 million coins in circulation. ∎

ENIGMA TRANSACTION EXAMPLE

ALICE wants to send coins anonymously to BOB.

ALICE (−10) CLOAK

Encrypted payment transaction
to BOB is sent to the network.

ENIGMA mixer nodes begin communicating.

CATHERINE

Every coin holder can announce
themselves as a Mixer Node,
also known as a "Cloaker".

Every participant remains
anonymous and communicates
through an encrypted channel.

ALICE's wallet is now connected to mixer nodes.

Each mixer node helps ALICE by
shuffling around the transaction.

This network of nodes creates
decentralized anonymization
similar to TOR Onion Routing.

Mixer nodes get rewarded for Cloaking ALICE's transaction.

CLOAK

A fee of the transaction
value is shared amongst all
participating Cloakers.

The system works seamlessly to
ensure complete anonymity and
total privacy.

BOB then receives ALICE's encrypted payment

BOB (+10) CLOAK

ALICE succesfully sent 10 CLOAK
to BOB anonymously.

AEON

A lightweight, blockchain-based currency, Aeon is designed to be used with mobile devices. The Aeon development team identified a need for a cryptocurrency that requires less computing power and storage space as more people move towards using light-weight mobile devices rather than more powerful desktop or laptop devices as their primary computers. Using a modified version of CryptoNite called 'Cryptonite Lite', Aeon aims to provide a fast, untraceable payment system that can exist entirely in the mobile ecosystem.

History

Aeon was first launched in June 2014. The development team believed in creating a coin that was fair, so Aeon was launched with no pre-mine or instamine. All users were given equal opportunity to accumulate coins from launch. The original code for Aeon was based on Monero. In October 2014, the original developers of Aeon abandoned the project, however, the project was revived through community support and in April 2015, a new development team was created. The lead developer for Aeon, known as 'Smooth', continues to develop for Monero.

Features

Aeon was developed from Monero, which uses an algorithm called CryptoNote. The CryptoNote algorithm was modified for Aeon, and is called CryptoNote Lite. CryptoNote Lite uses significantly less resources than CryptoNote, as it is designed primarily for use with mobile devices, which have significantly less computing power than desktop PCs, laptops, or custom-built mining rigs that are used commonly to secure blockchain networks.

Another feature of CryptoNote Lite is that it features blockchain pruning, which can significantly cut down on the storage memory needed for mining nodes whilst also permitting faster transaction speeds as the blockchain is not filled with unnecessary information. Perhaps, more importantly, the CryptoNote Lite algorithm manages to ensure that no important information is lost in the blockchain pruning process. Additionally, CryptoNote Lite allows non-obfuscated payments at a lower transaction cost, giving users the choice of showing transactions clearly on the blockchain at a lower cost rather than hiding transactions.

The CryptoNote algorithm was designed to create a blockchain where all transactions are clearly recorded and verified, but with the details of the sender, receiver, and transaction amounts hidden. In addition to this, CryptoNote uses pure CPU-based mining for their proof-of-work algorithm, which prevents miners of the currency from gaining more power over the network by investing in GPU-based mining rigs.

CryptoNote obfuscates transactions through combining several transactions together, which means that transactions can only be observed from the outside as a group. When a person tries to trace a specific transaction, they will see outgoing transactions from several possible wallets of differing amounts, and incoming transactions that go to several possible wallets. In effect, this means that any observer will not be able to pinpoint where a specific transaction originates from or is addressed to, as all wallets on the network are constantly observed as active and are possible parties to a transaction. In order to prevent double-spending, each transaction is signed with a one-time ring signature, and the blockchain automatically discards any duplicate transactions with the same signature. ∎

Currency Code:
AEON

Launch Date:
2014

Market Cap:
$124M

Max. Supply:
8,400,000 MUSIC

Circulating Supply:
14,651,140 AEON

Consensus Mechanism:
PoW

Hashing Algorithm:
CryptoNight Lite

Block Time:
4 minutes

URL:
aeon.cash

GROESTLCOIN

Groestlcoin is an all-in-one, multipurpose cryptocurrency that facilitates instant, private transactions with near-zero fees. Based on the proof-of-work (PoW) algorithm, the network is one of the safest and fastest platforms for digital money transactions. Groestlcoin also provides wallets for every possible platform, making it extremely accessible to anyone in any part of the world.

History

Groestlcoin was launched on March 22, 2014, with an aim to empower ordinary people to mine coins using an ordinary computer's CPU/GPU. The lead developer from the Netherlands known as 'Jackielove4u' claimed to be inspired after seeing Litecoin's blockchain being taken over, in their view, by ASIC developers and decided to make a coin *"for the people"* that wouldn't suffer from that problem. Another problem they saw was limited wallet options, which they pledged to address with Groestlcoin.

On December 25, 2014, the project introduced the Android wallet, going on to launch the updated version of the system Groestlcoin Core v2.11.0 on August 20, 2015. Groestlcoin made history as the first coin ever to activate SegWit on January 21, 2017. Groestlcoin is currently traded on major cryptocurrency exchanges such as Bittrex, Litebit, Cryptopia, Coinexchange, Bitsquare, and Livecoin. The currency has achieved impressive growth over the last three years, with a market capitalization as of January 25, 2018, exceeding $71 million.

Features

Groestlcoin supports SegWit and Lightning Network, and as such can offer fast transactions with minimal fees. The cost for transferring 10,000 GRS is just 0.000045 GRS, which is one of the lowest transaction costs of any of the current networks.

With top-notch encryption, as well as TOR and VPN support, users can conduct transactions with heightened anonymity via their Groestlcoin Samourai wallet. This anonymity, along with the cost and speed of the system, has led some analysts to describe Groestlcoin as the best-kept secret of the crypto world.

Groestlcoin is ASIC resistant, making mining distribution more balanced, and essentially maintaining the network's decentralization. The embedded GPU algorithm consumes a relatively low amount of power, minimizing mining costs, and allowing miners to earn a decent profit. Following the developer's vision, this arguably keeps the currency in the hands of "the people" as promised, as it prevents individual parties from controlling the hash rate. Groestlcoin also features multi-pool resistance, which reduces the possibility of a fork occurring in the blockchain, preventing anomalies and, once again, making distribution fairer.

The Groestlcoin network has many wallets on most platforms, making the currency accessible to anyone across the globe. Groestlcoin's algorithm also prevents loss of funds through accidental cross chain transactions. If users of other networks accidentally send coins to a Groestlcoin address, the transaction is denied immediately and the funds remain secure, solving a relatively common problem among crypto users.

Groestlcoin currently boasts an active development team releasing a new major update four times a year, along with a growing community, as awareness of one of the less-commonly known coins begins to spread. ∎

Currency Code:
GRS

Launch Date:
2014

Market Cap:
$123M

Max. Supply:
63,979,257 GRS

Circulating Supply:
69,164,832 GRS

Consensus Mechanism:
PoW

Hashing Algorithm:
Grøstl

Block Time:
60 seconds

URL:
groestlcoin.org

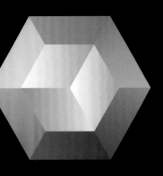

urrency Code:
OX

aunch Date:
015

arket Cap:
13M

ax. Supply:
0,000,000 VOX

irculating Supply:
0,000,000 VOX

onsensus Mechanism:
oW

ashing Algorithm:
crypt

lock Time:
5 minutes

RL:
oxelus.com

VOXELS

Voxels (VOX) is a coin associated with virtual reality technology and based on the Litecoin core. Through the Voxelus platform, the coin combines virtual reality and cryptocurrency technology to allow users to create, play, and share virtual reality games and experiences without having to code. The Voxelus platform features a collection of virtual reality assets that users can utilize to design 3D content.

History

Voxels was founded by Voxelus in 2015 under the leadership of Halsey Minor, the founder of CNET and Salesforce.com. The Voxelus team aims to increase cryptocurrency adoption across the globe. Over the years, Voxelus has grown to be one of the largest sources of 3D content globally, with over 500 virtual reality assets, 50 games, and an upcoming additional 7,000 content pieces via partnerships.

Voxels started trading in major coin exchanges in Q2 of 2016. In January 2018, Voxels' parent company announced plans to rebrand to RevolutionVR (RVR) in an effort to integrate more virtual reality possibilities. Following the rebranding, VOX will become RVR, which will be usable beyond the Voxelus platform.

Features

The Voxelus platform enables anyone in any part of the globe to create, experience, and share virtual reality games and content, without any knowledge of coding. It allows enthusiasts of virtual reality, gaming, graphic design, and art, to build and upload 3D content and environments. The platform comprises three core features: the Voxelus Creator, the Voxelus Viewer, and the Voxelus Marketplace. The Voxelus Creator is a 3D design application for both PC and Mac, and the Voxelus Viewer is a multiplayer application that supports desktop PCs as well as the Oculus Rift and the Samsung Gear VR.

The Voxelus Marketplace, an online 3D asset store compatible with the Voxelus platform, allows users to purchase 3D assets from designers around the world. Purchases can only be made using Voxels – the platform's inbuilt cryptocurrency. Voxels is fully premined and though mining is possible, it is not recommended.

Voxelus is set to partner with Flatpyramid.com, an online marketplace for finding as well as buying and selling 3D content. Following the partnership, Voxelus will add up to 7,000 virtual reality assets to its platform, making 3D content more readily accessible.

Voxels could be the future of virtual reality, as unlike many other coins, it is not just speculation-oriented. The coin allows users to buy and sell virtual reality assets using blockchain technology, as well as withdraw Voxels to use in whichever way they wish.

The Voxel platform has earned a reputation and acclaim for being the first virtual reality gaming platform with an inbuilt currency that is tradable on coin exchanges. It is estimated that the value of the virtual reality market will surpass $40 billion by 2020. Voxels may well be at the heart of this growth since both cryptocurrency and virtual reality are rapidly evolving technologies. ∎

SHIFT

Shift is a framework for decentralized web hosting on the Web 3.0. By combining decentralized applications, a delegated proof-of-stake blockchain and an interplanetary file system (IPFS), the project will allow users to monetize content, store data via the peer-to-peer system, safeguard content via the uncensored and decentralized blockchain and create smart contracts to deploy on the platform.

History

Shift was announced in August 2015 and was the first hard fork of Ethereum to take place. For its first twelve months, Shift was developed and mined on Ethereum's algorithm, however, due to a low hash rate for the blockchain and vulnerability, the developers decided to migrate to a customized fork of Lisk's codebase, changing from the PoS consensus method to the DPoS algorithm.

The Shift platform is built to make use of the IPFS protocol, created by Juan Benet. It is a network designed to create content-addressable, peer-to-peer methods of storing a sharing media in a distributed file system. IPFS transitioned to a free open-source project and Shift aimed to implement the protocol of the project.

Features

Phantom is the core product on the Shift network, a dApp dedicated to decentralizing web hosting. Phantom is the frontend for the underlying IPFS, allowing users to publish, exchange, and collaborate on ideas without the privatization of the internet interfering.

The Phantom interface provides a GUI with drag-and-drop functionality and allows users to implement IPFS on their web page by connecting IPFS hashes to top-level domains (such as ".com", ".org"), using the 'Jenga' DNS solution. Phantom and IPFS technology can be used as a file storage system without a single point of failure and can prevent DDoS attacks, due to content being distributed among nodes.

Jenga is the transparent layer that dynamically translates hashes to DNS (Domain Name System). This allows users hosting their websites on the Shift/ Phantom platform to use a "www" URL, without needing to install third-party extensions or browser plugins. Bridging these connections is achieved by having all nodes on the IPFS cluster monitored by Jenga.

It is possible for DNS records to point to an IPFS hash, however, that results in a specific server being targeted, removing the benefits of decentralization. Based on the information it receives, Jenga dynamically inserts and removes DNS records, meaning domain names can point to multiple storage nodes, therefore decentralizing the file storage.

The ShiftHub is a 'dashboard' for users to access Phantom's functionality. Registering domains, creating websites, communicating with other users, transacting funds and creating dApps are done through the ShiftHub. As Shift works on the Lisk codebase, the platform features the same functionality, however, with IPFS implemented, Shift aims at being a web hosting platform as opposed to Lisk's app platform. ∎

Currency Code:
SHIFT

Launch Date:
2015

Market Cap:
$112M

Max. Supply:
11,701,696 SHIFT

Circulating Supply:
11,418,841 SHIFT

Consensus Mechanism:
DPoS

Hashing Algorithm:
Dagger

Block Time:
27 seconds

URL:
shiftnrg.org

Currency Code:
FTC

Launch Date:
2013

Market Cap:
$109M

Max. Supply:
336,000,000 FTC

Circulating Supply:
187,526,070 FTC

Consensus Mechanism:
PoW

Hashing Algorithm:
Neoscrypt

Block Time:
60 seconds

URL:
feathercoin.com

FEATHERCOIN

An open source fork of the Litecoin blockchain, Feathercoin was the first altcoin to use the ASIC-resistant, NeoScrypt hashing algorithm. One of the first altcoins after Bitcoin, it languished for several years before being infused with new life, and with the return of its founder in January 2018, Feathercoin now faces a promising future.

History

Feathercoin was created by Peter Bushnell on April 16, 2013, as a successful fork of the Litecoin blockchain. Released back in the days when only a handful of altcoins existed, the team had big plans for its development, including even such things as laser etched physical coins and T-shirt wallets. These plans, however, fell by the wayside for reasons that remain unclear and Bushnell, a magistrate in Information Technology at the Brasenose College of Oxford University left the development team sometime in 2014.

Although the project was somewhat neglected for several years, it has recently gathered new momentum, culminating in the official return of Peter Bushnell to the team on January 1, 2018, with talk of imminent new developments, such as the integration of Lightning Network functionality and native SegWit support, as well as compatibility with BarterDEX to support atomic swaps.

Features

Feathercoin runs on an open source platform, based on the Litecoin protocol. The coin is ASIC resistant and allows mining with both CPUs and GPUs. It uses a proof-of-work protocol, that although considered by many to be time-consuming, is not only scalable and secure but considerably fast compared with its predecessors, with an average block time of just 60 seconds. For comparison, Litecoin takes 2.5 minutes and Bitcoin now takes around 10 minutes.

In order to keep their platform secure, Feathercoin has developed what they call the NeoScrypt algorithm to ensure secure digital transactions. The NeoScrypt protocols are also highly rewarding to miners who receive 80 coins per block; considerably more than other altcoins. For security purposes, in addition to the NeoScrypt algorithm, Feathercoin also makes use of a user-friendly multisignature (multisig) with a graphic user interface (GUI). A multisig is a simple security measure that requires another user or users to sign off on a transaction before it can proceed and be broadcast onto the blockchain. The Feathercoin multisig feature also allows for users to write comments into the Feathercoin blockchain with their transactions.

Apart from the standard features, the Feathercoin wallet also comes with certain extras, most of them in the form of compatibility with useful, third-party plug-ins, such as Bitmessage, Coinnector, and Shapeshift. Bitmessage is a peer-to-peer messaging platform that allows for users to exchange information such as invoices or addresses in an anonymous manner, without passing through any central servers. Coinnector is a real-time service that provides listings of FTC on the Alternate coin exchanges, while Shafeshift is a similar service with more advanced features. With these plug-ins, users can also trade their cryptocoins without the need for an account.

Other benefits of the Feathercoin wallet include the ability to obtain transaction reports, as well as the ability to send and receive FTC to stealth addresses, URI text documents or QR Codes. With imminent developments such as SegWit support, Lightning Network functionality and the ability to perform atomic swaps, Feathercoin looks set to re-establish itself as an important player in the volatile world of cryptocurrency. ∎

GULDEN

Gulden is a cryptocurrency project based in the Netherlands and named after the former Dutch currency, the 'guilder'. Gulden aims to improve the proof-of-work algorithm with their PoW² blockchain that improves transaction times and blockchain stability, as well as protecting against large-scale attacks on the network. Perhaps the most unique feature of Gulden is the ability to transfer money from the Gulden wallet to any bank account directly, using the account's IBAN number.

History

Gulden was announced and released in early 2014 after founder Rijk Plasman identified the complexity of Bitcoin as an obstacle towards wider adoption. Originally known as 'Guldencoin', the name of the project was chosen to appeal to Dutch nationals as something they previously knew, but now in a digital form. Gulden was initially focused on the Netherlands but due to the nature of crypto has now gone worldwide.

In May 2015, the DELTA algorithm was released to the Gulden blockchain, as a preventative measure against long block times. DELTA development began when block times were passing 3 hours, with a peak of 18.1 hours for one block.

After DELTA was deployed, block time was reduced drastically, however, it was not until December 2016, that block times reached the expected average of 2.5 minutes per block after a further update to DELTA. In 2018, Gulden will release proof-of-work 2 (PoW²) and Segregated Signature (SegSig), two major enhancements to the network, aiming to reduce transaction time and increase security via PoW², as well as reducing transaction size and increasing transaction throughput with SegSig.

Features

The PoW² consensus algorithm developed by Gulden is addressing shortcomings of the original PoW, PoS and PoS/PoW hybrid consensus methods as identified by Malcolm Macleod (lead developer for Gulden) in the PoW² white-paper. PoW² features two classes of miners - the PoW 'miner' and PoS 'witness'. The PoW miners mine new blocks and submit them to the network, however, they are not immediately added to the network - they must first be validated by the PoS witnesses. In the 'pre-witnessed' state, blocks may have additional transactions added by the witness which ensures a transaction fee paid to the witness for validating the block. When the valid witnessed block is created, it is then rebroadcast to the network and added to the blockchain.

These changes allow the network to run at almost full capacity, with empty blocks being filled with transactions from the witness, instead of waiting to be added to the next block. Miners can also no longer immediately mine the following block, providing a good resistance to side chains and 'selfish' mining. PoW² also reduces the chance to perform a >50% attack on the network, by increasing the amount of coin supply and hash rate needed to perform the attack.

Additionally, transactions require only 1 or 2 confirmations to occur securely, with a possibility for secure 0-confirmation transactions. A recent feature to be added is the result of a collaboration between Gulden and Nocks, the first company to be built upon the Gulden blockchain. By simply scanning a SEPA QR code or copying a bank account's IBAN number to the 'Pay from clipboard' function in the Gulden wallet, money can be transferred directly to any bank, worldwide. This represents a useful innovation in the world of crypto, helping to further bridge the gulf between crypto and fiat currencies. ∎

Currency Code:
NLG

Launch Date:
2014

Market Cap:
$104M

Max. Supply:
1,600,000,000 NLG

Circulating Supply:
389,866,605 NLG

Consensus Mechanism:
PoW²

Hashing Algorithm:
Scrypt

Block Time:
2.5 minutes

URL:
gulden.com

Currency Code:
POT

Launch Date:
2014

Market Cap:
$87M

Max. Supply:
420,000,000 POT

Circulating Supply:
219,131,433 POT

Consensus Mechanism:
PoS

Hashing Algorithm:
Scrypt

Block Time:
40 seconds

URL:
potcoin.com

POTCOIN

PotCoin is a community-based cryptocurrency focused on banking for the global legalized marijuana industry and is currently the industry-wide standard for payment. PotCoin aims "to empower, secure and facilitate the legal cannabis community", and to be "the digital currency that allows cannabis enthusiasts to interact, transact, communicate and grow together."

History

PotCoin was released on January 21, 2014, at exactly 4:20 pm (a number associated with the cannabis culture). Its popularity grew rapidly in the cryptocurrency community and in February 2014, PotCoin announced its first merchant support from a cannabis foods supplier, Chronic Star Medical, signaling a move towards wider adoption and pushing PotCoin's volume and price up dramatically. In 2015, however, the original development team disbanded and left the project. PotLabs, a group of developers from the early days of PotCoin, took over the project. After the transition, the new team started addressing issues within the currency and moved PotCoin from a proof-of-work (PoW) consensus system to proof-of-stake (PoS). In June 2017, PotCoin announced that they would provide financial support to former NBA player, Dennis Rodman, to return to the communist state, North Korea. The intention of the trip was to provide a "message of peace and understanding" to the regime. Potcoin also sponsored a second trip for Rodman later that year.

In December 2017, PotCoin announced a promotion with licensed Canadian medical cannabis producer, WeedMD, the first association between a cryptocurrency and licensed producer. Additionally, plans for the creation of the PotCoin Foundation were introduced – an intended parent group for businesses in the PotCoin ecosystem.

Features

PotCoin provides merchants a gateway to process payments outside the traditional cash-only practices that businesses are forced to use due to banks and credit card companies avoiding potential legal issues involved in the medical cannabis industry. Businesses accepting PotCoin will be listed on the interactive PotCoin map and will feature in regular updates to the PotCoin community.

The project aims to integrate with major cannabis growers as well as legal cannabis dispensaries and certain benefits will be afforded to customers using PotCoin to process transactions. Additionally, PotCoin will work to increase adoption with a 'PotCoin Go' campaign. The campaign will provide an instant wallet preloaded with PotCoins, created via SMS. PotCoin will also provide medical cannabis patients free PotCoins with purchases from partnered dispensaries.

The PotCoin Foundation will take fee profits from partnered businesses and reinvest them into the PotCoin ecosystem as well as provide rewards to the PotCoin community and fund the PotFund – a collection of supported partners who will be eligible for financial services such as loans and insurance that are not easily available to cannabis-related businesses. Additionally, the PotCoin Foundation will act as a platform for subsidiaries on the blockchain, to store transaction data, engage in e-commerce, crowdfund for new services and products, and will introduce a 'pegged value trading token' in an attempt to reduce volatility for transactions executed on the platform. PotCoin is built on a proof-of-stake (PoS) system, allowing users to act as active nodes for the network. The current interest rate from staked coins is approximately 5%. ■

BLACKCOIN

BlackCoin was created by Pavel Vasin (known in the community as Rat4) so as to provide an eco-friendly currency working on a pure proof-of-stake (PoS) consensus protocol, instead of the proof-of-work (PoW) protocols found in almost all previous cryptocurrencies. Anonymous and fast, BlackCoin has maintained a strong presence within the wider cryptocurrency community since its inception, helping drive development and approval for the PoS protocol.

History

BlackCoin was released to the public in early 2014 as a hybrid PoW/PoS system with a circulation of 75 million coins mined within the first week. With no pre-mine done by the developers and a 'fair' release (wallets available as source code and compiled binaries for multiple platforms), BlackCoin established itself as a viable product at a time when many coins were surfacing and enthusiasts were overwhelmed with choice.

Once the initial mining of the coins was complete, BlackCoin transitioned to pure PoS, allowing users to stake their holdings in order to help process transactions. Since then, BlackCoin has seen a number of upgrades, the most notable being the PoS 3.0 protocol. This implementation became the de facto standard codebase for many newer coins that sought to use the PoS protocol.

Features

BlackHalo and NightTrader are the smart contract and decentralized exchange services fueled by BlackCoin. BlackHalo differs from other smart contract solutions by using deposits to enforce a smart contract, thereby avoiding fraudulent contracts being executed. It makes use of the Python coding language, permitting users to draft smart contracts with any degree of complexity. Additionally, BlackHalo includes multi-signature wallets, joint accounts and encoded blockchain messaging.

NightTrader is a decentralized exchange built into the BlackCoin network. It prevents the need for intermediary coins and parties in trading supported currencies. NightTrader also supports the exchange of digital goods such as games and e-books.

To increase new user adoption, BlackCoin released their own software wallet, BlackCoin Lore, which has improved verification times by approximately 50% as well as reducing wallet synchronization speeds.

BlackCoin uses the PoS system that allows for 64 second confirmation times (compared to Bitcoin's estimated 10 minutes) and secures the network through a process known as "minting", which is less energy-intensive and cheaper than PoW "mining" protocols.

Open-source, decentralized, near instant transaction speeds and minimal transaction fees; BlackCoin aims to prove that PoS is a stable, secure and viable alternative to the PoW protocol. ∎

Currency Code:
BLK

Launch Date:
2014

Market Cap:
$86M

Max. Supply:
100,000,000 BLK

Circulating Supply:
76,592,566 BLK

Consensus Mechanism:
PoS

Hashing Algorithm:
Scrypt

Block Time:
60 seconds

URL:
http://blackcoin.co

Currency Code:
PURA

Launch Date:
2017

Market Cap:
$81M

Max. Supply:
350,000,000 PURA

Circulating Supply:
72,351,916 PURA

Consensus Mechanism:
PoA

Hashing Algorithm:
X11

Block Time:
2.5 minutes

URL:
pura.one

PURA

Based on Dash, Pura aims to provide secure, instant, and private international transactions using blockchain-based technology. It uses code from an already successful cryptocurrency in combination with a strategic plan for mass adoption, in order to create mainstream acceptance. As a community-based project, Pura allows users in its community to create their own rules for financial governance.

History
Pura is based on Dash which was originally released in 2014 as XCoin and then changed 10 days later to become Darkcoin. In March 2015, Darkcoin was then rebranded again, changing its name to Dash. Dash featured the use of masternodes, PrivateSend, and InstantSend. Pura was launched in August 2017, based on the Dash codebase, with a marketing strategy aimed at creating and funding socially-focused projects.

Features
Pura employs the use of masternodes in order to create a network that is fast, secure, and not reliant on mining hash power. The reward for running a masternode ensures that users are incentivized to help contribute to the security and usability of the network, while also increasing the value of the currency, as held tokens are effectively locked away, increasing the scarcity of the currency. Any user can contribute to the network as a masternode, as long as they have 100,000 PURA. Unlike other staking cryptocurrencies, Pura does not require users to hold their tokens in their own wallets but instead provides masternode service providers, which can hold tokens on the user's behalf. Users are able to withdraw their tokens and relinquish their masternode status at any time they choose.

The Pura network also allows its users to mine coins. The problem with mining with many other cryptocurrencies is that the rewards from mining are heavily dependent on the equipment used to mine, effectively creating a situation where users with more resources to purchase better mining equipment are rewarded heavily for their investments. This creates more centralization in the network. Another effect of this is that miners who have invested in specialized equipment tend to switch between different networks, depending on which coin is most profitable to mine at any given moment. This creates instability within the network, whereas the purpose of mining is to provide a consistent, secure support. Pura overcomes this problem by using a mining difficulty adjustment algorithm called DeltaDiff, which adjusts the mining difficulty by reviewing the time required to find blocks over the past 24 hours and adjusting accordingly. This means that miners are consistently rewarded, and have no incentive to 'jump' to mining for a different network when the mining becomes less profitable.

Pura has a focus on building projects for the common good of society. To achieve this goal, 10% of all Pura mined and gained through masternodes is donated to a community fund. The fund is then used for projects that help society and the environment. Pura has a Decentralized Autonomous Organization system which allows the community to propose and vote on projects which the communal funds are then spent on. ∎

I/O COIN

I/O Coin is a cryptocurrency and blockchain framework focused on market usability, merchant facilitation and advancing the adoption of global decentralized services. The I/O Digital development team's goal is to provide a secure, multi-functional, user-friendly blockchain platform that encourages users to support the network with a proof-of-stake (PoS) staking system.

History

I/O Coin was released by I/O Digital (a non-profit organization that supports and develops software for the I/O Digital ecosystem) and the genesis block was mined on July 23, 2014. After Scott Nadal and Sunny King released the white-paper for Peercoin (the first currency to make use of the PoS consensus method) the I/O Coin team, led by Joel Bosh, devised their own approach to PoS to steer away from the energy-intensive PoW method.

The I/O Coin team opted for a fair launch of their blockchain, which allowed equal access to miners instead of a pre-mine that would unfairly reward developers and those involved. Initially, the currency was mined for 14 days under the X11 PoW algorithm and was then transitioned to a PoS system. Since its inception, I/O Coin has maintained 100% uptime for their blockchain and 100% community consensus for their proposed upgrades.

In early January 2018, I/O Coin released a new version of their white-paper, outlining proposed upgrades to the ecosystem coined 'DIONS v2', which would introduce more privacy features, group messaging and the Chameleon project.

Features

DIONS (Decentralized Input Output Name Server) is an upgrade to the I/O Coin blockchain focused on updating the core platform algorithm with a new PoS algorithm named 'CiPher', with staking and security enhancements and the addition of an alias system, allowing messaging and encrypted data. DIONS provides a name/value key pair or 'alias' that offers users a human-readable name that is resolved directly from the blockchain. There are both private (encrypted) and public (unencrypted) aliases on the I/O Coin blockchain and these are only identified with one address on the IOC blockchain. While encrypted, private aliases are non-viewable on the blockchain and cannot receive IOC. The private aliases are used for file storage and secure file transfers via a secure channel constructed between two transacting aliases.

Peer-to-peer messaging can occur between public aliases who first exchange an encryption key that allows them to instantly message in a private channel. Each DIONS alias has the option to upload any binary data to the I/O Coin blockchain. The file is encrypted and compressed, then stored on the blockchain – accessible at any time by the user.

I/O Coin's Chameleon is a mechanism that allows separate peer-to-peer networks to interoperate with a lightweight API between them and without the need for a central coordinator. Chameleon provides the services of two different blockchains to a single user. The upgrade will also permit companies and users to create their own sidechain with a full portal to all the features of the IOC mainchain. Parties retain full control and privacy of their sidechain and any updates made to the IOC mainchain will not affect any private sidechains. ∎

Currency Code:
IOC

Launch Date:
2014

Market Cap:
$80M

Max. Supply:
16,500,000 IOC

Circulating Supply:
16,456,841 IOC

Consensus Mechanism:
PoS / PoW

Hashing Algorithm:
X11

Block Time:
60 seconds

URL:
iocoin.io

NAMECOIN

Namecoin is an experimental open source key/value pair registration and transfer system used to improve decentralization, security, and speed of certain components of internet infrastructure. Based on modified Bitcoin software, Namecoin uses the same proof-of-work (PoW) algorithm as Bitcoin but has the ability to store data within its own blockchain transaction database, therefore providing a decentralized DNS (domain name system) that is resistant to internet censorship.

History

The idea for Namecoin began in November 2010 on a Bitcoin developer IRC channel. A bitcoin-like DNS system was envisioned, and discussion of the project shifted to the bitcointalk.org forums. Pioneers of Bitcoin and cryptocurrency such as Gavin Andresen, Hal Finney, and Satoshi Nakamoto became involved in the conversation and sought to create a solution for the BitDNS/DomainChain system.

On December 4, 2010, a bounty of 3500 BTC was offered if a Bitcoin-like system for DNS allocation could be created and on April 18, 2011, a person named 'Vince' introduced a multi-purpose distributed naming system based on Bitcoin, known as Namecoin, which went on to become the first fork of Bitcoin. In October 2011, merged mining with Bitcoin began which allowed miners to process transactions for the Bitcoin and Namecoin networks simultaneously and receive NMC (the Namecoin currency) as block rewards.

Features

Namecoin allows the creation of TLDs (top level domains, i.e. '.com') that are not owned by anyone, with the DNS lookup tables stored on the Namecoin peer-to-peer network. This means rules cannot be imposed that affect the operation of the peer-to-peer TLDs. 'Dot-Bit' or '.bit' is the first TLD to be implemented on the Namecoin network.

Domains are created by users first initiating a transaction with a cost of 0.01 NMC that pre-orders a domain name for the network. Secondly, a transaction with variable costing is executed which registers the pre-ordered domain and makes it publically visible on the blockchain.

Finally, users must maintain their Dot-Bit domain with a zero cost transaction that updates, renews or transfers the domain, allowing it to exist on the blockchain for the next 36,000 blocks. By storing the domain registry on the user's personal computer, times taken to look up a Dot-Bit domain are reduced to around 3 milliseconds, compared to 100 milliseconds or more on a traditional DNS server. Additionally, Dot-Bit registries take approximately 40 minutes to update on the network, meaning switching website configurations is significantly faster than standard website hosts.

Namecoin's decentralized DNS provides inherent security by removing the requirement for centralized CAs (certificate authorities) to verify domain addresses on the internet. As CAs can be subject to hacks, mistaken entries, or being forced by third-parties, impersonators can assume control of a domain for their desired purpose. The Dot-Bit protocol provides CA security without relying on a CA to protect users. Additionally, the Dot-Bit protocol does not generate any network traffic when users look up addresses, as opposed to standard DNS which allows third-parties to deduce websites visited by users. ∎

Currency Code:
NMC

Launch Date:
2010

Market Cap:
$76M

Max. Supply:
21,000,000 NMC

Circulating Supply:
14,736,400 NMC

Consensus Mechanism:
PoW

Hashing Algorithm:
SHA-256

Block Time:
10 minutes

URL:
namecoin.org

EXPANSE

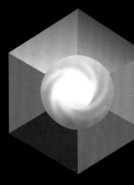

Expanse is a stable fork of Ethereum, that aims to bring funding through increasing the value proposition of the coin rather than through initial coin offerings. The development team focuses on expanding the capabilities of the Expanse platform through a democratic process by the community. Expanse allows smart contracts and a Decentralized Autonomous Organization system called Borderless Technology, which governs the development of the network.

History

Expanse was launched in September 2015. As a community-based coin, it was developed through community contribution and feedback. In late 2015, a Decentralized Autonomous Organization platform was launched which allowed development to be controlled democratically. Through this platform, many applications have been integrated into the Expanse system, for example, Votelock, which allows voting for projects within the Decentralized Autonomous Organization, and Tokenlab, which increases the application development functionality of Expanse. Development for Expanse has continued through the democratic platform it has produced, and it aims to become a serious competitor to Ethereum.

Features

The Decentralized Autonomous Organization allows community input into the development of the Expanse platform. It is funded through simple smart contracts that provide rewards for developers that contribute to coding for Expanse. The goal of this organization is for development to continue entirely through community support rather than through crowdfunding, as Expanse believes that the ecosystem in which it exists should be self-supporting.

TokenLab is a platform that allows users to create decentralized applications on the Expanse network. Similar to Ethereum, it allows users to create smart contracts and use tokens which can be traded to create value on these tokens. The decentralized applications are able to perform specialized functions and computations on the Expanse network.

One feature of TokenLab is that the tokens generated through decentralized applications can be time-locked. This means that once an initial coin offering has been created and sold off, the tokens can be set a mandatory holding period in which they cannot be traded, in order to prevent investors from dumping the tokens immediately after the sale.

Borderless Technology is a new self-governance system that has been built on the Expanse platform. Its goal is to develop a global, decentralized governance system that is able to provide services in regards to citizenship, identity, marriage, and other political issues that are central to creating a society. The project aims to be able to provide global decentralized governance for the world at large. Users are able to create cryptographically secure identities that can be verified through the blockchain, and this can replace current systems of identity and registry.

Using the same technology that Expanse is built upon, Borderless Technology will be able to fund socially-focused projects as more and more citizens join the globalized system. For example, in August 2017, it launched a project to help fund a program to aid families in helping their children attend schools. The Borderless Charity is a registered charity in the United States and donations to the charity are tax-deductible. ∎

Currency Code:
EXP

Launch Date:
2015

Market Cap:
$71M

Max. Supply:
31,400.000 EXP

Circulating Supply:
7,906,397 EXP

Consensus Mechanism:
PoW

Hashing Algorithm:
Dagger

Block Time:
30 seconds

URL:
expanse.tech

Currency Code:
GRC

Launch Date:
2013

Market Cap:
$71M

Max. Supply:
N/A

Circulating Supply:
390,312,753 GRC

Consensus Mechanism:
POS

Hashing Algorithm:
DPoR

Block Time:
90 seconds

URL:
gridcoin.us

GRIDCOIN

An open source network protocol using blockchain technology, the Gridcoin network is able to be used as a distributed computing network for scientific research. Instead of requiring a supercomputer to process data, scientists are able to use the Gridcoin network (based on the Berkeley Open Infrastructure for Network Computing; BOINC) to process data at a much lower cost. The project aims to further the capabilities of scientists worldwide by providing them with the computing power they need that otherwise might be completely inaccessible.

History
BOINC began development in 2002, its goal being to manage the SETI@home project started by the Berkeley SETI Research Center. SETI@home was one of the first distributed computing networks created. Its purpose was to analyze radio signals and search for signs of extraterrestrial intelligence, but before long, it had expanded the scope of its abilities to include other types of scientific computation. Gridcoin was launched in 2013 as a reward for participating in the BOINC network.

Features
BOINC is an open source distributed computing network system that is able to perform computations for multiple sciences. It is the largest computing grid in the world and runs on multiple operating systems. The network uses both CPU and GPU power to compute its algorithms, which means that Gridcoin is not ASIC averse like some other cryptocurrencies. There are currently 37 projects whitelisted for BOINC, with projects sponsored by universities from all over the world.

Gridcoin rewards are based on both proof-of-stake and proof-of-research algorithms. Proof-of-stake generates an interest rate of 1.5% per year on the staking coins while proof-of-research pays users for participating in approved BOINC projects. BOINC projects have a Cross-Project ID which is linked to computations that are completed, and if the computations are related to the ID then the user is rewarded for helping with the computation. Users are paid out in Gridcoin tokens, proportional to their Recent Average Credit score (RAC), which is determined by the number of helpful computations that the user has provided the network.

Gridcoin is decentralized, so the development of the coin is based on community consensus. A blockchain-based voting system exists where users can stay updated with current projects and vote on the development of the coin. Features such as the BOINC whitelist were developed through the voting system.

Other cryptocurrencies generally create coins and maintain their value through their distributed computing networks, however, this results in a lot of computing power being directed towards solving computations that are then discarded. Gridcoin aims to direct the wasted resources into producing results for research.

The project sees idle computing power and computing power used for discarded algorithms to be a waste. There is a large demand for computing power within the scientific community, and the cost of running a centralized network is quite high. By rewarding users to direct the computing power towards the Gridcoin/BOINC network, Gridcoin is able to create an energy efficient network that is also able to help further develop our knowledge. ∎

ELASTIC

Elastic is an open source project that aims to create a secure, trustless, decentralized, and programmable supercomputer. By using blockchain-based technology, Elastic is able to incentivize users to contribute to their decentralized network. Users who require access to a supercomputer to complete work are able to access the Elastic network at any time with reasonable fees, which is a huge advantage over locating, requesting access to, and paying for the use a physical supercomputer.

History

The Elastic project was announced in March 2016 as a community-based project with anonymous lead developers. In 2017, one of the lead developers vanished along with most of the funds raised in the initial coin offering, however, it is unclear whether this was due to malicious intent or health issues from the developer.

The developer in question was anonymous and had previously mentioned problems with his health. Prior to their sudden disappearance, they had paid out funds to other developers and contributing members of the community. As the project is open source, it continues to be developed by many members of the community.

Features

Elastic provides supercomputer computational abilities to anyone who wants to access the network by using cryptocurrency-based technologies. A proof-of-work protocol is used to generate computing power with miners contributing their processing power to the network - the more miners that contribute, the more powerful the network is. In order to incentivize miners to continue contributing, they are awarded XEL tokens, which can be traded for monetary value on exchanges. As the Elastic network expands and more people use the platform, the XEL tokens should rise in value, and more miners should be attracted to contribute to the network.

Users are required to pay for computational power using XEL tokens, so this creates an ecosystem where the coins mined are sold back to the people who require the use of the network. As the system is decentralized, there is no need to rely on any single entity in order to run.

The Elastic programming language enables users to program complex algorithms for the network to solve, in exchange for XEL tokens. The programming language is loosely based on C, however, there are no FOR, WHILE, or DO loops in order to prevent programs from running indefinitely on the network.

Elastic has replaced this with a REPEAT function, which will access the same functionality as a loop without causing congestion. The language is designed to be secure and without the possibility of malicious code, as any exploits would cause large problems to the network and all the computers that compose it. Issues such as endless loops and data leakage are not possible with the Elastic programming language.

The language continues to be developed, with the main focus being to provide a language that can complete a wide range of computational tasks without having the capability to cause damage to any miners' computers or to the network as a whole. ∎

Currency Code:
XEL

Launch Date:
2016

Market Cap:
$71M

Max. Supply:
100,000,000 XEL

Circulating Supply:
88,355,631 XEL

Consensus Mechanism:
PoS

Hashing Algorithm:
SHA256

Block Time:
N/A

URL:
elastic.pw

urrency Code:
MD

aunch Date:
013

larket Cap:
69M

lax. Supply:
,380,000 DMD

irculating Supply:
,591,624 DMD

onsensus Mechanism:
oS / PoW

lashing Algorithm:
roestl

lock Time:
0 seconds

JRL:
it.diamonds

DIAMOND

Diamond (DMD) is a form of digital currency designed to be used as a store of wealth. It has a low cost for transactions and there is a very limited supply of coins available. There is also a high annual interest rate for coin holders. Transaction times are very fast on the network and the coin also aims to lower the energy consumption of the network through using a proof-of-stake algorithm.

History

Diamond was originally released in 2013 and began mining coins using both proof-of-work and proof-of-stake algorithms. In 2014, the Diamond development team released Diamond 3.0. From 2017, the mining rewards began to decrease significantly, as planned by the team. The planned decrease in mining rewards is expected to continue, with a roadmap plan that extends beyond 2027.

Features

Diamond aims to be scarce, valuable, and secure. The development team has also planned to be able to use Diamond as a software platform in the future. In order to ensure scarcity, the maximum supply of Diamond is limited to 4.38 million coins. In order to combat inflation, Diamond is designed with a coin burning system called 'Treasure Digging' that will activate in 2027, after most of the coins are mined and available.

Treasure Digging will allow users to search for wallets with amounts that have not been spent for over 10 years and 'burn' the coins. Users who discover these wallets receive a portion of the wallet as a reward. The Diamond Wallet will have a feature to easily help users keep track of their wallets and quickly change wallets to reset the 10-year time limit. Wallets containing over 10000 Diamonds will not be included in Treasure Digging. Diamond also burns transaction fees and will be introducing services and apps which will continue burning coins, so that miners will still continue to be rewarded.

Diamond creates value through a high annual interest rate for users who stake their coins. When users leave unspent coins in their wallet for 9 days, they will start accumulating more coins as a reward through the proof-of-stake algorithm. The number of coins that users receive is based on a number of factors, for example, how long the coins have been in the wallet, the number of coins already held, and how many other wallets are currently staking their coins. In 2017, the reward for staking coins was over 25%.

The proof-of-stake algorithm that Diamond uses has been modified to fix a few of the problems that previous proof-of-stake systems encountered. Previous systems used mainly the coin's age as a factor for receiving rewards which resulted in many stakers holding coins, as the coins were more valuable unspent.

However, another effect of this was that nodes became dormant as they were still rewarded as long as they had staked coins. Diamond's proof-of-stake system prevents these problems by only allowing active nodes to receive rewards. As the reward rate is standardized (for example at 2.35DMD per block at launch), this incentivizes more nodes to continue running to claim their share of rewards. ∎

CROWN

Crown is a masternode-based coin that combines features from Bitcoin and Dash, while adding extra features, such as the ability to mine coins concurrently with multiple blockchains. As a community-based coin, Crown development is heavily based on feedback from its users. Users are able to develop applications for use on the Crown network, and Crown has released APIs (Application Programming Interface) that allow developers to easily access the functionality of the Crown blockchain. Crown openly does not support anonymous features.

History

Crown was launched as Crown Coin in 2014 as a fork of the Bitcoin code that integrated features from Dash, namely the masternode features (as Crown does not believe in anonymity with their cryptocurrency). There was no premine for the launch of Crown Coin. In 2016, Crown Coin implemented masternode features and rebranded to its current name, Crown. Major updates to its core code were introduced in 2017, allowing an implementation of its current governance system, as well as its current node structure.

Features

Merge mining allows multiple cryptocurrencies with the same base algorithms to be mined concurrently, allowing networks to expend fewer resources without sacrificing the security or speed of the network. Crown uses merge mining coupled with Bitcoin, as Crown believes that proof-of-work mining expends too many resources, which is harmful to the environment. Crown will also introduce a form of proof-of-stake mining called Chronos in order to lessen the environmental impact and increase the security speed of the network.

A masternode system comprised of three types of nodes is used to secure the Crown network. Service Tron nodes will be able to process basic transactions for users over the network while specialized Tron nodes are responsible for deploying and running decentralized applications. Chronos nodes exist to monitor time on the network, which is essential in order to expand the capacity of the network without compromising security. As more and more transactions are processed, more precise time-monitoring is needed to ensure that transactions are legitimate and that double-spending or counterfeiting is not possible.

Crown allows developers to create applications and tokens, similar to Ethereum's development platforms and an easily accessible API is available for developers to access the functionality of Crown's blockchain network. The API was designed with ease of use in mind, allowing developers to create applications on the network without the need for a deep understanding of blockchain technology. Smart contracts are enabled on Crown, allowing users to interact with other users through trustless transaction technology.

Anonymity has been purposefully removed from Crown, even though Crown is developed from Dash technology. Crown developers believe that in order for mass adoption and widespread use, Crown needs to be open and auditable. Anonymity may cause governments to be wary of the use of the currency as it can bring up legal issues such as money laundering. The Crown development team has hired a high profile law firm in order to comply with US and EU regulations, with the goal of creating a government approved cryptocurrency. ∎

Currency Code:
CRW

Launch Date:
2014

Market Cap:
$67M

Max. Supply:
42,000,000 CRW

Circulating Supply:
16,668,940 CRW

Consensus Mechanism:
PoW

Hashing Algorithm:
SHA-256

Block Time:
60 seconds

URL:
crown.tech

Currency Code:
FAIR

Launch Date:
2014

Market Cap:
67M

Max. Supply:
53,000.000 FAIR

Circulating Supply:
53,193,831 FAIR

Consensus Mechanism:
PoC

Hashing Algorithm:
N/A

Block Time:
minutes

URL:
fair-coin.org

FAIRCOIN

FairCoin is a community-based, collaborative effort to introduce a cryptocurrency into Europe that is tied to a stable value. This value is determined by the community who regularly hold open forums to reassess the true value of the coin. FairCoin is a core element of the FairCoop project. At the moment of writing, the value of 1 FairCoin is equal to 1 Euro.

History

FairCoin began development anonymously in 2014, but was soon abandoned and then later revived. The initial offering of FairCoin was made through an 'airdrop', where 50 million FairCoins were distributed to members of the community who registered for the event. FairCoin has always focused on reaching a common consensus for the price of the coin, however as the adoption of the coin becomes more widespread, the value of the coin naturally increases. Therefore, rather than be left purely to market demand, the value of the coin is reassessed constantly in order to determine its price. When FairCoin was released, it was worth 0.05€. Since then, its value has increased consistently up to its current price of 1€ per coin.

Features

FairCoop is the community that supports FairCoin. The aim of the FairCoop cooperative is to create an alternative global economic system. This is to be achieved through following the ideals of the community and through community contributions, with consensus on the direction of the cooperative always required for the implementation of any proposals or changes.

One of the core features of FairCoin is its price stability. This was implemented in order to ensure the sustainability of the cryptocurrency and to prevent potential investors from altering the price for their own gain. Price stability is accomplished by limiting the maximum size of a transaction, increasing the confirmation time of transactions to discourage trading, and by the support of the community that holds and use the currency. Creating a community that cooperates to use FairCoin at an agreed-upon price, means that participants within the community can use the cryptocurrency without having any concerns regarding price fluctuations. The goal of this feature is to increase acceptance by businesses, as this would have the intended effect of the cryptocurrency being used as a replacement to fiat.

Instead of using algorithms which require miners to hold coins or compete for rewards, such as proof-of-work or proof-of-stake, FairCoin uses a proof-of-cooperation algorithm which utilizes collaboratively validated nodes to secure the network. Coin-generating algorithms are not used, as the number of coins within the ecosystem is limited to what the community agrees upon in order to control inflation. Proof-of-cooperation means that the network designates an individual node to create a block of transactions which is then verified by the rest of the network signing the data.

The development for FairCoin is community-based, with rewards given for individual tasks, paid in FairCoin. The community helps to decide on the direction of development as well as in the creation of the FairCoin economy. An example of this can be seen in the FairCoin marketplace - FairMarket - that was created to list the goods and services of businesses who have accepted FairCoin. ∎

OMNI

Omni (Omni Layer), formerly known as Mastercoin, is an open source crypto-currency and communication protocol based on the Bitcoin blockchain. It is a software layer that facilitates the creation and trading of digital assets and currencies. Launched in 2015 as a continuation of Mastercoin, the platform exploits Bitcoin's blockchain to offer extra distributed services such as decentralized currency trading, smart contracts, as well as digital assets trading.

History

Omni began as Mastercoin in 2013, however, the idea of Mastercoin was conceptualized in January 2012 by J. R. Willett in his paper "The Second Bitcoin Whitepaper" (Version 0.5). Willett proposed that the existing Bitcoin blockchain could be used as a software layer to facilitate the creation of new digital assets and currencies without changing the blockchain or developing a new one. Willett's idea aimed to address three key issues: 1) enhance Bitcoin's stability via the creation of new currencies; 2) add value to the existing Bitcoin network to the benefit of Bitcoin holders, and 3) provide a platform for financing software development and new protocol layers.

On July 31, 2013, Version 1.0 of the initial white-paper was released, calling for funding of the Mastercoin project. This was the first ever ICO in cryptocurrency history. A Bitcoin address - Exodus Address - through which the public could send Bitcoins in exchange for Mastercoins was provided with 1 Bitcoin equivalent to 100 Mastercoins. The first Mastercoin transaction was recorded on August 15, 2013, and the offer remained open until August 31, 2013. At the end of the offering, 4,740 Bitcoins were received, an equivalent of approximately 563,162 Mastercoins.

In September 2013, the Mastercoin Foundation was created with seven volunteer members, including J. R. Willet, and Ron Gross as the Executive Director. On October 15, 2013, Mastercoin held the first code contest valued at $25,000. In 2015, Mastercoin rebranded to Omni, aiming to enhance its distributed offerings. Today, Omni is one of the more popular names in the cryptocurrency world.

Features

Omni offers two types of wallets: Omni Wallet and Omni Core. Omni Wallet is a free, hosted web wallet. Three key features of the wallet include; private keys, usability, and multi-currency support. The Omni Wallet allows users to easily create custom assets or currencies and trade them through the Bitcoin blockchain, whilst private keys guarantee users high-level security. The Omni Wallet also facilitates decentralized crowdfunding by allowing crowdsale participants to send tokens directly to an issuer's address. From there they can be automatically conveyed to the sender as required, all without the need for a third party.

Omni Core is a desktop wallet that allows for the peer-to-peer trading of tokens. This occurs through Omni Layer's distributed exchanges, which allow Omni users to trade tokens or Bitcoins directly on the blockchain without requiring a third party. Omni Core is based on Bitcoin Core and is supported by Windows, Mac OS, and Linux. Users of Omni can also view all Bitcoin-based Omni transactions via Omniexplorer.info. The website provides users with information relating to Omni deals, addresses, distributed exchanges, and wallets, as well as Omni Layer and Bitcoin usage. ∎

Currency Code:
OMNI

Launch Date:
2013

Market Cap:
$66M

Max. Supply:
616,782 OMNI

Circulating Supply:
560,403 OMNI

Consensus Mechanism:
PoW

Hashing Algorithm:
Scrypt

Block Time:
3 minutes

URL:
omnilayer.org

ION

A gaming-oriented, proof-of-stake cryptocurrency, ION is based on decentralized blockchain technology. Since the advent of cryptocurrencies, it has been quite difficult for digital currencies to achieve widespread adoption due to scalability issues and the sometimes complex investment and transaction process intimidating potential users. ION seeks to eliminate this barrier by making it easy for anyone to enter and understand the crypto world.

History

The development of ION started in November 2015. The founding company, Ionomy, aimed to ease cryptocurrency adoption via mobile gaming and social engagement. The initial round of funding, a crowdsale offering, raised $125,000. This funding enabled the development of the ionomy.com platform. On April 4, 2016, Ionomy launched an ICO at a price of $0.20 per coin, targeting to raise an additional $500,000 for further development and deployment of the platform. The ICO concluded in May 2016, paving the way for the official launch of the coin. As of January 31, 2018, ION's market capitalization was approximately $91.2 million, trading at $4.70 per coin. This represents a 2,250% growth compared to the ICO price.

Features

ION was designed to be inviting and user-friendly and is accessible on both desktop and mobile devices. The platform is easy to learn and use with features that encourage fun, social engagement, and investment. The network appeals to crypto fans, traders, investors, gamers, and developers alike.

Active players on the ionomy.com platform are awarded tokens called 'Electrons' for their successes in solo games and competitions. The Electron tokens are intended to increase engagement since players can use them on the platform. A coveted prize is also offered to help players earn coins more quickly. As players use the platform and engage via games, their reputation builds up, consequently opening more opportunities for incentives and rewards.

The ionomy.com platform offers easy-to-use web-based wallets. Both ION and Bitcoin wallets allow users to easily send, receive, and store coins. Users have an option of depositing ION into their wallets at a fixed rate of return, paid on a daily basis, and the platform also allows users to trade ION and Bitcoin on a live exchange, with users being able to convert most cryptocurrencies to ION instantly and directly. Multiple payout avenues give users a level of flexibility that is not available in most other cryptocurrencies. Besides the web-based wallets, users can accumulate their ION coins on local private wallets, which are supported by all major operating systems. Local private wallets allow users to earn staking rewards by storing ION in their wallet and keeping the wallet connected to the internet. Users holding 20,000 ION or more can host masternodes in exchange for rewards (at the time of writing this amount is valued at approximately $83,200). Both wallets and masternodes are crucial for maintaining the security of the network.

By combining gaming and cryptocurrency investment, ION attracts users with varying levels of interest and experience, and the coin's gaming focus is valuable for game developers as well as gaming enthusiasts. Game developers can use the network to conduct crowdfunding and to beta-test new products, allowing ION to fill in quite a specific niche in the gaming community. ∎

Currency Code:
ION

Launch Date:
2016

Market Cap:
$60M

Max. Supply:
9,706,034 ION

Circulating Supply:
8,841,071 ION

Consensus Mechanism:
PoS

Hashing Algorithm:
N/A

Block Time:
70 seconds

URL:
ionomy.com

WHITECOIN

Whitecoin is an open source, community-driven cryptocurrency, designed to be fast, anonymous, and secure. The Whitecoin Foundation is the community-based organization that develops and promotes the use of Whitecoin. Development for Whitecoin began in 2014. By the end of 2017, Whitecoin was listed on 9 exchanges, with a trading volume of over $3 million a day. WhiteOS is an operating system developed by the Whitecoin community as a way to increase anonymity and security when accessing and using Whitecoin.

History

Whitecoin began development in 2014 and the coin was an immediate success, reaching the top 5 in volume trading of all cryptocurrencies within a week of release. The original code, however, was flawed, which resulted in the formation of the community (later identifying as the Whitecoin Foundation) to repair the coin and continue development. The problems with the coin were repaired within a week. During this period, miners received no rewards and the platform was completely community supported. Whitecoin continues to be very community-focused, with a well-defined vision for the development of the cryptocurrency.

Features

One of the core components of Whitecoin is how the community is structured to further the development and market growth of the coin. Whitecoin is completely crowdsourced, so all the work is done by volunteers, even though there are occasionally fundraisers to support the Whitecoin project. Decisions on the coin are made based on a loose consensus decision-making model, which means that any changes require a majority support. Work done for the project is evaluated through peer review, and there is near flat power-structure to the Whitecoin Foundation. The common ideals of the Whitecoin Foundation guide the community in terms of decision-making, and members can raise a review of the direction of the coin at any time provided certain criteria are met.

Whitecoin uses a proof-of-stake 3.0 algorithm, which allows users to gain between 0.5-6% interest per year on their held coins. Using a proof-of-stake algorithm allows the network to gain interest and also helps keep the network energy efficient.

As with most other cryptocurrencies, Whitecoin offers the ability to anonymously create wallets to send and receive currency. Users do not require any identifying information to use Whitecoin, however, nodes may still be able to track IP addresses from which transactions are broadcasted. All transactions are displayed transparently on the blockchain.

WhiteOS was created in order to help users become completely anonymous when using Whitecoin. WhiteOS is a complete operating system which is run from a USB and uses a customized version of Ubuntu. The operating system allows users to keep their Whitecoin safe in cold storage while also increasing anonymity.

WhiteOS ensures that connections are routed through the TOR network, which prevents nodes from tracking user transactions through their IP addresses. Another security feature of WhiteOS is that it is able to wipe any trace of it being run on the host computer, which means that users can rest assured that their personal keys are safe and their funds are secure. ■

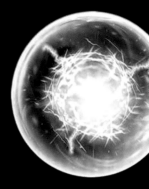

Currency Code:
XWC

Launch Date:
2014

Market Cap:
$59M

Max. Supply:
248,720,145 XWC

Circulating Supply:
248,618,793 XWC

Consensus Mechanism:
PoS

Hashing Algorithm:
Scrypt

Block Time:
60 seconds

URL:
whitecoin.info

Currency Code:
MC

Launch Date:
2017

Market Cap:
$51M

Max. Supply:
Unlimited

Circulating Supply:
546,115,084 MUSIC

Consensus Mechanism:
PoW

Hashing Algorithm:
ETHash

Block Time:
60 seconds

URL:
www.musicoin.org

MUSICOIN

Musicoin is a decentralized platform using blockchain technology to give power to musicians, allowing them to control the ownership of their content and finances. Its blockchain is founded upon those already used by Bitcoin and Ethereum and uses pay per play (PPP) smart contracts to ensure that all musical content and services are reasonably compensated.

History
As a standalone cryptocurrency with its own blockchain as the public ledger, Musicoin began with no presale or ICO and with no funds pre-allocated to project development. Instead, it has allowed its community to mine 100% of the coins right from inception.

Musicoin officially launched its project on February 11, 2017, with the mining of the first block of MUSIC; a fork of the Ethereum blockchain, strongly supported by a community of users and Musicoin developers.

The coin has continued to grow in value, with current capitalization close to $50 million. Since Musicoin is able to track individuals' listening history, the developers are now working towards using artificial intelligence to help music lovers select the right playlists in real time.

Features
Musicoin is redefining the often complex relationship between musicians, managers, record labels and listeners to create a more sustainable and equitable model that honors the creators of content and does away with much of the redundancy of the classic model. One of its co-founders, Isaac Mao calls it a *"Musiconomy built on the foundation of sharism."*

The idea of the Musiconomy is to create a basis to help musicians release their work and at the same time, define the terms, while consumers have access to it without any restrictions. The 'Sharism' functionality makes it easy for users to share their creations online and at the same time get paid; a far cry from the practice of having one's music released via streaming sites with little or no monetary compensation.

Musicoin utilizes several templates from which creators can choose to automatically run smart contracts. The most important of these is called Pay-Per-Play (PPP), which enables the automation of the unit consumption of music once a playback occurs. This contract ensures payment to the content creators and each transaction that occurs is embedded into the network's blockchain as a lasting record.

Although the Musicoin (MC) currency used on the platform can be mined by individuals, most mining is effected via pools using proof-of-work (PoW) protocols, where all the users in the mining pool cooperate to create new coins.

Listeners also enjoy certain benefits including free listening, access to global music, direct interaction with artists as well as the participation in an equitable and sustainable musical economy. ∎

PHORE

Phore is a proof-of-stake-based currency with near-instant transaction times and a focus on privacy and anonymity. It is based on Bitcoin, with Zerocoin protocols built in for anonymity. The master node system employed by Phore allows users to send transactions almost instantly by requiring zero confirmations for payments. Phore plans to create an ecosystem where users can create decentralized applications, and Phore will be providing their own decentralized marketplace where users can trade items for Phore. As a community-based currency, Phore aims to continue its project with transparency and community as the principal guiding forces.

History

Phore was originally called KryptKoin and launched in May 2014. The coin was distributed fairly amongst those who were qualified to stake the coin, and there was no pre-mine. There was no initial coin offering, and instead, a total of 500 stakes were distributed evenly, with the original developer receiving the same stake as all other participants in the launch. In 2015, KryptKoin launched a marketplace with PayPal integration, which sold digital items such as Wordpress themes.

In 2017, due to the need to integrate new features into the protocol, the KryptKoin code was completely rewritten and rebranded as Phore. There was a 2-month window in which KryptKoin holders were able to swap their tokens at a 1:1 ratio for Phore, after which all 7 million remaining unexchanged tokens were destroyed, leaving a supply of around 11 million Phore.

Features

Phore (PHR) is a proof-of-stake coin, which requires users to hold PHR in running wallets in order to secure the network and generate value. This encourages users to support the network and they are incentivized to contribute by being rewarded just by being connected. Using proof-of-stake also creates a more decentralized system, as all users can contribute to the network, not just those who are able to invest energy and resources into mining the currency. Transaction fees are very low with Phore, and these fees are burned as they are used, which increases the value of the coin. The team envisions that as network use increases, the burning of transaction fees will create deflation, increasing the value of the currency. Random open wallets that are contributing to the network are rewarded Phore every 60 seconds, with users who are holding more tokens more likely to receive a reward.

Masternodes are used to process private transactions and for handling the Phore budget governance process. 10,000 PHR are required in order to start a masternode, which is operational 24/7, as it can run on a virtual private server, or on personal computers if certain requirements are met. Users can dismantle their masternode and withdraw their held coins at any time. Masternodes also receive more rewards for their contribution to the network. The Phore budget governance process provides 10% of mined coins to developers, and masternodes are able to vote on the direction of the development of Phore.

Phore employs the Zerocoin protocol in order to provide transactions with privacy and anonymity, however, these protocols are optional for users, as they may desire for their transactions to be publicly listed on the Phore blockchain. ∎

Currency Code:
PHR

Launch Date:
2014

Market Cap:
$48M

Max. Supply:
11,840,585 PHR

Circulating Supply:
8,108,332 PHR

Consensus Mechanism:
PoS

Hashing Algorithm:
N/A

Block Time:
60 seconds

URL:
phore.io

Currency Code:
HUSH

Launch Date:
2016

Market Cap:
$42M

Max. Supply:
21,000,000 HUSH

Circulating Supply:
2,242,500 HUSH

Consensus Mechanism:
PoS

Hashing Algorithm:
Equihash

Block Time:
2.5 minutes

URL:
myhush.org

HUSH

Hush is a fork of Zcash that replaces the Zcash founders' reward (a percentage given to the developers and founders through mining) with a fixed amount of premined coins. There are also additions to the Zcash codebase, such as implementing secure messaging within the network, and the ability to create smart contracts. Hush combines Zcash protocols with components from Counterparty and Komodo.

History
Hush was originally released in November 2016 as Zdash, a fork of the Zcash currency. The development of Zdash changed hands in May 2017, with the previous lead developer Joseph Stuhlman stepping down and introducing David Mercer, citing that the project deserved to be coded correctly. In July 2017, Zdash was rebranded to Hush after consultation with the Hush community. Rebranding was necessary as there was a lot of negative association with the Zdash name as it was too similar to its predecessor, Zcash.

Features
Zcash features privacy protocols which encrypt transaction information between senders and receivers. Records on the blockchain are still public, however, the specific sender, receiver, and transaction amount information are hashed, so only the participating parties can access the information. This provides privacy for the users of the protocol. Although the protocol does not provide anonymity – as a user's IP addresses are still accessible by mining nodes – the protocol is compatible with anonymizing services such as TOR.

Hush was originally developed in response to Zcash's funding scheme, as Zcash required miners to donate a percentage of their mining rewards to the original investors of Zcash. As Hush still required funds for development, the funding scheme was modified so that instead of an ongoing mining tax for using the protocol, there was a limited premined amount that was donated to developers. This encouraged developers to continue to add value to the protocol and was designed to be more attractive to contributors to the network while still rewarding the developers.

Users can create smart contracts and assets on the Hush blockchain using the Counterparty protocol. The Counterparty protocol allows data to be encoded within transactions on the Hush blockchain, without the need to use a specialized decentralized platform like Ethereum. Transactions made using the Counterparty protocol appear on the blockchain as normal transactions for a small amount that the Counterparty interpreter will recognize and interpret as data, processing the instructions based on specific rules. Counterparty uses an encoding method that is able to be discarded from the blockchain after being used, which means that using the protocol will not cause too much data bloating. Smart contracts that are programmed in Solidity and Serpent for the Ethereum Virtual Machine are compatible with Counterparty. Counterparty data is able to be completely transferred to different blockchains in the event of a particular blockchain becoming obsolete.

Hush provides a fast and secure messaging platform called Hushlist. Users are able to send up to 50 messages at once and allows users to remain anonymous when sending or receiving them. As Hushlist is blockchain-based, messages can be easily verified for authenticity and are non-retractable. ∎

STEALTHCOIN

Stealthcoin focuses on providing anonymity and ease of use. It routes transactions through the Tor network and allows users to transfer currency directly to another user through a variety of methods, including using a text message routing system. Stealthcoin uses a proof-of-stake mining algorithm to secure the network and verify transactions. The application, Stealthtext, makes sending currency easily accessible to new adopters by using a system that they are already familiar with.

History
Stealthcoin was launched in July 2014 featuring an energy efficient algorithm, X13. It was originally a fork of Novacoin. There was a 1% premine to raise funds for developers prior to release, after which mining was opened to the public. In late 2014, the Stealthcoin and Stealthtext wallets were released.

Features
X-Algorithms were originally introduced to prevent ASIC mining (specialized hardware designed to mine coins), as this was causing cryptocurrencies to become more centralized by favoring users who had the resources to invest in specialized equipment.

ASIC mining also resulted in users switching between mining pools for different coins, which caused networks to become less secure as less power was directed towards securing the networks when the mining difficulty was too high. X13 was designed to be more energy efficient and less taxing on the equipment, resulting in less heat generated and lower operational costs. Stealthcoin started off using proof-of-work to generate coins but later changed to a proof-of-stake method as this was more energy efficient and adequate for the purpose of securing the network.

In order to generate Stealthcoin through staking, users must have coins in their wallet for a minimum of 3 days. Users with more tokens in their wallet receive a higher chance of staking, and wallets are only rewarded if they are open and connected, in order to encourage users to contribute to the security of the network. Users can gain 20% of their staked amounts annually. Tor is a network built to create anonymity on the internet. Users who connect to the internet through the Tor protocol have their connections routed through multiple Tor nodes, which in effect makes it almost impossible for anyone to track the user's original IP address and location.

Stealthcoin requires users to connect to the Stealthcoin network through Tor, so that all transactions are untraceable. In combination with pseudonymous wallet addresses, the only way that users are able to be identified when using Stealthcoin is if they explicitly give out their personal information when making transactions (for example, giving out a mailing address).

Stealthtext is a method in which users can send Stealthcoin through SMS messaging. Users are able to link their Stealthcoin wallets with a text messaging service (eg. Google Voice) and send transactions directly to wallet without a connection to the internet.

Transactions sent this way are routed through their text messaging service, converted to email which is read by their wallet, and then sent through the Stealthtext network. Using this method users can easily transact with each other securely through a familiar medium. ∎

Currency Code:
XST

Launch Date:
2014

Market Cap:
$42M

Max. Supply:
N/A

Circulating Supply:
27,793,882 XST

Consensus Mechanism:
PoS

Hashing Algorithm:
X13

Block Time:
60 seconds

URL:
stealthcoin.com

Currency Code:
GEO

Launch Date:
2015

Market Cap:
$40M

Max. Supply:
3,406,438 GEO

Circulating Supply:
3,373,266 GEO

Consensus Mechanism:
PoW

Hashing Algorithm:
Qubit

Block Time:
60 seconds

URL:
geocoin.cash

GEOCOIN

A virtual currency combining geocaching technology and the blockchain, the GeoCoin project aims to bring Geographic Information Systems (GIS) and Geo-technologies to the blockchain with a MapBox interface, providing a game-like experience to users.

History

GeoCoin was announced in January 2015, while still in its early stages of development. Although originally intending to use the X11 algorithm, the team first consulted with the community to determine the best algorithm for the project. GeoCoin was subsequently released with the Qubit algorithm instead, to encourage adoption by miners and an initial pre-mine took place as a means to pay the developers.

After an initial attempt to create an in-house system for discovering and 'mining' new GEO, GeoCoin instead announced a plan in mid-2017 to migrate to the Ubiq blockchain to allow for further technological innovations (such as proof-of-location) to be implemented.

A full token swap occurred in early 2018. The market was paused and the PoW mining phase ended. All balances mined on the GEO PoW chain up until the blockchain snapshot were credited to the UBQ network and created as a new ERC20 token. The previous PoW blockchain, while still able to be mined, was considered abandoned. With the transition to the new blockchain, the total supply of tokens available was reduced from 6.8 million to 4 million.

Features

GeoCoin is powered by the Mapbox Interface that provides a game-like experience. Users can see clusters of coins and zoom to a 3D street-view level to see the coin locations. GeoCoin holders can pin GEO to the environment, allowing other users to travel to the location in order to collect them.

In planned updates to the GEO Mapbox Interface, GeoCoin will offer the ability to drop large amounts of coins at a particular location for events or promotions and will even offer the ability to drop other cryptocurrencies by paying GEO as a fee. It will also feature GEO that are tied to certain environments as well as GeoHunter achievements and statistics. The camera perspective controls on the interface will be able to be shared via Facebook, allowing users to show others where to find GeoCoins.

The project will implement street-view into the app so GEO can be seen in augmented reality, allowing for possibilities in AR gaming and geo-dashing events, where users visit geo-points around the world and can receive GEO as a prize.

With GeoCoin transitioning to the UBQ blockchain, it will be able to make use of Proof-of-Location technology, meaning users must physically travel to a location to create new coins, thereby providing a monetary benefit to users for geocaching. Proof-of-location will take over the traditional mining aspect of the currency by having the UBQ blockchain mint the GEO through a smart contract and then automatically scatter the GEO randomly across the world. ∎

DEEPONION

Deep Onion is an anonymous digital currency that routes all its transactions through the TOR network. The DeepSend protocol is used in order to make tracing transactions impossible within the Deep Onion network. The aim of Deep Onion is to provide a means of transferring wealth that is free from observation and scrutiny by government bodies and malicious individuals.

History

Deep Onion was first announced in July 2017. Distribution of Deep Onion was done through free airdrops to members of the BitcoinTalk forums who signed up on the Deep Onion website, with 12.5 million Onions given away over 40 airdrop rounds. DeepVault, a data storage platform on the Deep Onion network, was launched in late 2017. Future releases of Deep Onion will integrate DeepSend, a protocol which will further obfuscate transaction information, and VoteCentral, a method in which the Deep Onion community can voice their opinions and decide on the direction of development for the project.

Features

Deep Onion has a strong focus on providing anonymity for its users, as the team believes that wealth should not be controlled by the government and security is of paramount importance. Using traditional cryptocurrency technology where all transactions appear transparently on the blockchain, any user can see the amount of wealth a person has, and where they spend the wealth as soon as the user reveals their ownership of a particular wallet address. This can create problems, for example, malicious users are immediately aware of the wealth and identity of the individual, or users may end up being associated with illegal activities by possessing coins which were previously used by criminals, even if they are innocent.

In order to create anonymity for their currency, the TOR network is used. TOR obfuscates a user's identity by making their IP address untraceable to nodes. Any person trying to identify a user connected to the TOR network will only see that the user is connecting from the TOR network, but will not be able to see the original IP address, and no parties within the TOR network are able to identify the original IP address either. Deep Onion further anonymizes transactions with DeepSend technology.

DeepSend uses a combination of Zero Coin, CoinJoin, and Ring Signature technology borrowed from other anonymity based cryptocurrencies to make transactions untraceable and unidentifiable within the Deep Onion network. Even if the TOR protocol fails to anonymize a user's connection, the DeepSend protocol will make it impossible to identify the exact details of any particular transaction.

Deep Onion has a feature called DeepVault, which utilizes blockchain technology to verify the legitimacy of files uploaded to the network. A feature of the blockchain is that once information is uploaded and propagated across the network, it is immutable - it cannot be changed. This is due to the network constantly verifying the integrity of the information shared. Using this feature, users can upload a hash of a particular file and use that to check whether a particular file has been tampered with. ∎

Currency Code:
ONION

Launch Date:
2014

Market Cap:
$38M

Max. Supply:
25,000,000 ONION

Circulating Supply:
4,732,432 ONION

Consensus Mechanism:
PoS / PoW

Hashing Algorithm:
X13

Block Time:
48 seconds

URL:
deeponion.org

Currency Code:
PINK

Launch Date:
2014

Market Cap:
$35M

Max. Supply:
383,201,150 PINK

Circulating Supply:
377,491,065 PINK

Consensus Mechanism:
PoW / PoS

Hashing Algorithm:
XEVAN

Block Time:
3 minutes

URL:
getstarted.with.pink

PINKCOIN

Pinkcoin is a cryptocurrency-based charity platform "inspired by the pursuit of philanthropy", offering a transparent and secure alternative to traditional closed charity models. The coin advocates community involvement, giving everybody "a part to play" in spreading their "altruistic spirit and gratuitous mentality".

History
Since being launched in May 2014, Pinkcoin has undergone many pivotal changes. Originally abandoned by its creator, Pinkcoin was taken over by enthusiasts, backers, investors and community leaders with the vision of "changing the landscape" of charity donations and campaigns.

In April 2017, shortly after it transitioned to a new blockchain, Pinkcoin activated the first pools of the Donate 4 Life (D4L) campaign. This campaign was created as a platform to facilitate donations to a variety of charitable causes. It also allowed for staked rewards to be directed back to the Pinkcoin platform and community.

Around mid-2017, Pinkcoin founded the Pink Foundation LLC, allowing Pinkcoin to partner with real-world organizations and charities, legitimizing the use of this world first donation-based currency.

Features
Pinkcoin is a triple hybrid PoW/PoS coin which implements a new technology known as 'flash-staking', where the stake rate and reward structures increase at pre-selected peak hours in the day, reducing overall block count over time but retaining confirmation speed. This system allows smaller wallets to participate in staking without being dwarfed by larger staked wallets.

Additionally, Pinkcoin pioneered a system known as 'side-staking', which allows block rewards to be shared automatically, allowing users to choose their preferred method of supporting the currency, community or charities via the Donate4Life campaign.

D4L currently consists of 9 different pools which are split into 2 categories. The regular category contains 6 different funding pools: Humanitarian (funds sent to certified organization's representatives), Charity (funds sent directly to certified charity representatives), Administrative (funds for the marketing and development of Pinkcoin), Environmental Stewardship (dedicated to helping preserve the environment), Education (minted coins are sent to an educational program or school) and Relief (providing funds for those in need).

The 'Rain Forest' category contains 3 different pools: Rain Cloud (sends its stakes to a random staking address on the network every hour), Elder Tree (every stake goes to a random address supporting the network) and Acorn (coins minted here are sent to the smallest wallets on the network). Their purpose is to reward the community for supporting the network, as well as to provide incentives for smaller accounts so that they too can play a supporting role. ∎

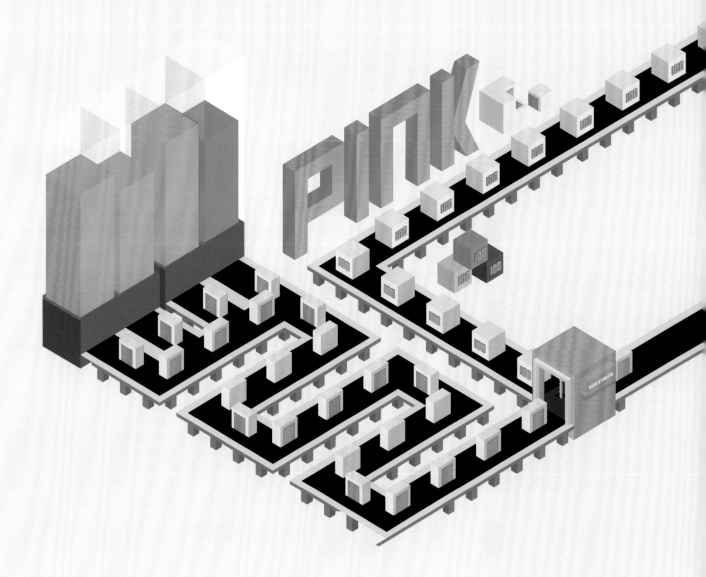

 Micro Tip - Micro Impact.

"The aim for Pinkcoin is: simple, trustless transactions between individuals and public facing businesses with user friendly controls that emulate what one might expect from a private credit card or checking account. Making the process of donating fun, easy, and effortless, Pinkcoin's exhilarating new blockchain is crafted to encourage altruism!" – Pinkcoin blog.

getstarted.with.pink

Currency Code:
IOP

Launch Date:
2014

Market Cap:
$33M

Max Supply:
21,000,000 IOP

Circulating Supply:
3,295,367 IOP

Consensus Mechanism:
PoW / PoS

Hashing Algorithm:
SHA-256

Block Time:
120 seconds

URL:
iop.global

IOP

IOP is the token of the Internet of People (IoP) project, a fully decentralized infrastructure for apps and payments. IoP runs its own blockchain, and in collaboration with the Libertaria decentralization movement has created a node-based communication and transaction network, which can run on almost any device. IoP's decentralized and private person-to-person technology allows users to communicate, do business and use familiar apps, cutting out all middlemen and anyone who might try to control, censor, or steal users' data.

History

IoP was founded by Luis Molina in 2014 as Fermat — an open-source project aiming to provide a free, secure, decentralized communications and payment network to protect users' data and eliminate middlemen. IoP began as a covert project, but by its second year, it had over 100 collaborators from around the world, with many members forming local chapters. The mining software and IoP blockchain were released publicly in November 2016 and have been running stably since then.

In June 2017, chapter members voted to split from Molina's leadership and the project rebranded, changing its name and structure. The Fermat local chapters became the IoP Community, while the company, IoP Ventures, was established to guide IoP's development into a decentralized autonomous organization (DAO). IoP now works in close collaboration with the Libertaria project, using Libertaria technologies as the foundation to build a new internet.

Features

IoP's decentralized peer-to-peer server network is made up of hardware nodes running on a wide range of devices, including PCs and Raspberry Pis. Nodes can message each other and create peer-to-peer connections and are incentivized via IOP tokens to provide decentralized services such as storage, location services, and maintaining IoP's blockchain.

This network is the foundation for fully decentralized apps, powered by IOP tokens. Users will retain full control of their personal data via a social graph and profile system, with no data stored on centralized servers. Users can revoke data permissions at any time. As of late 2017, the network has been launched and is running smoothly.

IoP has a unique regional membership structure, with contributors receiving IOP tokens for their work. Anyone can buy and trade IOP tokens and use IoP apps, but only members can acquire a license to mine IOP tokens, with mining capped to ensure poorer regions can participate. In addition, IoP's blockchain-based governance system allows members to vote on project issues using IOP tokens.

With first-stage development complete, plans for 2018 include a decentralized app store, support for micro- and nano-payments, a peer-to-peer multi-wallet chat app, the release of the governance and smart contract system, and the establishment of offices in Germany and Hungary. ∎

The IOP Token

The Internet of People's IOP token is a multi-purpose crypto-token intended to support a fully decentralized Internet without middlemen. It's used as a currency, an incentive for node operators, payment for project contributors and will power IoP's dApps. IOP is traded on exchanges and is compatible with Komodo (KMD) atomic swaps.

The IoP blockchain is built on a version of the bitcoin core code, with modifications to enact a licensed mining system for a fairer and more resource-efficient distribution of tokens.

Several modifications and improvements to the IOP token will be implemented in 2018, including a voting system, micro- and nano-payment support (coffee on chain), faster block times and windows and a transition to a hybrid PoW and PoS system.

IOP: Building a new Internet without middlemen

Decentralizing Everything

dApps & Services

Social Graph

Servers

Community

Research

Libertaria

IoP works closely with the Libertaria movement, creatin technologies to enable fully decentralized societies. Io technology is built on several of these, including:

Mercury: A true P2P communications protocol with profile system which allows full social med functionality with complete data privacy.

Hydra: A next-generation ledger protocol providin multichain support and atomic swaps betwee currencies.

Themis: A decentralized smart contract protocol t support higher economic functions.

Titania: A decentralized OS powering an uncensorabl and undisruptible node network.

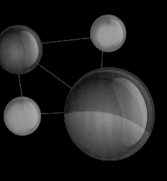

Currency Code:
CURE

Launch Date:
2014

Market Cap:
$29M

Max. Supply:
23,000,000 CURE

Circulating Supply:
23,830,695 CURE

Consensus Mechanism:
PoW / PoS

Hashing Algorithm:
SHA-256

Block Time:
10 minutes

URL:
curecoin.net

CURECOIN

An open source, decentralized cryptocurrency, Curecoin combines computational biology research and blockchain technology. By mining Curecoins, participants are contributing to funding efforts in researching cures for diseases such as cancer, Alzheimer's disease, influenza, diabetes, and Parkinson's disease. The overarching objective of the project is to contribute to society by rewarding participants who advance medical research.

History
Curecoin was founded in May 2014 by John Smith. The initiative was a partnership between Stanford University's Folding@Home program and the Curecoin Forum. The Folding@Home program is the brainchild of Stanford University professor, Vijay Pande, who conceived a program that would simulate protein behavior on users' computing devices and forward the resulting data to Stanford University to aid in scientific research.

The program also allows participants to earn an income for their efforts. A few months after the launch, Curecoin was recognized for its computational research speed, and today it is one of the largest contributors to the Folding@Home disease research program.

Features
Unlike other cryptocurrencies, Curecoin is a hybrid of proof-of-work (PoW) and proof-of-stake (PoS). Established as a non-profit initiative, the coin is both a cryptocurrency and a tradable embodiment of scientific research. The initiative deals specifically with research into protein folding, a process through which medical scientists find cures for diseases.

CureCoin can be mined using CPU/GPU or SHA-256 ASIC hardware, making it possible for virtually anyone to mine Curecoins. By folding proteins, folders earn a proportional amount of coins. The currency works the same way carbon offsets work - the amount of Curecoins purchased represents a proportional amount of medical research. Individuals with technical expertise contribute to protein folding by performing the technical work, consequently earning some income. As the amount of protein folding increases with time, the network and the amount of medical research represented by each coin grow as well.

Curecoins are distributed to three groups of participants: folders, miners, and developers. Folders get 76% of all the coins mined, while miners and developers get 19% and 3%, respectively. The remaining 2% goes to people who donated funds for project development.

Curecoin is not necessarily restricted to protein folding; the project is open to other types of medical research and crowd-aided simulation as well, and as the network grows, more scientific computing projects can be readily incorporated.

Curecoin has received acclaim for its efforts and status as a cryptocurrency that allows investors to profit while aiding life-saving medical research - something that casts a good light on the cryptocurrency community overall. The practical and beneficial utility of the currency arguably gives it a more intrinsic value compared to other altcoins. As the driving force of what is widely viewed as a good cause successfully executed, the coin has the potential to bring awareness to the world of cryptocurrency and inspire similar projects to follow in its footsteps. ∎

BITSEND

Bitsend, formerly known as LimecoinX, is a cryptocurrency built on the Xevan algorithm whose main function is to handle online payments. It is a unique fully-incentivized peer-to-peer network that is based on Bitcoin Core 0.14.

History

Bitsend was launched in 2014 as LimecoinX but was later abandoned before it was taken over by the current team. Since it was renamed and transformed, its value has continued to rise exponentially, gaining various partner projects like ERC Europecoin, IOC coinstorm, Machinecoin, and DMD Diamond.

The PoW period of the coin is expected to last for 33 years during which 210 million coins are to be supplied, with 4.3 million of them mined per year, in addition to the current 14.6 million. The main factors responsible for its rapid growth are – its low fee, its masternode network, and its fast transaction speed.

Features

A number of features set Bitsend apart from other cryptocurrencies. Apart from the fact that it runs on blockchain technology, which ensures its privacy, security, and decentralization, the coin comes with a fast confirmation time of just 3 minutes.

In addition, Bitsend has a medium block size of 10 MB, giving it a high potential transaction capacity. This translates to consumers being able to carry out transactions for a minimal fee compared to Bitcoin and many other altcoins.

Its simplicity of use has also contributed immensely to its growth. Using Bitsend does not require passing through security checks or background checks and creating an account is quick and easy to do.

One other advantage that Bitsend has is that it runs on specialized cloud computers that ensure the privacy and safety of all transactions as well as reducing the vulnerability of hacking since it is difficult for hackers to have access to the cloud to wreak havoc on the system. This has been largely responsible for the confidence users have in the cryptocurrency.

Moreover, the masternode network allows participants to provide a level of service to the network and ensures that collateral is provided before one can take part. Since collateral is safe and never forfeited, investors are given the confidence to offer their service to the network and earn interest, thereby minimizing the digital currency's volatility. This sense of belonging and the assurance of not losing one's collateral helps to boost investors' confidence in the coin, thereby ensuring that participants invest with peace of mind.

The Bitsend team are currently directing their efforts towards three main tasks: the development of the Bitsend Core 0.14 wallet (that implements SegWit technology), the SPV Wallet (Simplified Payment Verification) as well as other gaming related technologies. ■

Currency Code:
BTX

Launch Date:
2014

Market Cap:
$28M

Max. Supply:
21,000,000 BTX

Circulating Supply:
17,761,682 BSD

Consensus Mechanism:
PoW / PoS

Hashing Algorithm:
XEVAN

Block Time:
3 minutes

URL:
bitsend.info

Currency Code:
ATB

Launch Date:
2017

Market Cap:
$27M

Max. Supply:
52,386,429 ATB

Circulating Supply:
40,139,917 ATB

Consensus Mechanism:
PoS

Hashing Algorithm:
ECDSA / SHA-256

Block Time:
45 seconds

URL:
atbcoin.com

ATBCOIN

ATB Coin (Alternate Technology Base) is a project whose aim is to create a blockchain-based currency that is fast, secure, cost-effective, and anonymous. It implements best practice methods used in other cryptocurrencies such as SegWit and op. ATB Coin uses a proof-of-stake algorithm and cryptography to secure its network.

History
ATB Coin was announced in June 2017 and the Initial Coin Offering ran from June to September of that year. The ATB wallet began testing in July 2017 and in early 2018, ATB Coin recruited more team members to continue developing the project.

Features
Like with most other blockchain-based cryptocurrencies, no single entity has ownership or control over ATB Coin. The developers can only improve upon the code, however, the network still needs to reach consensus in order for changes to take effect. Coins are created when users hold ATB Coin with their wallets online and uses a proof-of-stake algorithm. Cloud mining allows users to generate ATB Coin without running the wallet on their system by allowing them to deposit their holdings into a joint cloud account, which then mines the currency on their behalf. In this way, users can invest in the network through providing funds, without having to use their own resources.

Segregated Witness, or SegWit, is a method of optimizing block sizes within the blockchain to increase network scalability. It decreases transaction fees, commission fees, transaction times, and network efficiency. ATB Coin implemented SegWit early in development in preparation for widespread adoption and use of the currency.

ATB Coin is part of the Lightning Network, a protocol which reduces transaction fees and transaction times, while increasing the security of the network. The Lightning Network also allows multi-signature addresses, which permits users to make transactions that will only be approved when two or more predetermined private keys sign to confirm it. This means that users can perform peer-to-peer transactions with the comfort of knowing that their funds are secure until they are satisfied with the conditions of the transaction. Another feature of the Lightning Network is the ability to exchange currencies directly through the blockchain. This means that users are able to easily swap between currencies which creates flexibility to choose which payment methods they want to use or receive.

ATB Coin aims to be used as an effective means for micropayments due to the low transaction fees and fast transaction times it provides. Smart contracts are also being developed to enable users to detail conditions in which payments are transferred. For example, a user can make a payment with the condition that it is sent after a certain period of time, or when they receive another payment. This allows users to securely transact with others and maintain trust, without having to rely on any third-party brokers or escrow services. These features allow ATB Coin to be used effectively as a transfer of value with built-in trust-less security measures. ■

CREATIVECOIN

A decentralized platform for digital content distribution and registration, the Creativechain platform acts as a public record which keeps the information transacted by digital content creators and consumers. This public record of information can be consulted and verified at any point in time. Creativechain makes the certification of licensing and authorship permanent, secure, and tamper-proof. The team at Creativechain aim to empower artists and creatives by giving them a tool for presenting their work, with the use of blockchain technology.

History

The idea of Creativechain was conceived on May 7, 2015, and in the third quarter of 2016, the existing team began developing the concept. Later that year, the official landing page was launched. In 2017 they released an initial coin offering for Creativecoin along with a white-paper describing the end goal and details of the platform being developed.

Features

Creativechain makes use of the technology of the blockchain and its power of attorney to create an incorruptible timestamp which cannot be modified by anyone. This allows for the certification of authorship and the licensing of use and distribution of all forms of digital work or content. The platform issues authors with a digital certificate of authenticity which can be used as a means for defending their rights.

Creativechain also offers an openly accessible database of direct legal advice, as well as access to specialized copyright lawyers who will be able to aid users when necessary. The Creativechain platform is also capable of releasing smart contracts which can be used for the creation of work assignment protocols. These contracts can be either public or encrypted and can guarantee users a secure and reliable agreement. Creativechain also allows for the creation of decentralized applications which store and index content using the Creativechain blockchain.

Other platform features include - the ability to send and receive donations of either Bitcoin or Creativecoin to the digital content producers, the ability to create limited edition content where creators can limit their works' broadcasting or sell only a certain number of reproductions, thus limiting the supply and increasing the overall value of the content, and the ability for equity crowdfunding where the author offers investors a percentage of participation. Creativechain believes that digital content producers deserve more freedom and control over their work and that they are not provided this through most third-party corporations.

For this reason, Creativechain has set out to dedicate their efforts to providing digital creatives and authors with a platform where they can truly express themselves, without any borders or repercussions, and at the same time, maintain complete control over their creations. It also provides its users with a strong sense of security, knowing full well that their content will be in the safe hands of trustworthy blockchain protocols. ■

Currency Code:
CREA

Launch Date:
2017

Market Cap:
$10M

Max. Supply:
115,000,000 CREA

Circulating Supply:
13,093,295 CREA

Consensus Mechanism:
PoW

Hashing Algorithm:
Scrypt

Block Time:
120 seconds

URL:
creativechain.org

Currency Code:
EO

Launch Date:
2014

Market Cap:
$22M

Max. Supply:
1,000,000,000 LEO

Circulating Supply:
96,955,338 LEO

Consensus Mechanism:
PoS

Hashing Algorithm:
Scrypt Jane

Block Time:
60 seconds

URL:
leocoin.org

LEOCOIN

LEOcoin is a decentralized, peer-to-peer network, designed for faster and more secure transactions. It comes with the ability to carry out private wallet-to-wallet chat, as well as anonymous transactions. It is maintained by the LEOcoin Foundation but largely supported by the LEOcoin community.

History
LEOcoin was developed by Learning Enterprises Organisation Limited (LEO) and launched in June 2014. LEOcoin received acceptability almost immediately after being introduced to the crypto market, mainly due to its decentralization, security, and user-friendliness. It has also carried out a major upgrade to ensure that users' rights to privacy are fully respected.

The initial plan of the developer was to help in minimizing business costs for its members, however, it soon evolved into a community of over 300,000 people across 190 countries, making it a positive force to reckon with in the world of cryptocurrency and finance.

LEOcoin also launched proof-of-stake in 2016, promising to reward users based on their holdings. This may have contributed to increasing the number of users interested in growing their coins in the long term.

Features
LEOcoin has a chat function which makes it easy for users to communicate in a private manner without being traced. The chat interface enables users to interact with community members in order to get regular updates about trading strategies, price behaviors as well as LEOcoin development news.

In 2016, LEOcoin moved to a proof-of-stake mining method. By reducing entry obstacles, members were now able to mine coins in a democratized manner.

In addition, LEOcoin offers a number of other related services to users. Some of these services include a trading platform (LEOxChange), and a crowdfunding site (LEOcrowd), which assist potential entrepreneurs in realizing the fundraising goals for their project, as well as allowing them to accept payments with digital currency.

LEOcoin uses advanced cryptography and encryption methods in carrying out transactions, making it a truly anonymous digital currency, able to shield the identity of users and safeguard them against fraudsters and identity theft.

In a world where the right to privacy is regularly violated, even though highly cherished, LEOcoin helps to bring back hope to major stakeholders in online transactions, by providing a system with enhanced security to make sure people can transact business with the level of privacy they seek.

The final feature worthy of note is that LEOcoin does not charge a commission for intermediaries. This has helped in getting rid of the middlemen and reducing the cost of doing business with the cryptocurrency. In order to increase its flexibility, the coin has launched wallets for various operating systems such as Linux, Windows, MacOSX, and mobiles. ∎

The LEO Philosophy

"...wake up every single day determined to change the ... by delivering an unbeatable service. LEOcoin is ... than just a new way to make purchases. It's even ... than a protocol for exchanging value over the inter- ...ithout an intermediary. We put our Members' best ...sts first and foremost. They drive everything we do. ...e in constant pursuit of innovation and strive con-...tly to exceed expectations. We believe in complete ...parency, deep collaboration and we never forget ...eople come first. Having this mindset allows us to ...and advance at a rate which others cannot."

...nderson
...of LEOxChange and Founder of LEOcoin.

LEOXCHANGE

LEOxChange is designed for holders of cryptocurrency including, but not limited to, LEOcoin, to allow them to trade their cryptocurrencies in the open market.

LEOxChange is the official exchange for trading LEOcoin It offers advanced trading tools, a sophisticated user interface, robust technical security and is fully compliant with the relevant regulations.

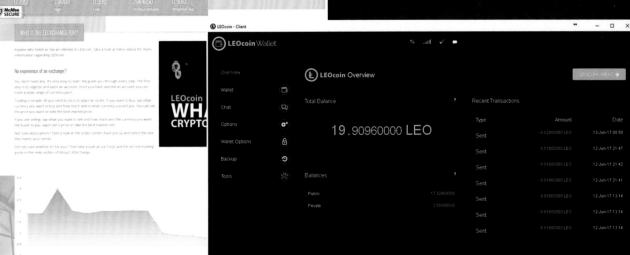

THE EASIEST WAY TO BUY CRYPTOCURRENCIES WITH FIAT.

OXYCOIN

Oxycoin is a cryptocurrency, mobile exchange, and decentralized application software platform created through the collaborative effort of blockchain professionals. Their mission is to build a "platform that has everything cryptocurrency investors need, right at their fingertips" as well as to "enable 'non-blockchain developers' to build decentralized applications using JavaScript" so as to integrate dApps into the mobile and web world.

History

Oxycoin is based out of the Hague in the Netherlands and has an experienced core and support team, many of whom run delegates for other DPoS systems.

Oxycoin ran its Early Supporter Program (ESP) from August 21 to August 31, 2017, which offered investors the chance to receive 25% to 50% bonuses depending on the size of their investment, before launching its ICO on September 1, 2017. The ICO campaign was funded by a pre-mine of 100 million Oxycoins and had a target figure of 700 BTC with BTC, BCC, ETH, SHIFT, LISK, RISE, and ARK all accepted as payment.

Features

Oxycoin is primarily focused on providing solutions in two major areas in order to accomplish its goal of bringing cryptocurrency to the masses. The first of these is the Oxycoin mobile application which is intended to provide everything an investor in cryptocurrency needs - enabling its users to exchange cryptocoins and FIAT directly, manage all their wallets and passwords, as well as give them access to a user-friendly Global Address Book; an information hub where they can access all the information they need to make intelligent, informed investments.

The Global Address Book also aims to tackle the problem of multiple addresses for different cryptocurrencies by allowing users to create a searchable username that links to all of their various wallets. Using the Global Address Book, users will be able to type in a username and send funds to them via the various cryptocoin wallets they use, doing away with the need for managing long strings of alphanumeric codes in the process. There are also plans to integrate the use of QR Codes as another means of transferring funds.

The second solution that the team are currently working on comes in the form of the Enhanced Decentralized Application Software Development Kit (dApp SDK), which is designed to *"remove the limitations which have kept non-blockchain developers from using blockchain technology"* and will, according to its white-paper, *"allow Mobile and Web applications to make use of decentralized applications for the first time in the history of blockchain."*

An interesting recent development is a partnership that has been forged between Oxycoin and the ING Bank. In order to do this, five of the founding members have been required to fully identify themselves and provide their financial backgrounds - something very rare in the world of cryptocurrencies, due to the general emphasis on privacy and anonymity. Through this partnership, Oxycoin aims to directly link the cryptocurrency markets with the financial markets without the interference of third-parties. ∎

Currency Code:
OXY

Launch Date:
2017

Market Cap:
$22M

Max. Supply:
105,638,930 OXY

Circulating Supply:
85,511,932 OXY

Consensus Mechanism:
dPoS

Hashing Algorithm:
N/A

Block Time:
15 seconds

URL:
oxycoin.io

KORE

Kore is an experimental, decentralized, peer-to-peer digital currency whose primary focus is on providing privacy and anonymity. Utilizing a proof-of-stake (PoS) wallet incorporated into the TOR browser, its features include anonymous phone calls and a secret, decentralized marketplace with the option of no transaction history.

Currency Code:
KORE

Launch Date:
2017

Market Cap:
$14M

Max. Supply:
12,000,000 KORE

Circulating Supply:
2,022,465 KORE

Consensus Mechanism:
PoSv3

Hashing Algorithm:
Momentum

Block Time:
60 seconds

URL:
kore.life

History
Kore was officially launched on October 14, 2017, as a blockchain transfer from an older project initially begun in June 2014 called KoreCoin. The original project was taken over by a new team put together and headed by MikeMike. At the time of the change-over, the roughly 2 million coins already in circulation were moved to the new chain and made accessible to their owners. The team seems to be highly motivated and passionate about the project – with the mission *"to provide an entire ecosystem that facilitates privacy and security."*

Kore has recently become involved with the 'Silvana Lima-Surf & Stand Up' school foundation helping impoverished children, created and run by the world-renowned pro-surfer Silvana Lima.

Features
Kore is a coin that aims to revolutionize the way people communicate, use the internet and spend their money; providing users with software that allows for online privacy, a marketplace that protects its users as well as encrypting communication, and transactions that are almost instantaneous with virtually negligible fees. Transactions are in the process of providing full anonymity through the future implementation of processes such as the POBA, 'anonymous proof-of-burn' (PoB) protocol. PoB simply means that after tokens are sent to a specific address, the coins are destroyed by a technique called 'Anonymous Burn Destroy'. Another of its unique features allows users to hide the source of their coins by sending them to a special address while still targeting the receiving address. The receiver accepts newly burned or mined coins which originate from a newly generated, never used address. The original, sent coins are locked in the KORE special address and cannot be spent. Instead, they will be subtracted from the total coins in existence.

After 100,000 coins were mined, Kore moved away from proof-of-work towards a proof-of-stake (PoS) protocol. Now coins are minted instead of mined – allowing for a lower expenditure of energy and reduced costs to keep the network secure and active. Kore is in the process of developing their own ecological consensus algorithm that best suits security and fairness. Kore will reintroduce KoreVoIP, an anonymous calling platform built into the wallet. The calls are 100% anonymous and are also untraceable.

The Kore wallet has a built-in anonymous browser that works directly through the TOR network. Simple in its functioning and user-friendly – a single click on the browser link within the wallet allows users to securely browse the internet anonymously. In development is KOREbay, a secure shopping platform allowing users to buy goods, services, and barter through a decentralized and anonymous marketplace. KOREbay utilizes all aspects of the Kore security suite.

The long-term goals for Kore are to further enhance the user's experience by allowing for higher levels of privacy in people's personal lives as they work on their own Aether OS, KorePhone, and corresponding Mesh Network. Beyond this, the team is working on providing ATM machines for the public, making it even easier to buy and sell Kore as well as Bitcoin. ∎

Privacy Is Freedom

KORE believes that every human on this planet is born with the inalienable right to transact and communicate in complete privacy if so desired. More and more these rights are being eroded by bloated corporate entities and corrupt governments.

The KORE platform provides all people in the world the ability to securely and privately communicate with one another, acquire information on the web, engage in commerce and run their business on the blockchain without the interference of intrusive third party agents.

The KORE platform and projects are centrally focused for the greater good of humanity.

The KORE Platform

KOREsurf

TOR browser built into the KORE wallet. Surf the web in complete privacy with a click of your mouse.

VoIPA

Secure, private digital voice and video DApp built directly into the KORE wallet.

KOREphone

The only way to be truly private on mobile is to make sure your smart phone is secure. KORE is doing that.

KOREbay

Shop with complete privacy in the KORE P2P marketplace. Runs directly on KOREsurf.

Æther OS

Revolutionary privacy-focused operating system built from the ground up to resist malware and support future KORE DApps.

KORE ATMs

Physical ATMs provide real-world access to KORE without the need for centralized exchanges.

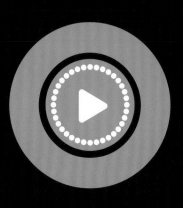

Currency Code:
ADC

Launch Date:
2013

Market Cap:
$9M

Max. Supply:
N/A

Circulating Supply:
838,864,017 ADC

Consensus Mechanism:
PoS

Hashing Algorithm:
Scrypt

Block Time:
60 seconds

URL:
audiocoin.eu

AUDIOCOIN

Audiocoin is a cryptocurrency focused on changing the music industry's pay model. The coin works on a proof-of-work and proof-of-stake algorithm, meaning that people who hold the coin are rewarded interest. It is a derivative of Peercoin but with a much higher proof-of-stake interest rate of 18% per year.

History
Audiocoin was created in 2013, based upon Peercoin protocols. Originally it required the use of a proof-of-work algorithm, but since around block 525000, it has been using a proof-of-stake algorithm. In 2015, the Aurovine music distribution platform adopted the use of Audiocoin. Since then, its popularity has grown with even the artist, Bjork, becoming involved, offering a bonus of 100 Audiocoins for each purchase of her album 'Utopia'. In November 2017, the third version of the Audiocoin wallet was released for all platforms.

Features
Audiocoin aims to change the music industry through empowering music-lovers through breaking down barriers (such as region locking) and rewarding both music producers and fans for contributing to their ecology.

Music producers are able to receive funding directly to their own wallets, without going through a third party distributor. This means that artists are able to gain more rewards by directly marketing to their listeners. Listeners can also pay for music without using credit cards or giving away private information, and also benefit from the cost savings by producers who no longer have to pay distributors for content.

The higher proof-of-stake interest in this coin was designed around the sharing culture of the music industry — this allows producers (who hold more Audiocoin) the ability to generate Audiocoins to give to fans as incentives thereby stimulating the Audiocoin economy.

An example of how Audiocoin can be used effectively is through the 'direct to fan' music delivery platform called 'Audiovine'. Audiovine allows users to upload and listen to music, and for listeners to pay the producers directly for their content. An added bonus is the fact that both artists and fans are given coins upon signing up (250 and 50 Audiocoins, respectively). Also, artists and users are both rewarded when streaming music (when over half of the song is streamed and then shared), with both parties gaining an equal amount of coins (0.5 each).

Users can also alternatively opt to pay for music (which doesn't require music to be shared), and both artist and listener are also rewarded for this transaction at 2.5 coins each. For complete albums, this reward is increased to 10 coins each. Alternatively, artists can opt for songs to be free downloads, which results in the same rewards as streaming. When streaming or downloading, a small amount is transferred to a bonus wallet, which is divided between the top 50 artists on the platform depending on their ranking in the system.

The Audiovine platform incentivizes users to interact with the system and share music, and the high proof-of-stake rewards enable the platform to generate bonuses for their users without having to use their existing holdings. The platform also allows Audiocoin to be used as a currency, increasing the usability of the coin. ∎

APPENDIX

Glossary

Address - a code used to send, receive or store cryptocurrency. These addresses consist of a combination of letters and numbers with 26-35 characters. The address can also refer to the public key, a pair of keys needed to sign their digital transactions.

Airdrop - the process of freely distributing a new cryptocurrency, usually when a new crypto is being launched or as a means of ongoing promotion.

Algorithm - a series of mathematical steps that will solve a problem. In cryptocurrencies, algorithms are generally used to hide and reveal information.

Alphanumeric - something made up of both letters and numbers.

Altcoin - short for 'alternative coin' - this is any cryptocurrency other than Bitcoin.

Anti-Money Laundering (AML) - a set of laws designed to prevent the conversion of illegally earned money into what appears to be legally earned money.

API (Application Programming Interface) - a set of subroutine definitions, protocols, and tools for building application software.

ASIC - Application-Specific Integrated Circuit, commonly known as ASIC. 'Application-specific' means 'built for one specific purpose' and an 'Integrated Circuit' is a computer chip. An ASIC is used in cryptocurrencies to help record transactions on the blockchain in a process known as mining.

ATH - short for 'All Time High'.

Atomic Swap - technology that allows the exchange of different cryptocurrencies directly.

Auxiliary Proof-of-Work (AuxPoW) - in merged mining, this is the relationship between two blockchains for one to trust the other's work as their own and accept AuxPOW blocks.

Bitpay.com - an online Bitcoin payment service provider allowing online stores to accept Bitcoin as payment.

Block - a recording of information on the blockchain. The data is typically a collection of transactions that describe changes to the data. It can also contain the record of a transfer of assets from one owner to another or the record of some personal information being updated.

Block Height - the number of blocks in the chain between the one you are looking at and the very first block in the blockchain.

Block Reward - the amount of crypto given to the computer that solved the math problem required to discover a new block.

Blockchain - technology for creating permanent, decentralized, secure digital recordings.

Blockchain Agnostic - this is something that can be applied to public blockchains such as Bitcoin and Dash as well as private blockchains.

Bot - short for 'robot', a bot is a computer program that automatically carries out any task that it has been programmed to.

Botnet - a number of internet-connected devices, each of which is running one or more bots. Botnets are often used to perform distributed denial-of-service attacks (DDoS), steal data, send spam, and allows the attacker to access a device and its connection.

Central Processing Unit (CPU) - the electronic circuitry within a computer that carries out the basic arithmetic, logical, control and input/output (I/O) operations specified by the software.

Centralized - a system or organization that is controlled by one person or group.

Chain Split - a break in the digital recordings of the blockchain. When a network of users managing cryptocurrency technology disagree on how the blocks should be made, they may split off, each forming their own chain of recordings.

Chatbot - a computer program that conducts a conversation via auditory or textual methods.

Circulating Supply - the number of coins currently available and in the people's possession. Coins that are locked, reserved or unable to be sold and traded are not included in the circulating supply.

Coinbase.com - a cryptocurrency exchange that allows people to trade regular money like US dollars for cryptocurrencies.

Confirmation - the successful act of hashing a transaction and adding it to the blockchain.

Consensus - an agreement from the majority of people about something. Consensus requires at least 51% of the people agree on something and is a very important part of cryptocurrency technology. It can also be used to refer to a strategy method used by nodes in a distributed ledger and defined by the blockchain to determine the correctness of the chain. The most common consensus strategies are proof-of-work, proof-of-stake, and delegated proof-of-stake.

Contract - a spoken or written promise between two or more people for some mutual benefit.

Core - the group of individuals that are most active in developing a cryptocurrency.

Core Wallet - a wallet that contains the entire blockchain as opposed to a piece of it and allows users to not only receive, store and send digital money but also to program with it.

Crowdfunding - a way of raising money by getting small amounts of money from many people.

Crowdsale - the issuing of coins or tokens that represent shares or equity in a company or cryptocurrency.

Crypto - short for cryptography or cryptocurrency. 'Crypto' comes from the Greek word meaning 'hidden'.

Cryptocurrency - electronic money created with technology controlling its creation and protecting transactions, while hiding the identities of its users.

Cryptography - the study of making information unreadable so it can be kept secret.

Currency - a system and its units for exchanging value.

DAG (Directed Acyclic Graph) - a structure that is built out in one single direction and in such a way that it never repeats.

DAO (Decentralized Autonomous Organizations) - these are leaderless organizations supported by a network of computers. They are decentralized as they have no central location and they are autonomous, or self-governing, as they have no single leader or controller.

dApp (Decentralized Application) - a software application that has its technology running publicly on a network of computers.

Dark Gravity Wave (DGW) - an open source difficulty-adjusting algorithm for Bitcoin-based cryptocurrencies that was first used in Darkcoin/Dash and has since been adopted by other digital currencies.

DDoS (Distributed Denial-of-Service) - a computerized attack on a website or other online service that causes the service to slow or shut down.

Decentralized - a system or organization that has no single person or executive group controlling it.

Delegated Proof-of-Stake (DPoS) – a variation of proof-of-stake in which the responsibility of the creating blocks is delegated to third-party nodes, known as 'witnesses'.

Digital Signature - permission and proof done through a computer that an authorized person has agreed to something.

Distributed Ledger - a digital record of money being received and spent, maintained simultaneously by a network of computers.

Distributed Network - a type of network where processing power and data are spread over the nodes rather than having a centralized data center.

Double Spending - the action of spending digital money twice usually meant to cheat the first person out of their money before they have received it.

Ecosystem - any system or network of interconnecting and interacting parts.

Encryption - the process of locking information in an unreadable form so it can be kept secret.

Enterprise-Grade - an application that has the features necessary to support enterprise customers who have unique requirements because of their scale and risk profiles.

Escrow - a part of the transaction process where the buyer and seller store money or other valuables with a third-party to minimize risk. The escrow service holds onto the valuables and will not release them until the agreement has been fulfilled by both parties.

Exchange - a place where something of value can be traded.

Faucet - a website or application that provides small, free amounts of new cryptocurrencies to help increase awareness of a particular coin.

Fiat Currency - money that has been declared to be valuable by a government.

Forging - the name giving to the process in proof-of-stake blockchains where there is no block reward. Forgers keep transaction fees instead.

Fork - a split in the digital recordings, leaving two blockchains to run simultaneously on different parts of the network.

Fungible - a positive quality where two or more of the same thing have identical value. That is to say, one of a group of things can be a substitute for another without changing the value. For example, a $20 bill is worth the same as any other $20 bill, however, a car doesn't have the same value as another car and so is not easy to substitute and is therefore non-fungible. Some cryptocurrencies like Bitcoin are not fungible coins. This can be a problem when the coins are used for illegal transactions because with enough research, some of the coins can be linked to the illegal activity.

Gdax - short for General Digital Asset Exchange, it is a cryptocurrency exchange company owned by Coinbase.

Genesis Block - the first block in the chain. It is created when a blockchain is first deployed, serving as the anchor to which all other blocks link.

GitHub - having started as a developer's collaborative platform, GitHub is now the largest online storage space of collaborative works in the world.

GPU (Graphical Processing Unit) - a computer chip that creates 3D images on computers but is often used as processing power by miners.

Hacking - the process of using a computer to manipulate another computer or computer system in an unauthorized and unapproved way.

Halving - the reduction of a cryptocurrency's mining reward by half.

Hard Cap - the maximum amount of money a cryptocurrency can receive from investors in its Initial Coin Offering (ICO).

Hard Fork - a radical change to the protocol that makes previously invalid blocks/transactions valid (or vice-versa), and as such requires all nodes or users to upgrade to the latest version of the protocol software.

Hardware Wallet - a specially designed device to lock away access to your cryptocurrency. The device is extra secure because it is disconnected from the internet and other computers and is virtually virus-proof.

Hash - a value that is computed by an algorithm, which uniquely identifies the input data without revealing the contents of that data. Hash values are used to ensure the veracity of data on the blockchain. The block headers contain the previous block's hash, which enables the integrity of the entire chain to be quickly verified.

Hash Function - a computer program that takes information and turns it into letters and numbers of a certain length, used to make storing and finding information quicker. Hashes also make information unreadable and so they become a secret.

Hashrate - the speed that a computer can complete a mathematical program that takes any set of information and turns it into letters and numbers of a certain length.

Hidden Cap - an unknown limit to the amount of money a cryptocurrency can receive from investors in its Initial Coin Offering (ICO).

HODL - a misspelling of 'hold' that evolved into a shortened form of 'Hold On for Dear Life'. It is used in the crypto community when referring to keeping, i.e. holding onto a particular cryptocurrency rather than selling it.

IBO (Initial Bounty Offering) - the limited-time process by which a new cryptocurrency is made public and distributed to people who invest their skills and time to earn rewards in the new cryptocurrency. Unlike an Initial Coin Offering where the coins are sold, an IBO requires more mental commitment.

Initial Coin Offering (ICO) - a method of raising funds for the development of a new cryptocurrency project. Investors are offered units of the new cryptocurrency in exchange other cryptocurrencies. It is also known as a token sale or crowdsale.

JOMO - short for Joy of Missing Out. This is the pleasure of doing what you are doing and not worrying about anything worthwhile you might be missing out on.

Key - a secret string of letters and numbers that must be used to make hidden, unreadable information readable.

Kimoto's Gravity Well (KGW) - a modification to Bitcoin's difficulty adjustment algorithm that was first developed for the altcoin Megacoin and has since been implemented in many other altcoins, both in its initial incarnation as well as in modified fashions.

KYC (Know Your Customer) - a set of laws where financial organizations must request government-issued identification from their customers before allowing them to use their services.

Ledger - the principal book or computer file for recording and totaling economic transactions.

Leverage - the use of borrowed capital for an investment, expecting the profits made to be greater than the interest payable.

Lightning Network - a 'second layer' payment protocol that operates on top of a blockchain and enables trustless, potentially free, and instant transactions between participating nodes.

Market Capitalization - a way to rank and judge the size of a cryptocurrency or stock in a company and calculated by taking the total supply and multiplying it by the price of the coin.

Masternode - first used to describe Dash masternodes, these are nodes in the currency's network that fulfill a specific function beyond simply relaying transactions.

Max Supply - the maximum number of coins that will ever exist for a cryptocurrency.

Merkle Tree - a way to organize data so it is more efficient and secure, named after Ralph Merkle, a computer scientist, who created a patent for Merkle trees in 1979. A Merkle tree uses computer technology known as 'hashing' to convert large amounts of written information into smaller and smaller chunks of information.

Merklized Abstract Syntax Trees (MAST) - a proposed addition to Bitcoin that allows for smaller transaction sizes, more privacy, and larger smart contracts.

Microtransaction - an online purchase or exchange worth very little money.

Mining - the computer process of recording and verifying information on the digital record known as the blockchain.

Mining Difficulty - a measure of how hard it is to record information onto the digital record, known as the blockchain.

Mining Pool - the pooling of resources by miners, who share their processing power over a network and split the reward equally, according to the amount of work they contributed to the probability of finding a block.

Mining Rig - computer technology used to record information on the digital record known as the blockchain.

Mixing Service - also known as a 'tumbler', it allows a user to send cryptocurrency and get the same amount back, minus fees, from other people. The purpose of this is to improve the privacy and anonymity of digital money by making it harder to track what the cryptocurrency was used for and who it belongs to.

Mtgox.com - one of the first websites where Bitcoin could be exchanged for regular fiat money. In 2014, Mt. Gox closed after roughly 850,000 Bitcoin were declared lost or stolen.

Multisignature - this is when more than one signature or approval is required before a transaction can take place. This increases the security for cryptocurrencies so that one person cannot take all of the money for themselves without approval from the others.

Node - a host in a network that is capable of adding blocks to the chain. The way nodes are able to do this varies based on the needs of the chain.

Open Source - any type of technology that is made public and can be seen, shared and changed. The term is usually used for computer technology that has been made available to anyone and is not protected by a standard copyright.

Orphan - a block that has been abandoned and will not be built upon.

P2P - see 'peer-to-peer'

Platform-as-a-Service (PaaS) - a category of cloud computing services that provides a platform allowing customers to develop, run, and manage applications without the complexity of building and maintaining the infrastructure typically associated with developing and launching an app.

Paper Wallet - a piece of paper containing the information needed to access and spend your cryptocurrency.

Peer-to-Peer (P2P) - a connection between two or more computers that allows them to share information.

Permissionless - a positive quality where anyone is permitted to join and participate in an activity.

Poloniex.com - a digital cryptocurrency exchange company that allows people to trade their various coins with each other.

Premine - a condition of some new cryptocurrencies, where the maximum supply has already been created before being made publicly available, meaning that no new coins will be created during the mining process.

Private Key - a string of letters and numbers known only by the user that allows them to spend cryptocurrency.

Proof-of-Burn (PoB) - a method of investing in brand new cryptocurrencies where, in order to get 1 coin of the new currency, you must burn/destroy another currency.

Proof-of-Developer (PoD) - any verification that provides evidence of a real, living software developer who created a cryptocurrency. PoD is used when launching a new cryptocurrency to prevent an anonymous developer from collecting and stealing money without actually providing a workable cryptocurrency.

Proof-of-Capacity (PoC) - see 'Proof-of-Space'.

Proof-of-Importance - a consensus strategy introduced by NEM that functions similarly to proof-of-stake. Nodes need to 'vest' an amount of currency to be eligible for creating blocks and are selected for creating a block roughly in proportion to some score.

Proof-of-Space (PoSpace) - also called proof-of-capacity (PoC), this is a means of showing that one has a legitimate interest in a service (such as sending an email) by allocating a non-trivial amount of memory or disk space to solve a challenge presented by the service provider.

Proof-of-Stake (PoS) - a consensus strategy that relies on nodes which hold collateral to participate in contributing blocks to the chain. With proof-of-stake, blocks may be added to the chain more quickly.

Proof-of-Work (PoW) - a consensus strategy that relies on a computationally difficult challenge to solve in order to find the hash of a new block. Although the original block hashing algorithm is difficult to solve, the discovered solution is easy for others to verify, allowing the other participating nodes to quickly agree that the new block is correct.

Public Key - a string of letters and numbers that allows cryptocurrency to be received. Although it is called a 'public key', it is not publicly visible until a user has shared it or sent money out.

Pump and Dump - an illegal manipulation tactic where people increase the price of a stock (the pump) so that they can sell it at those high prices for a profit (the dump).

Pumping - to promote an investment for the purpose of increasing prices, usually so it can be sold at a profit.

QR Code - a barcode in the shape of a square that contains information. Like a wallet address, QR codes can be used to tell others where money is to be sent to.

Roadmap - a plan with estimated completion dates that show what an organization wants to achieve in the long term.

Return on Investment (ROI) - a percentage used to measure how profitable an investment is.

Ring Signature - a type of digital signature that can be performed by any member of a group of users that each have keys.

Satoshi - the smallest amount of Bitcoin at one-billionth of a Bitcoin or 0.000000001 Bitcoin.

Satoshi Nakamoto - the name used by the unknown person or group of people who designed Bitcoin and created its original reference implementation.

Schnorr Signature - a digital signature produced by the Schnorr signature algorithm whose security is based on the intractability of certain discrete logarithm problems. The Schnorr signature is considered the simplest digital signature scheme to be provably secure in a random oracle model.

Scrypt - an alternative proof-of-work system to SHA-256, designed to be particularly friendly to CPU and GPU miners, while offering little advantage to ASIC miners.

Secret Key - see 'Private Key'.

Secure Hash Algorithm 256 (SHA-256) - a cryptographic hash that acts like a 'signature' for a text or a data file. SHA-256 generates an almost-unique 256-bit (32-byte) signature for a text.

Segregated Witness (SegWit) - the process by which the block size limit on a blockchain is increased by removing signature data from transactions. When certain parts of a transaction are removed, this frees up space or capacity to add more transactions to the chain.

Shapeshift.io - a website that allows for the quick and easy conversion of one type of cryptocurrency to another.

Shuffling - an effective privacy feature that enables users to mix their funds quickly and efficiently with other users' funds by creating a random mapping between existing user accounts and new recipient accounts provided by the users.

Side Chain - a group of recordings added to the main group, the blockchain, in such a way that data can travel in either direction between both groups of data. A side chain is a separate chain built to upgrade the technology with extra features.

Smart Contract - an agreement made between two or more people and recorded in the permanent, transparent digital record known as the blockchain.

Soft Cap - the minimum amount of money a cryptocurrency can receive from investors in its Initial Coin Offering (ICO).

Soft Fork - a change to the blockchain protocol wherein only previously valid blocks/transactions are made invalid. Since old nodes will recognize the new blocks as valid, a soft fork is backward-compatible.

Software Fork - the act of taking the technology from one group, and changing it to create an entirely new technology. This was done with Bitcoin technology to create other cryptocurrencies like Litecoin.

Software Wallet - a computer program and interface designed to secure cryptocurrency while allowing only its user to access it.

Tangle - a technology created by the cryptocurrency Iota, to record its transactions instead of the blockchain. The tangle is created using directed acyclic graphs (DAG) which is a structure built out in one single direction and in such a way that it never repeats.

Testnet - software that is identical to the software used by a cryptocurrency, built to experiment with new ideas without disturbing or breaking the main net.

Token - a unit of digital value with programmable potential built into it.

Token Sale - A token sale is a method of raising funds for the development of a new cryptocurrency project. Investors are offered units of the new cryptocurrency in exchange other cryptocurrencies such as Bitcoin and Ethereum. It is also known as an ICO or crowdsale.

Tokenize - the process of converting valuables in the real world into something of digital value called a token.

Total Supply - the complete amount of coins currently available for a cryptocurrency not including any coins that were burnt.

Transaction - a record of a change to the data set typically based on rules defined by the blockchain.

Transaction Fee - a payment made to people using their computers to verify transactions.

Trustless - a positive quality where a user is not required to trust the person they are transacting with. A trustless system is so secure and smooth in handling transactions, that both people can safely hand over money and other valuables without the risk of being cheated.

TX - short for 'Transaction'.

Unregulated - something that is not managed and controlled according to rules.

User Interface (UI) - an information device with which a person may interact. This can include display screens, keyboards, a mouse, and the appearance of a desktop, as well as the means through which a user interacts with an application or a website.

Volatility - the measurement of how much the price of an asset is likely to change over a period of time. Stocks for established companies have a much lower volatility than cryptocurrencies which may change a lot even in one day.

Wallet - software that interacts with the blockchain and lets users receive, store, and send their digital money.

White-Paper - a document that explains the purpose and technology used in a cryptocurrency. Usually, a white-paper is released when a cryptocurrency is just starting to help people understand what it has to offer.

Witness - A node in a DPoS blockchain that performs the task of creating new blocks.

Zero-Knowledge Proof - a method by which one party can prove to another party that a given statement is true, without conveying any information apart from the fact that the statement is indeed true.

index

Acknowledgments

Picture credits
Adobe Licensed Stock.

Illustrations
Bitcoin Future infographic by Raconteur.
Blockchain infographic Licensed by Adobe Stock.

Contributors
Jason Brett Serle
Eliot Eden
Jinia Shawdagar
Michael Oni
Mark Gill
Marc Gilbert
Jared Robinson
Conor Maloney
Jesse Cox

Normal Books would like to thank the following people and organizations who have all helped in some way to make this book possible.

Lokesh Patel, Evgene Shumilov, Steve Lee, Kristina Kalcheva Jason "Bitbender", Jason Lee, Stephen Chia, Sinone, Darkjon, Imran, Veronica Torras, A. Papargyris, MxRider, Mikemike, Munti, Dieter, Nolan Dedrik, Alina Razumova, Reuben Yap, Jan, Seatrips, Kryptowerk, Imyb, Sidi25, Manuel, Metakid, Sebastian Senff, Rosario Pabst, Marios Mamzeris, Harold Budd, Marina and Marcello, Claudia and Oscar, Dr. Bergmann, Nem Foundation, Digibyte Foundation.
— THANK YOU ALL! 💙

Alphabetical index of Cryptocurrencies.

Notes

Notes

Notes